Government and Politics in Virginia
The Old Dominion at the 21st Century

Edited by Quentin Kidd   with a Foreword by Larry J. Sabato

SIMON & SCHUSTER
CUSTOM PUBLISHING

Printed in the United States of America

10 9 8 7 6 5 4 3 2 1

Please visit our website at www.sscp.com

ISBN 0–536–01888–X

BA 98610

SIMON & SCHUSTER CUSTOM PUBLISHING
160 Gould Street/Needham Heights, MA 02494
Simon & Schuster Education Group

Contents

Section Three: Public Policy Issues

Appendix

Foreword

This textbook, *Government and Politics in Virginia: The Old Dominion at the 21st Century,* is timed to meet several important needs.

As the federal government continues to pass responsibility for governmental services and programs to the states, the importance of understanding state government is increasingly highlighted. This textbook, written by many of the state's experts on government and politics, provides a solid understanding of Virginia state government in this regard.

It is a nationally recognized concern that many Americans lack an understanding for and appreciation of their civic responsibilities. Whatever the cause of this, it is at least partially the responsibility of educators to deal with the problem. One way that citizens might be able to better understand their civic responsibility is to better understand their state government. This textbook, along with the reader *Virginia Government and Politics* that I put together with Thomas R. Morris, are excellent resources for educators to use in helping students understand Virginia government and politics.

Finally, Virginia politics, and therefore Virginia government, is in a historic period of change. The party system in Virginia has been shifting over the last decade from a firm Democratic Party–dominated system to a competitive two-party system. As the party system shifts, so does state government, and this textbook documents these changes very well.

Any class on state and local politics, or Virginia government and politics, would benefit greatly from this textbook.

Lawrence J. Sabato, Director
University of Virginia Center for
Government Studies

Preface

It is without question that state government is becoming much more important to our lives and will continue to be so as we move into the 21st century. Indeed, since the mid-1980s, Americans have been living through what politicians, policy makers, pundits and political scientists call "devolution." Devolution is a process whereby the federal government devolves responsibility (including to a certain extent financial responsibility) for a policy to the states. For example, part of the recent "welfare reform" involved devolving some responsibility for welfare to states. The result is that states have more responsibility for financing the welfare system than they ever had before, and they also have more control over welfare policy than they ever had before.

Our purpose in putting this textbook together is to provide for students a resource to better understand Virginia government. We believe that this textbook, along with Morris and Sabato's *Virginia Government and Politics*, will do just that. It is our hope that as students pass from college to positions of responsibility in communities across the Commonwealth, the information contained in this textbook will help them to be better citizens. Specifically, we would like the 21st century's leaders to have a solid understanding of how their state government works, for it is only by understanding how one's government works that one can understand how to effectively participate in governance.

This textbook is organized in three major sections: Structure of Government, Instruments of Political Power, and Public Policy Issues. In the first section, Structure of Government, students learn about the nuts-and-bolts of Virginia government. The section starts with a summary of the Virginia constitution, an important document that provides the framework for state government. The next four chapters look at the important "pieces" of state government: the governor, the General Assembly, the judiciary, and the bureaucracy.

The second section looks at the Instruments of Political Power. Since "government" is really a political institution, chapters in this section look at the various instruments used in the political struggle of governance. Chapters in this section focus on political parties, the media, the internet as a political and governmental tool, the state budget, and inter-governmental relations.

The final section focuses on selected Public Policy Issues. There are obviously many different policy issues important to Virginians at any given time. In this section, we look at five that have been particularly important in recent years: taxes, crime, ethics, the environment, and Virginia's role in the international economy. We expect these to be important policy issues into the next century.

The primary purpose of this textbook is to serve the educational needs of our students. Without that purpose, there would be little need for a textbook like this. To that end, I greatly appreciate Simon and Schuster Custom Publishing, and especially our Acquisitions Editor John O'Brien, for taking on this project. Custom Publishing is a very welcome development as it makes smaller projects such as this feasible.

Finally, no textbook can cover everything that needs to be covered. I am certain that there are topics that are important that do not appear in this textbook. To this end, I would encourage faculty, as well as students, who use this text to contact me with comments or suggestions. My address is: Department of Government and Public Affairs, Christopher Newport University, 1 University Place, Newport News, VA 23606, or e-mail me at: qkidd@cnu.edu.

Quentin Kidd, Ph.D.

About the Contributors

David Coffey is an associate professor of social science and Program Director for Administration of Justice at Thomas Nelson Community College. He is a former deputy district attorney for Los Angeles County and has collaborated on several publications.

Tom Dempsey is an assistant professor of government and Director of Criminal Justice Programs at Christopher Newport University. He is the author of several journal articles and a textbook entitled *Contemporary Patrol Tactics*.

Stanley Hash is a doctoral student in the Graduate Program in International Studies at Old Dominion University and an instructor of government at Christopher Newport University.

Connie Jorgensen is an instructor of political science at Piedmont Virginia Community College.

Quentin Kidd is an assistant professor of government at Christopher Newport University. He has authored or co-authored articles in the *American Journal of Political Science, Social Science Quarterly* and *PS: Political Science & Politics*.

Tom Lansford is A.B.D. in the Graduate Program in International Studies at Old Dominion University. He has authored articles in *Defense Analysis, European Security* and t*he Journal of Conflict Studies*.

Wayne Lespearance is A.B.D. in the Graduate Program in International Studies at Old Dominion University. He has authored articles in *European Security* and the *Notre Dame Science Quarterly*.

Stan Livengood was recently awarded a Master's in Public Administration degree from James Madison University. He has served as a precinct judge and campaign manager in elections in San Antonio, Texas, and the Mississippi House of Representatives.

Steven Medvic is an assistant professor of political science at Old Dominion University. He has published articles in *Legislative Studies Quarterly, PS: Political Science & Politics*, and is working on a book about political consultants in congressional elections.

Dan Palazzolo is an associate professor of political science at the University of Richmond. He has authored numerous articles and a book entitled *The Speaker and the Budget: Leadership in the Post-Reform House of Representatives*.

Patrick Lee Plaisance is a senior writer with the *Daily Press* in Newport News who covers Virginia politics and government issues. He also has taught writing and journalism courses at Thomas Nelson Community College and at Norfolk State University.

Robert N. Roberts is a professor of public administration at James Madison University. He is the author of *White House Ethics: The History of the Politics of Conflict of Interest Regulation* (1988) and with Marion T. Doss, *From Watergate to Whitewater: The Public Integrity War* (1997), and has written numerous articles on public service ethics law which have appeared in *Public Administration Review* and the *International Journal of Public Administration*.

Alan Rosenblatt is an assistant professor of government and politics at George Mason University. His research and teaching focuses on political persuasion and communication technology.

Larry Schack is A.B.D. at the University of Virginia. His dissertation is a critical study of Virginia executive/legislative relations. He has published articles in the *Journal of Law & Politics, Southeastern Political Review* and *Virginia Review*, as well as an entry in the upcoming edition of *Virginia Government & Politics Reader*.

Douglas Skelley is an associate professor of public administration at James Madison University. His research interests include public management innovation, organizational theory, and local government administration.

Glen Sussman is an associate professor of political science at Old Dominion University. He has authored or co-authored articles in the *Western Political Quarterly, Congress and the Presidency, Political Communication, American Review of Politics*, and *Journalism and Mass Communications Quarterly*.

Laura Van Assendelft is an assistant professor of political science at Mary Baldwin College. She has recently published a book entitled *Governors, Agenda Setting, and Divided Government*.

John Whelan is a professor of political science at the University of Richmond where he teaches in the area of American governments and directs the Department's State Legislative Internship program.

SECTION ONE:

Structure of Government

CHAPTER ONE

The Virginia Constitution: Continuity From 1776 to 1971

Stanley Hash
Christopher Newport University

It is the same English political heritage that both shaped the first Virginia constitution and made it necessary. The first Virginia constitution was written by a committee of Virginia elite in May and June, 1776 in Williamsburg. That constitution known as "The Constitution or Form of Government" was ratified by the Virginia Assembly on June 24, 1776 . . . nearly two weeks before the Declaration of Independence. The chief architect of the first Virginia constitution was George Mason, a prominent Fairfax County planter, politician, political liberal, and member of the House of Burgesses, with George Washington, a close friend and political ally.

The American Revolution was a long time coming, and the Virginia constitution was the first to emerge from the former colonies. It served as a model for other former colonies, and most of its basic parts remain intact in today's Virginia constitution. Much of the language and basic political philosophy found in the first Virginia constitution later appear in the U.S. Constitution and Bill of Rights.

This chapter provides a brief look at the political philosophy and heritage that led to the first Virginia constitution. Specifically, in this chapter we will look at the events leading to the writing of the constitution, the form of the constitution with emphasis on George Mason's "Declarations of Rights"—later to become the core of the U.S. Constitution's first ten amendments, early disagreements over the validity of Virginia's first constitution and subsequent changes to the original. The chapter concludes with an examination of the 1971 Constitution.

Influences of British Political Philosophy and Early Colonial Constitutional Experience

Colonialists in Virginia were accustomed to representative self-government. The influences of John Locke played a central role in their attitudes toward government. Natural law and natural rights were fundamental to the colonialists' political philosophy. Stressing individual rights over excesses of the crown, Virginia colonialists expected political rights and freedoms. "The guarantee to an Englishman who emigrated to Virginia that, once there, he would enjoy the same 'liberties, franchises and immunities' that would have been his in England set the English colonialist apart from colonists of other countries. . . . by terms of the charter of [the Virginia Company of London] of 1606, the English colonialist would carry with him the protections and privileges that the common law would have accorded him in England" (Howard 1974: 2). Distance from the London government and internal political upheaval in England reinforced the habit of self-government.

Virginians considered themselves loyal subjects of the crown. In fact, early colonialists far preferred the King's direction to that of the Virginia Company of London. The arrival of Governor Sir George Yeardley in April 1619 at Jamestown marks the earliest formal recognition that the Jamestown colonialists would enjoy some modicum of self government. Under Yeardley's direction, the first Virginia General Assembly assembled several months later.

This meeting of the first Virginia Assembly in Jamestown conducted by a royal governor represented recognition from the crown to the right of self-government

Figure 1.1 Statue of George Washington inside the Virginia state capitol. Courtesy of The Library of Virginia.

albeit ultimately limited under the authority of the King. Sir Francis Wyatt, succeeding Sir George Yeardley, brought with him the new "Ordinance and Constitution," dated July 24, 1621. This document is the first charter of free government in America. In 1624, King James ordered the confiscation of The London Company records and arrested its deputy treasurer. The Company had challenged the King's authority in Virginia, even though the King had previously issued it broad authority to govern and represent the crown. The crown prevailed at the ensuing trial in King's Bench and the company was dissolved. The import of this action was that Virginia colonialists attained even greater political freedom. "King James issued a new commission for the government of Virginia continuing Sir Francis Wyatt in office with eleven counselors empowering them to govern 'as fully and amply as any Governor and Council resident there, at any time within the space of five years now last past.' The term of five years was precisely the established period of representative government and so the continuance of popular assemblies was formally sanctioned" (Smith 1901: 22).

The excesses and abuses of the crown and royal governors and the events that led to the American Revolution are well documented. Virginians from the outset expected and demanded political freedom and representative government. While initially loyal to the crown and prosperous when left alone to self-administration, colonialists rebelled when they perceived betrayal. The early Englishmen were used to and preferred the rule of law and such law was expected in written form. In the earliest days, royal charters provided the form and they eagerly participated in the first colonial constitution in the form of the "Ordinance and Constitution" of 1621 delivered by Sir Francis Wyatt. However, the first post-colonial constitution was drawn up both from habit and from necessity, there being no central document or constitution to provide the framework for a new government in Virginia. Before the final convention of 1776, when the decision was made to break with England, four Virginia revolutionary conventions had taken place, all of which focused on accommodation with Great Britain. There was a great deal of disagreement about breaking with England but by May 1776 the die had been cast. The delegates from Buckingham, Charlotte, Cumberland and James City counties had been instructed to vote for independence.

Virginia's Bill of Rights and First Constitution

While departing from the British tradition of constitutional law as a body of documents rather than a single document, the colonialists followed the British tradition of rule of law. When the House of Burgesses was dissolved by Governor Dunmore on May 26, 1774, its same members reconvened at the Raleigh Tavern in Williamsburg and continued its habit of self-government, still in the English form. It was on May 15, 1776, that the convention ordered a committee be appointed "to prepare a Declaration of Rights, and such a plan of government as will be most likely to maintain peace and order in this colony, and secure substantial and equal liberty to the people" (Van Schreeven 1967: 2).

The Declaration of Rights

The committee began work immediately. It was made up of the most distinguished members of the convention. James Madison took his seat on May 16 and George Mason took his seat on May 18. Mason proposed a bill of rights known as "Declaration of Rights" that was later re-named the "Bill of Rights." Mason was also the primary author of the first constitution of Virginia. The preamble of the first constitution was taken from Thomas Jefferson's proposed constitution. In many major ways the Declaration of Rights was a restatement of the basic principles of the English liberty documents, such as Magna Carta, the Petition of Right, and the Bill of Rights. To this English heritage were added statements of natural rights philosophy such as power derives from the people, men have certain inherent rights which they retain in civil society, and that a majority of the people have the right to alter or abolish an existing form of government (Howard 1974, 7).

The Convention adopted Mason's Declaration of Rights on June 12, 1776. More than British heritage, the Declaration of Rights provided the framework for the constitution that was adopted on June 29, 1776. The declaration was different from the British documents that preceded it. The Magna Carta and (British) Bill of Rights of 1689 were lists of grievances and remonstrations directed toward a known rule, while the Declaration of Rights was written without knowledge of either future form of government or ruler. Mason's declarations, rather, were intended to serve as negative limitations—tempered by experiences with excesses of the Crown and British

Figure 1.2 Colonial Williamsburg. The hall of the Virginia House of Burgesses where the oldest legislative assembly in America met from 1704–1780. Courtesy of the Colonial Williamsburg Foundation.

Parliament and also to serve to provide the outline and form of a new government. Mason intended this Declaration of Rights as a framework for future government.

On June 29, 1776, the convention adopted "The Constitution or Form of Government" of Virginia and almost immediately selected Patrick Henry as the first governor of the Commonwealth of Virginia. Features of the new constitution included:

- There would be three separate branches of government: the executive, the legislative and judiciary.
- The legislature, the General Assembly, would consist of two houses, the Senate and the House of Delegates. The senators would be chosen one from each of newly drawn districts. The House was to be made up of delegates; two chosen from each county and one from each of certain cities.
- Members of both houses would be freeholders.
- All legislation was to originate in the House.
- The powers of the Senate were limited to veto power of bills and amendments; however, money bills could only be accepted or rejected without amendment.
- The governor would serve for three years and was to be selected jointly by the Senate and House. The governor could not succeed himself.
- The governor's duties, weakened by design, were limited to exercising power with the advice of the Council of State. The governor could grant pardons, commission justices and officers of the militia, and call for extra sessions of the legislature (but not dissolve or adjourn it). The governor was subject to impeachment by the House for mal-administration.
- The privy council, whose president was to be the lieutenant governor and eight members elected by joint ballot of the Senate and House, was to act with the governor in the conduct of the Commonwealth's business.
- Other constitutional officers including the Treasurer, judges of high courts, the Secretary of State and the Attorney General were similarly to be elected by joint session of the Senate and House. Constitutional officers and ministers were barred from sitting on either the Privy Council or in the Assembly.
- All revenues formerly going to the crown would go to the Commonwealth government.
- The boundaries of Virginia were defined and former Virginia lands that had become Maryland, Pennsylvania, North Carolina and South Carolina by royal charters were excluded.

In short, nearly all power was in the hands of the legislature—the Senate and House of Delegates. There was no direct vote for governor or other high officers of the Commonwealth. Judges were nominated and selected by the Assembly. The arrangement, while seemingly ineffective in today's context, is understandable in the context of the post-colonial period. The constitution was purposely written to make the executive ineffective much as the same framers would have made the King of England ineffective had it been possible through constitutional change—to avoid the tyrannies of the executive.

Objections to the First Constitution

From the outset, there were strong objections to some aspects of the new constitution. Thomas Jefferson led with the four primary objections. First, that the convention that formed the committee to write the constitution had no original authority because the delegates were not sent to the convention with that mandate to write a constitution. Second, that suffrage was far too narrowly limited to the freeholders and unfairly excluded others–especially those who had fought in the militia against the British. Third, that "all powers of government, legislative, executive, and judiciary result to the legislative body." Fourth, that the system of representation to the House was unfair–that it gave undue advantage to smaller counties (Van Schreeven 1967: 104).

Jefferson was not without allies. No less a political luminary than Edmund Randolf remarked, "[b]y a further analysis of the Constitution a lesson will be taught, that the most expanded mind–as that of George Mason's was, who sketched the Constitution–cannot secure itself from oversights and negligence in the tumult of heterogeneous and indistinct ideas of government, circulating in a body, unaccustomed to much abstraction" (Hill 1966: 150).

In July, 1776 the members of the convention were far more interested in getting on with positive business of founding Virginia and probably had little patience with Jefferson's early objections. Patrick Henry of the Movement Party was the winner in the gubernatorial contest with Thomas Nelson, Sr., of the Conservative Party. George Mason was the chairman of the committee responsible for notifying Henry of his

Figure 1.3 The Governor's Palace at Williamsburg. Courtesy of the Colonial Williamsburg Foundation.

victory by a vote of 65-45, and installed him in Governor's Palace just previously occupied by Lord Dunmore, the last British governor.

The 1971 Constitution

Other than the 1776 Convention, there have been almost a dozen conventions, commissions and revisions made to the original constitution, the most recent resulting in the 1971 Constitution. In his opening address to the General Assembly in January, 1968, Governor Mills Godwin "noted the 'inexorable passage of time' on Virginia's Constitution and called upon the Assembly to create a Commission on Constitutional Revision" (Howard 1974: 21).

In 1969, the commission added by ordination to Article III (Division of Powers) a section that recognized the power of the General Assembly to create administrative agencies and provide for judicial review of the actions of such agencies. The constitution produced by the commission was approved by the voters of Virginia in November, 1970 and took effect on July 1, 1971. The definitive work on the 1971 constitution is by A. E. Dick Howard, the Executive Director of the Virginia Commission on Constitutional Revision and University of Virginia Professor of Law. In *Commentaries on the Constitution of Virginia,* Howard defines the Commission's purpose and guiding principles. Among the more important principles was the recognition that a constitution embodies fundamental law. The commission felt that a constitution was not a code of laws and that unnecessary detail, not touching on fundamental matters, should be left to the statute books. Related assumptions were that the Constitution should be brief and to the point, expressed in simple, intelligible language. In particular, the Commission thought that state government ought to make possible "healthy, viable, responsible state government" and, given the pace of social and other changes, to make it possible to deal with future problems as they arise. Throughout, the Commission's report was tempered with an understanding of the need to write, not a "model" or "ideal" constitution but rather one suited to the needs and circumstances of Virginia (Howard 1974: 22).

Curiously, much arcane old English language appears in the 1971 constitution—no doubt in respect to the original framers. With some very minor changes the wording of many of the sections in the Bill of Rights (Article One) are nearly identical to George Mason's first draft version of his proposed Declaration of Rights. The General Assembly called into special session in March, 1969 to consider the commission's recommendations was receptive to most. However, the General Assembly demurred on three major points: (1) the recommendation that all cities and counties with populations over 25,000 be permitted to adopt and amend their own charters upon approving referenda; (2) the recommendation that counties and cities be able to exercise all powers not otherwise expressly denied; and (3) the recommendation that the governor be invested with the power to administratively reorganize the executive branch. The General Assembly added to the commission's recommendations in three major areas: (1) annual sessions of the legislature; (2) strengthening the education article (Article VIII) by imposing on localities the responsibility to pay for their share of public schools; and (3) strengthening the conservation articles (Article XI).

Both the commission and the General Assembly were aware that constitutional revisions submitted by referenda in other states had failed because of the "take it or leave it" single propositions; therefore, the main body containing most of the non-controversial changes were included in the first question and the other more controversial issues were contained in three more questions. The campaign for ratification was undertaken not by state government but rather by a private organization, Virginians for the Constitution. Opposition to the new Constitution centered on several charges, as described by Howard, "that it would result in the creation of regional governments, that it would lead to the busing of children for the purpose of racial integration, that it would permit the creation of $1 billion in state debt, and that, because not drafted by a convention, the whole revision was unconstitutional" (Howard 1974: 24). Virginia voters approved all four questions by substantial margins.

Outlined below is an article-by-article summary of the 1971 Virginia Constitution with mention of the most recent or major amendments. A copy of the constitution appears as an appendix. No attempt is made to lay out every detail of the constitution; rather, the primary features are generalized and any pertinent or important changes are noted.

Article I: Bill of Rights

There are seventeen sections in the Bill of Rights. Most are nearly identical in text if not intent to George Mason's original Declaration of Rights with a notable exception being the deletion of "God" in Section Two changing Mason's "That all power is by God and Nature vested in, and consequently derived from, the people . . ." to "That all power is vested in, and consequently derived from, the people . . ." Section Eight (Criminal Prosecutions) is considerably elaborated from the original with the most notable change being Section Eight-A (Rights of Victims of Crimes) being added by amendment approved by voters in November, 1996 and made effective January 1, 1997. An addition made to the original is Section 17 (Construction of the Bill of Rights), quoted here in the complete text: "The rights enumerated in this Bill of Rights shall not be construed to limit other rights of the people not therein expressed."

Article II: Franchise and Officers

Freeholders, in the original Virginia Constitution, were the only Virginians entitled to vote. As mentioned above, Thomas Jefferson objected to the narrowly defined and restrictive language of the first constitution and sought to change it. These changes came over times as the U.S. Constitution was amended. Specifically, the 15th Amendment to the U.S. Constitution gives all men the right to vote, the 19th Amendment gives women the right to vote, and the 24th Amendment changes the minimum age of voting to 18. Restrictions in the 1971 Virginia Constitution disallow voting by convicted felons, non-U.S. citizens, or those judged mentally incompetent. In addition, amendments to this article prohibit discrimination based on gender or race. Changes to Virginia code were made to comply with *The National Voter Registration Act of 1993* (Public Law 103-31-May 20, 1993) commonly known as the "Motor Voter Law."

This law requires easy and convenient voter registration procedures allowing registration by mail, and at public offices.

Interestingly, the 1971 Constitution still contains language reminiscent of 'Jim Crow' law literacy tests. Section Two, Article Two reads: "Nothing in this article shall preclude the General Assembly from requiring as a prerequisite to registration to vote the ability of the applicant to read and complete in his own handwriting the application to register." In any case, Article Two must be in compliance with the "Voting Rights Act of 1965."

Article III: Division of Powers

This article is an elaboration of Mason's original concern about separation of powers. Officers of the state government are not permitted to hold office in more than one branch of government. Also, a notable addition is: ". . . administrative agencies may be created by the General Assembly with such authority and duties as the General Assembly may prescribe. Provisions may be made for judicial review of any finding, order, or judgement of such administrative agencies [created by the General Assembly]." The section pertaining to administrative agencies was added in a 1969 revision to the Constitution.

Article IV: Legislature

This article provides organization, procedure and limitations to the General Assembly. The article provides for a two-house chamber—the Senate and House of Delegates, stipulates terms of office, lays out powers of the legislature, qualifications for holding office, compensation, session length and dates, provides a 'rules' outline for quorum, grants immunity to legislators, and contains housekeeping requirements. Its larger purpose, however, is to provide a framework for the primary work of the legislature-making laws. Section 14 details limitations on the legislature.

Article V: Executive

As with the previous article, this article lays out a framework defining powers of the governor, qualifications for office, compensation, election procedures, rules of succession and other defining details. Unlike in the original Virginia Constitution, today the governor is popularly elected and has a four-year term of office. Some notable features of this article include: (1) the governor may not succeed himself; (2) the governor has "line item" veto power in appropriation bills; (3) the governor is empowered to conduct state business with foreign states; and (4) the governor appoints all administrative heads and constitutional officers with the exception of the lieutenant governor and attorney general (both of which are also popularly elected).

This article treats more separately the offices of lieutenant governor and attorney general, the only other popularly elected state-wide offices aside from the governor. It provides that candidates for the governor and lieutenant governor offices run separately, which can result in the governor being of one political party and the lieutenant governor of another.

Article VI: Judiciary

Along with Thomas Jefferson, John Marshall argued for the separation and distancing of the Virginia judiciary from the legislature. Such a separation of powers took years to evolve. In fact, early colonial Virginia courts found appeals proceeding to the King in Council in London–effectively losing control of jurisdiction. Another item of contention was the right of the Supreme Court to judicial review. Virginia courts were instrumental in evolving the doctrine of judicial review—a power claimed by the U.S. Supreme Court in the landmark *Marbury v. Madison* case. This article defines powers of the judiciary, qualifications for office, compensation, selection procedures, rules of succession, and the organization of the Virginia judicial system. The article provides for a distinct separation of power from other branches of government. Some limitations still exist such as the power of the General Assembly to determine the original and appellate jurisdiction of the courts of the Commonwealth.

    The article provides that justices of the Supreme Court ". . . shall be chosen by the vote of the majority of the members of elected to each house . . . for a term of twelve years." Other judges are similarly selected but their terms run for eight years.

Article VII: Local Government

As provided by Dillon's Rule, all local governments are "creatures of the state." This article of the Virginia constitution defines organization, powers and restrictions of local government. Virginia has 95 counties, 39 cities and nearly 200 incorporated towns. In Section Two, the article provides specific definitions for county, city and town, and provides for general law to provide "organization, government, powers, change of boundaries, consolidation and dissolution of cities, towns, and regional government."

    Under the constitution, cities and counties are independent of each other in contrast to the common practice of cities and towns being subordinate to counties. In general, counties are administrative subdivisions of the state, while cities are more often organized under state charters to further the common interests of their residents. One of the distinctions made in this article concerns the power of cities and counties to issue bonds or other interest-bearing obligations. Cities are given the authority to issue bonds and obligations up to ten percent of the assessed real estate value of the political district. Counties are limited in this regard to education and literary purposes and only with the consent of the General Assembly.

Article VIII: Education

This article provides for compulsory elementary and secondary education. It also requires a board of nine members and Superintendent of Public Instruction be appointed by the governor and confirmed by the General Assembly for the purpose of providing an "educational program of high quality . . . and maintained." This article removes some traditional powers of local school boards by empowering the State board with authority to approve text books, instructional aids and materials. Further, the article stipulates that public funds may not be used to fund anything other than 100 percent owned and controlled schools or institutions except for non-sectarian private schools and institutions when approved by the General Assembly. The General Assembly may provide funds for loans and grants to students attending non-religious and non-theological, non-profit institutions of higher education whose purpose is collegiate or graduate education.

Article IX: Corporations

Until the railroad corporations began to dominate commerce, the prevailing economic philosophy in a largely agrarian society was *laissez faire*. In the beginning, states like Virginia promoted development of large-scale private businesses such as railroads and canal operators; however, as growth occurred abuses soon followed and it was necessary to regulate corporations. This article addresses the need and provides for a framework of regulation and monitoring in the form of the "State Corporation Commission." The board has three members, all of whom are elected by the General Assembly and serve for six years.

The State Corporation Commission issues charters to domestic corporations and licenses to foreign corporations wishing to operate in the state, and is charged with enforcing state laws. Powers include the setting and regulation of privately owned utilities and railroads. The constitution gives the commission broad powers to investigate and enforce compliance. Section Five stipulates that the commission may not allow foreign corporations operating in the state to do anything not allowed domestic corporations.

Article X: Taxation and Finance

This article defines the state tax and financing system, and provides for the methods in which the state may exercise its power to tax and borrow. Section One begins: "All property, except as hereinafter provided, shall be taxed. All taxes shall be levied and collected under general laws and shall be uniform upon the same class of subjects . . ." The article provides definitions of property and defines exceptions. It grants authority to local government to exempt or reduce taxes for those over sixty-five years old or disabled.

The article stipulates that the state may not collect more revenue than it needs to operate efficiently, and includes a provision for a 'stabilization fund' to allow for shortfalls. Also, the constitution prohibits the state from incurring debt except in the event of certain emergencies and to fund capital projects and, in any case, is self limiting to 1.15 times the average tax revenues of the state. The final section provides that the state will maintain a state employees' retirement system subject to restrictions and conditions of the General Assembly.

Article XI: Conservation

This article was added with the 1971 Constitution, and was made necessary by the realization that natural resources were not limitless and the environment not forgiving. The central thrust of this article is to address issues of quality of life and to provide management of natural resources. In short, the article provides the legal authority for the state to act on conservation and environmental issues. The article stipulates that "oyster beds, rocks and shoals in the waters of the Commonwealth shall not be leased, rented or sold but shall be held in the trust of the people . . ."

Article XII: Future Changes

This article provides for future changes. The 1776 Constitution made no provision for change. Thomas Jefferson argued that the delegates to the convention that produced the first constitution had no mandate and hence the constitution itself was invalid. In 1793, the five judges who heard a case challenging the validity of the first constitution held that laws could not be tested against that constitution because it did not have the status of a true constitution (Howard 1974: 1167). An attempt was made to include an amendment provision in the 1830 Constitution, but the effort failed. It was not until the mid-Nineteenth Century that provisions were made for amendment and not until the 1870 Constitution that explicit provisions were made in the constitution itself for changes.

This article provides two ways to amend the constitution by referendum or by convention. In short, proposed amendments to the constitution may originate in the House or Senate and if approved by majority vote will be submitted to the voters by referendum conducted in the next scheduled election. A simple majority vote is required to approve the amendment. The second method is by constitutional convention. By a vote of two thirds, members elected to both houses may call for a convention where either a new constitution or amendment(s) may be considered as stipulated by the bill. The General Assembly will provide for election of delegates to the convention. A simple majority vote of those delegates may approve a new constitution or amendment(s).

The last section of the 1971 Constitution provides implementing instructions.

Conclusion

From the early and sometimes painful efforts of the colonists to exercise freedom as Englishmen to the modern Virginia constitution, fundamental underlying American principles of civil governance remain unaltered and consistent. The United States, with its 1787 Constitution intact today, are beneficiaries of the very capable work of Virginia's patriots who lent their best political minds to the noble effort of capturing the spirit and essence of the Union and the American political system we enjoy today. The modern Virginia Constitution is a model that has endured and provides direction for Virginia's next generations.

Bibliography

Brenaman, J. N. 1902. *A History of Virginia Conventions.* Richmond: J.L. Hill Publishing Company.

Bruce Jr., Dickson D. 1982. *The Rhetoric of Conservatism: The Virginia Convention of 1829–30 and the Conservative Tradition in the South.* San Marino, CA: The Huntington Library.

Federal Election Commission. 1997. *The Impact of the National Voter Registration Act of 1993 on the Administration of Elections for Federal Office 1995–1996.* Washington, D.C.: Federal Election Commission.

Hill, Helen. 1966. *George Mason—Constitutionalist.* Gloucester, MA: Peter Smith.

Howard, A. E. Dick. 1974. *Commentaries on the Constitution of Virginia.* Charlottesville: University Press of Virginia.

Kramnick, Isaac, ed. 1998 [1788]. *The Federalist Papers.* New York: Penguin Books.

Mayer, J. P., ed. 1969. *Alexis de Tocqueville Democracy in America.* Garden City, NY: Harper & Row Publishers.

Pate, James E. 1930. "Constitutional Revision in Virginia Affecting the General Assembly." *William and Mary Quarterly and Historical Magazine* 10 (2).

Pelliam, David L. 1901. *The Constitutional Conventions of Virginia from the Foundation of the Commonwealth to the Present Time.* Richmond: John T. West Publisher.

Peterson, Merrill D., ed. 1977. *The Portable Thomas Jefferson.* New York: Penguin Books, Inc.

Senese, Donald J., ed. 1989. *George Mason and the Legacy of Constitutional Liberty.* Fairfax: Fairfax County, Virginia.

Smith, Margaret Vowell. 1901. *A Few Notes Upon the History of the Constitution or Form of Government of Virginia.* Glen Falls, NY: Glen Falls Publishing Company Co.

The Constitution of the State of Virginia Adopted by the Convention of 1901–2. 1902. Richmond: Virginia Government.

VanSchreeven, William J. 1967. *The Conventions and Constitutions of Virginia, 1776–1967.* Richmond: The Virginia State Library.

CHAPTER TWO

Virginia's Governor: Curator of the Political Museum Piece

Laura Van Assendelft
Mary Baldwin College

Quentin Kidd
Christopher Newport University

Much has changed in Virginia since V.O. Key's description of the "political museum piece," especially in the executive branch. The executive office has grown to become one of the most powerful in the nation. The state constitution grants extensive appointment and legislative powers to the governor. Statutory provisions further enhance the governor's administrative powers as chief budget and personnel officer. Party control of the governor's office has shifted from the conservative Byrd Democrats in the 1960s; to the Republicans throughout the 1970s; to a younger, more liberal Democratic Party in the 1980s; and finally back to the Republicans in the 1990s. Along with this change, however, there has also been continuity. Virginia remains steeped in conservative traditions that both define the opportunities for success and the limits on gubernatorial power.

This chapter will examine the Virginia governor in two ways. First, we will look at the formal, or official governor; that is, the requirements for office and the limitations and powers of the Office of the Governor, as well as the role of governing the Commonwealth. Then we will look at the personal and political governor; that is, the legacy of Harry F. Byrd on Virginia's gubernatorial politics, and recent shift in control of the governor's mansion among Democrats and Republicans.

The Formal Governor

Requirements, Limitations and Powers of the Office

Virginia's constitutional and statutory provisions grant the governor extensive appointive, legislative and budgetary powers. A quick review of the requirements and responsibilities of the office reveal the governor's great powers in this area. Ultimately formal powers must be combined with persuasion to increase the potential gubernatorial success. In this respect, the governor also benefits from Virginia's tradition of high public esteem for the office.

There are actually few formal requirements to become governor. The Virginia constitution stipulates that a candidate must be a U.S. citizen, be a resident of the Commonwealth and a registered voter in the Commonwealth for five years prior to seeking office, and have attained the age of thirty years. Formally, any individual who meets those three qualifications is eligible to run for governor.

The constitution limits the governor's term to four years, and makes the governor ineligible to run for this office again until a subsequent term has expired. Virginia is the only remaining state to limit the governor to a single consecutive term. The tenure limitation is a constraint on both the size and scope of the governor's agenda. In addition, the governor loses influence over the legislature much faster than a governor who is able to run for reelection. These disadvantages may be offset, however, by the short legislative session in Virginia. The General Assembly meets for sixty days during even-numbered years and only thirty days in odd-numbered years. Power naturally gravitates toward the governor's office because the legislature is out of session for most of the year, while the governor works year-round.

Another potential disadvantage to the governor is the independent election of the Lieutenant Governor, who presides over the Senate. The governor's influence over the legislature potentially increases when both officials represent the same party and work together on policy. Until recently, Democrats controlled both houses of the General Assembly. As the two parties have reached parity in numbers, however, the role of the Lieutenant Governor as a tie-breaker has become much more significant.

Aside from the limit on tenure, and the independent election of the Lieutenant Governor, the Virginia governor's powers are substantial. The Constitution vests the governor with the executive power of the Commonwealth and the responsibility to "take care that the laws be faithfully executed." The Governor's legislative powers include the responsibility to report to the General Assembly on the state of the Commonwealth and the authority to convene the legislature into special session. The State of the Commonwealth Address, given annually, provides the governor an opportunity to publicize his agenda and direct the General Assembly to focus on particular issues that he might be concerned with. For example, Governor Gilmore used part of his State of the Commonwealth address to direct the General Assembly to fulfill his campaign promise to end the personal property tax on automobiles.

Once a piece of legislation has been passed by the General Assembly, the governor has several options. He may sign the bill into law or allow the bill to become law without his signature if the legislature is in session. If the legislative session has ended, unsigned bills are vetoed automatically. During the legislative session the governor may veto an entire bill or veto line items in an appropriations bill. He may also amend bills and return them to the legislature. A two-thirds vote of those present in the legislature is required to override a veto. Executive amendments also require a two-thirds vote in each house and may be considered individually or en bloc. Executive-legislative negotiations are enhanced by these provisions because they facilitate compromise. The simple threat of an executive veto can often result in compromise. Likewise, the executive amendment forces the legislature to consider the governor's changes. The state constitution requires that the General Assembly reconvene on the sixth Wednesday after adjournment for consideration of executive amendments and vetoes of appropriations bills.

Implementation of the governor's legislative programs is facilitated by influence accrued through the appointment power. The governor has the power of appointment and removal of principal officers in the executive departments and agencies and all members of the state boards and commissions. There are approximately 4,000 appointments during a governor's term of office, all of which are subject to confirmation by the General Assembly. The governor does not have appointment power over positions in the state judiciary; the General Assembly appoints state judges. However, if a vacancy occurs while the legislature is not in session, the governor has the power to fill the office until the General Assembly reconvenes. Statutory provisions also designate the governor as chief personnel officer, granting the governor control over allocation of positions, ranks, and salaries of staffing within departments, agencies, and institutions. The governor's expansive appointment powers, and particularly the power to remove officials, are an asset in planning and implementing policy.

A further enhancement of the governor's ability to influence public policy is in his role as chief budget officer. The Executive Budget Act of 1922 gave the governor the responsibility for preparing the biennial budget to be submitted to the General Assembly. Although the legislature can amend the budget, the governor can use the executive amendment and line item veto. Furthermore, the governor retains oversight power with the authority to stop the disbursement of funds.

Formal powers do not guarantee gubernatorial success in policymaking. However, the substantial powers granted to the Virginia governor increase his potential influence in the policymaking process from agenda setting to policy implementation. Ultimately the governor's popularity, personality, and powers of persuasion are the keys to a successful administration.

The Roles Involved in Governing the Commonwealth

As we have already learned, in Virginia, the governor's powers are considerable. This is why Virginia is known as a "strong governor" state. However, what does it mean to govern the Commonwealth? The governor has several specific powers granted to him by the state constitution. These formal powers are granted to the office of the governor, regardless of who controls the office. In other words, the formal powers exist during good economic times and during bad economic times, during periods of Democratic control of the governor's mansion and Republican control, and during times when the legislature is in-session as well as out of session. In short, the formal powers and responsibilities granted to the governor are what make the governor the state's chief administrative officer, and thus make the governor ultimately responsible for governing the Commonwealth. However, in carrying out these formal responsibilities, the governor plays numerous roles.

The roles that the governor plays in carrying out his formal responsibilities include Chief of State, legislative agenda setter, Chief Administrator, chief military officer, leader of his party, leader of public opinion, ultimate judge, and crisis manager (Harrigan 1998, 243).

As Chief of State, the governor represents the Commonwealth to the rest of the nation. When called for, for example, the governor may go to Washington, D.C. and represent the state in a ceremony marking the anniversary of some historic document such as the signing of the Declaration of Independence. Another way that the governor represents the state as Chief of State is by being a member of the National Association of Governors, an organization designed to bring governors from across the nation together to discuss the common problems of governing states.

The governor is also the legislative agenda setter. The constitution requires that the governor "communicate to the General Assembly, at every regular session, the condition of the Commonwealth." In addition, the constitution requires that the governor recommend to the General Assembly ways of handling issues that he deems necessary and important. Thus, when Governor Gilmore recommended to the General Assembly that it reduce the tax on cars, he was carrying out one of the constitutional requirements of his office.

As Chief Administrator of the state, the governor appoints the officials of most state agencies, including the Boards of Trustees of the state's colleges and universities, as well as members of state regulatory commissions and advisory boards. He also requires all of these state administrators to report to him about their activities on a regular basis. Finally, as Chief Administrator, the governor has come to be responsible for preparing at least the first draft of the state's budget.

The governor is also the state's chief military officer, or the commander-in-chief of the state National Guard. Every state has a National Guard, which is often called out to keep peace and order during time of emergency. For instance, if a hurricane were to heavily damage the Hampton Roads area, the governor would probably call out the National Guard to protect private property (namely homes and businesses) while the owners were off to safety. The state constitution says "The Governor shall be commander-in-chief of the armed forces of the Commonwealth and shall have power to embody such forces to repel invasion, suppress insurrection, and enforce the execution of the laws."

The governor is also the leader of his political party. Virginia has a thriving two-party political system, and the governor is nearly always the most prominent leader of his political party. As leader of the party, the governor uses his office to provide patronage and political assistance to build support among his party for his programs and goals. The governor will also use the resources available to him to help other members of his party get elected to the General Assembly and to other elected posts. The reason for doing all of this is to make his job as leader of the state easier. With more members of his own party in the General Assembly, the fewer members of the other party there are to resist his legislative agenda.

The governor is also the leader of public opinion in the state. As the public opinion leader, the governor often travels the state making speeches and giving interviews trying to build support for his initiatives and programs. The governor (actually his staff) will also spend a great deal of time corresponding with citizens for the same reason. The ultimate objective as leader of the state's public opinion is to facilitate public support for causes that the governor favors.

The governor is also the state's ultimate judge. The state constitution gives the governor the ability to remit fines and penalties, grant reprieves and pardons after conviction, and to commute capital punishment. In every case, the governor must justify his reasons for remitting, granting, or commuting to the General Assembly.

Finally, the governor is the state's crisis manager, when the state is in crisis. Aside from being able to call out the National Guard when a crisis such as a hurricane hits the state, the governor is expected to organize the state's response, which includes coordinating with the Federal government and other organizations and agencies any aid they might provide. Ultimately the governor is expected to solve the crisis.

The Political Governor

The Byrd Legacy

Because we choose our governor through a political process, personality and politics are very important in deciding who the governor will be and what issues the governor will focus on. Although the days when the Byrd machine essentially hand-picked Virginia's governors are long gone, understanding the Byrd legacy sheds insight into the politics of the contemporary governor's office. Harry Flood Byrd's leadership dominated politics in the state of Virginia from 1925–1965. Virginia's Democratic Party was the Byrd "organization" according to Byrd allies, the Byrd "machine" according to his foes. Perhaps "organization" is the more accurate term, as the Byrd machine does not fit the standard description of the political machine by any means. As many political scientists and commentators since have reminded us, V.O. Key (1949) described the unique political apparatus of the Virginia Democratic Party as a political museum piece.

In contrast to the typical political machine which relies heavily on specific and material inducements—money, patronage, services and friendship in exchange for votes—the Byrd machine was founded on a set of principles. Comprised of a group of like-minded people, who believed in frugal management of state government finances, the organization provided purposive incentives. Although there were certainly opportunities for patronage and corruption through the extensive appointive powers of the governor, organization members abhorred scandal; they were united by a genuine interest in providing Virginia with good policy and honest politicians.

Appointed state party chairman in 1920 by Senator Thomas S. Martin ("boss" of the Martin machine), Byrd cultivated personal friendships and support across the state, leading to his own rise to power. Byrd used his political resources to win a debt controversy in 1923 through a state referendum. Byrd favored a gasoline tax, a "pay-as-you-go" policy, as an alternative to the bond proposed by the legislature to construct new roads. Byrd launched a massive media campaign and organized his forces to register voters and get them to the polls. Byrd's victory on the issue represented a mandate for the pay-as-you-go policy and secured his leadership position.

The success of the Byrd organization relied upon a small electorate. Urbanization, the elimination of the poll tax, and the Voting Rights Act increased the size of the electorate and eroded the Democratic stronghold in the state. The civil rights movement also left the Democratic Party divided into factions. While Byrd had preferred to close schools rather than integrate them, Democratic Governor Lindsay J. Almond (1958–1962) put an end to massive resistance. When Byrd resigned from the Senate in 1965 and died a year later, the organization was left without leadership. Although the inflexible pay-as-you-go philosophy ended with the demise of Byrd's domination of state politics, the Byrd legacy to Virginia is continued support for fiscal conservatism. As illustrated in Virginia's gubernatorial election politics, the electorate consistently rebels against proposals for expanded social welfare services. Although Virginia is a relatively wealthy state, political culture limits gubernatorial policy agendas.

Election Politics

Changes in state politics are most rapidly reflected in gubernatorial elections. Unlike the state legislator, who can run for reelection, the governor is not able to run for immediate reelection. The gubernatorial elections in Virginia provide a colorful picture of how the power vacuum was filled after the Byrd machine died. There are also noticeable trends in the factors that influence the election outcomes. Sabato (1996) identifies ten "keys to the governor's mansion." These keys are shown in Table 2.1 and include the economy, party unity, scandal, campaign organization and technology, campaign money, candidate personality and appeal, prior office experience of candidates, retrospective judgement on the previous governor, presidential popularity, and special interests and dominant circumstances. In Sabato's analysis of gubernatorial elections from 1969–1993 the party with the most "keys" in its favor won the governorship. A brief review of gubernatorial electoral politics since the end of the Byrd machine illustrates both change and continuity in Virginia politics.

In 1965 the Byrd organization saw its last victory with the election of Governor Mills E. Godwin over the Republican candidate Linwood Holton. The issue of massive resistance to segregation disappeared as each candidate contended for the growing number of black voters. Democrats invited blacks to their Jefferson-Jackson Day fundraising dinner. Holton called for an end to the poll tax. The two candidates ran almost identical campaigns, except that Godwin called for an unprecedented increase in spending for education and state mental institutions, to be financed by an increased sales tax if necessary. Godwin also capitalized on his association with President Lyndon B. Johnson. The Republican campaign proved to be poorly financed and Godwin ultimately won the election.

Table 2.1 The Ten Keys to the Governor's Mansion: A Comparison of Virginia Gubernatorial Elections, 1969–93 (Sabato 1996)

Electoral Conditions in Virginia

Year Gubernatorial Winner	1969 Linwood Holton (R)	1973 Mills Godwin (R)	1977 John Dalton (R)	1981 Charles Robb (D)	1985 Gerald Baliles (D)	1989 Douglas Wilder (D)	1993 George Allen (R)
[Winning %]	[52.5%]	[50.7%]	[55.9%]	[53.5%]	[55.2%]	[50.1%]	[58.3%]

Prevailing Conditions—General Election for Governor

Which party had the advantage? D=Democrat R=Republican N=No strong advantage to one side

	1969	1973	1977	1981	1985	1989	1993
Economy[a]	D	R	R	N	D	D	R
Party Unity	R	R	R	D	D	D	N
Scandal	N	D	N	N	N	N	R
Campaign Organization/ Technology	N	R	R	D	D	N	N
Campaign Money	N	N	R	N	N	N	D
Candidate Personality/ Appeal	R	N	R	D	N	D	R
Prior Office Experience of Candidates[b]	N	R	N	N	D	N	D
Retrospective Judgment on Previous Governor[c]	D	R	R	R	D	D	R
Presidential Popularity[c]	R	D	R	R	R	R	R
Special Issues and Dominant Circumstances	R	D	R	D	D	N	R
	("Time for a change" mood plus extreme factionalism among Democrats propelled Holton.)	(Watergate helped Henry Howell reach his high watermark —but it wasn't enough.)	(Democrats' divisive primary and campaign errors took their toll.)	(Democrats moderated while GOP factionalism emerged.)	(Diverse Democratic ticket attracted "new Virginia" suburban support.)	(Abortion issue helped Wilder in campaign, but race hurt him on election day.)	(Crime issue and yearning for change from the Robb/Wilder/ Clinton Democrats aided Allen.)
Net Advantage	R(+2)	R(+2)	R(+8)	D(+2)	D(+5)	D(+3)	R(+4)

Note: The Democratic party did not nominate a candidate for governor in 1973, but independent Henry Howell was given a de facto endorsement by the party's leadership. For our purposes here, Howell is considered the Democratic candidate.

[a] As measured by changes in per capita family income and the unemployment rate in the twelve months prior to election day.

[b] Prior statewide elective office is given more weight than district or local office.

[c] As measured by public opinion poll ratings in the six months prior to election day.

In 1969, however, the tides changed when Linwood Holton was elected the first Republican governor in Virginia since the 1880s. Holton played his Nixon association and successfully convinced the electorate that it was time for a change. The Democratic nominee, William C. Battle, had pushed his connection with John F. Kennedy. Battle's support had been damaged in a bitter primary struggle between three factions within the Democratic party: Fred G. Pollard of the Byrd organization; William C. Battle, a moderate; and Henry Howell, a liberal. Although the centrist candidate won the nomination, the party was torn by the struggle and was unable to reconcile its differences in order to win the election. In the general election specific issues were hard to identify as both candidates promised to increase the participation of blacks in state government and both opposed the continuation of the state sales tax. The Republicans emphasized Nixon's endorsement of Holton as part of the "Southern Strategy," whereby the president agreed to help Republican governors win election in an attempt to increase his own chances for reelection in that state. Since Virginia traditionally voted Republican in presidential elections, Holton benefited from the association. Holton's win marked the end of the Byrd organization's dominance in Virginia politics.

As the Byrd organization died, its conservative advocates had to find a new home. The new liberalism of the Democratic Party was not the answer. Given the choice, they sided with the conservative Republicans even though they were nominally Democrats. It was some time before the Democratic Party moderated its views and began to attract conservative Democrats once again. Meanwhile, the Republicans capitalized on the disunity of the Democrats, enjoying a winning streak that would last more than a decade.

After eighty-four years of success in gubernatorial elections, the Democrats failed to nominate a candidate in 1973. Both candidates were in fact former Democrats turned Republicans. Party labels essentially lost their meaning and voters were forced to sort things out by voting for the candidate rather than for the party. Mills E. Godwin, previously elected governor as a Democrat, ran as a conservative Republican. Henry Howell joined the race as an independent. Godwin came from the "old Virginia school" and fit the traditional gentleman image conservative Virginia voters prefer. Howell's flamboyant character provided a contrast that turned the race into a battle between personalities. Howell attempted to run a populist campaign, preaching at factories and country stores about keeping the big boys honest. In contrast, Godwin attended more formal events and ran a quieter, more conservative campaign. Godwin won, making history as the longest serving governor in Virginia and the only governor to serve under both party labels.

"Howlin' Henry" returned in the 1977 campaign, this time as the Democratic candidate with Jimmy Carter's endorsement, although Carter was not popular in Virginia at the time. Howell took liberal positions on such issues as desegregation, gun control, and the right-to-work law. The Republican candidate John Dalton campaigned for business stability, fiscal responsibility, and maintaining the course. Howell ran a mudslinging campaign, calling Dalton the "caviar candidate" for raising so much money, and a "mean junkyard dog." When Howell lost the election, he refused to call and congratulate Dalton. Virginia voters rebelled against the negativity of Howell's campaign and the liberalism of his platform, electing the more conservative candidate again.

In the 1981 campaign, Chuck Robb was able to unite the Democratic Party's bickering factions with a "something for everyone" campaign. Robb attempted to win the election by appearing more conservative than the Republicans, emphasizing Virginia's past with a campaign slogan, "Keep a Good Thing Going." The Republican candidate Marshall Coleman ran a mudslinging campaign in which he personally criticized Robb and his Texas in-laws as being part of the "Great Society." Marshall nicknamed Robb "Chucky Bird" and accused him of only play-acting conservatism. Furthermore, Godwin, campaigning on behalf of Marshall, turned off voters with racist remarks in one of his speeches. Once again personalities became a major campaign issue and Robb's victory brought Democrats back to the Governor's Mansion after a twelve-year absence. In office Robb proved to be more liberal than his campaign image, appointing women and blacks to top cabinet positions and the State Supreme Court and pushing for increased spending on education. A serious, quiet man with the traditional demeanor of the old Byrd candidates, Robb's popularity as governor helped his party maintain its hold on the governor's office in the next election.

In 1985 the Democratic Party nominated Gerald Baliles for governor along with L. Douglas Wilder for Lieutenant Governor, and Mary Sue Terry for Attorney General. The Republican candidate, Wyatt Durrette, had been defeated by Baliles for

Figure 2.1 Douglas Wilder greets supporters on election night 1989 after declaring himself winner. Courtesy of Associated Press/Wide World Photos.

Attorney General. The media labeled the candidates "Tweedledee" and "Tweedledum" in what proved to be a lackluster campaign. Baliles' pro-choice abortion stand and Wilder's candidacy became the only real issues. The Republicans accused the Democrats of using Wilder to win the black vote. All three Democratic candidates won, despite predictions that Virginia was not ready for such changes. As governor, Baliles successfully passed a transportation program funded by a gas tax and bonds. Clearly much had changed in Virginia since the days of Byrd's "pay-as-you-go" philosophy.

The 1989 gubernatorial election proved to be historic for Virginia. Lieutenant Governor Wilder secured the Democratic nomination and won popularity by shaking hands and giving speeches across the state. He cultivated an image slightly more conservative than Baliles and benefited from favorable press coverage. The major issue was abortion. Like Baliles, Wilder's pro-choice stand won him support mainly in Northern Virginia and Tidewater. He defeated Republican candidate Marshall Coleman by a narrow margin to become the first black governor.

In 1993 Attorney General Mary Sue Terry won the Democratic nomination and began campaigning for governor as the favored candidate. Terry's campaign was poorly managed, however, and she quickly lost support in the face of several obstacles. Among them was the unpopularity of the Democratic President Bill Clinton and the negative public response to infighting between Chuck Robb and Douglas Wilder. Terry also failed to respond adequately to allegations about her personal lifestyle. Allen used his popular image as the married man with children to stress family values in contrast to Terry's status as a single female. Terry was even unable or unwilling to court

Figure 2.2 Governor James Gilmore. Courtesy of the Office of the Governor, State of Virginia.

the women's vote. Expecting to win support with a five day waiting period for the purchase of a handgun, Terry was upstaged by Allen's pledge to abolish early parole for violent criminals. In the end Terry was blamed for the negativity of the campaign and Republican George Allen, a pro-life conservative, won the election by a wide margin.

Abortion arose again as an issue in the 1997 gubernatorial election. Democratic nominee Lieutenant Governor Don Beyer used his pro-choice stand to cultivate support in his homebase of Northern Virginia. Republican nominee James Gilmore retaliated with a proposal to end personal property taxes on automobiles. Beyer later joined the bandwagon, proposing a moderate tax credit for needy families. Both candidates offered comparable education plans to increase teacher salaries and reduce classroom size, however, education was overshadowed by the economy. Unemployment rates fell to record lows during the election campaign, while revenues continued to increase. Beyer simply could not compete with the Allen record or the popularity of Gilmore's car tax proposal. The Republicans won an unprecedented sweep of Virginia's three statewide offices.

The economy, crime, education, and personalities are the perennial issues in Virginia gubernatorial electoral politics. Traditions that cannot be breached include conservative fiscal policy and "gentlemanly" conduct during the campaign. The voters rebel against negative campaigning, scandal, and party infighting. Typically the most conservative candidate wins, whether by party platform, issues, or personality.

Conclusion

The Virginia governor is, as we have seen, a very powerful actor in state politics. Indeed, Virginia is known as a strong executive state because of the many constitutional and administrative powers that the governor has at his disposal. However, as we have also seen, the formal powers are not the only tools that the governor has available to use. Indeed, in order to be successful, the Virginia governor must also make extensive use of his political powers as well.

Bibliography

Atkinson, Frank B. 1992. *The Dynamic Dominion: Realignment and the Rise of Virginia's Republican Party Since 1945.* Fairfax: George Mason University Press.

Baker, Donald P. 1989. *Wilder: Hold Fast to Dreams.* Washington, D.C.: Seven Locks Press.

Bass, Jack and Walter De Vries. 1976. "Virginia: Out of the Byrd Cage," in *The Transformation of Southern Politics.* New York: Basic Books.

Berman, David R. 1997. *State and Local Politics,* 8th ed. Armonk, NY: M.E. Sharpe.

Edds, Margaret. 1990. *Claiming the Dream: The Victorious Campaign of Douglas Wilder of Virginia.* Chapel Hill: Algonquin Books.

Eisenberg, Ralph. 1972. "Virginia: The Emergence of Two-Party Politics," in William C. Havard, ed., *The Changing Politics of the South.* Baton Rouge: Louisiana State University Press.

Harrigan, John J. 1998. *Politics and Policy in States & Communities.* New York: Longman.

Heinemann, Ronald L. 1996. *Harry Byrd of Virginia.* Charlottesville: The University Press of Virginia.

Key Jr., V. O. 1949. "Virginia: Political Museum Piece," in *Southern Politics in State and Nation.* New York: Vintage Books.

Morris, Thomas R. and Larry J. Sabato. 1990. *Virginia Government and Politics: Readings and Comments,* 3rd revised edition. Charlottesville: The University of Virginia and the Virginia Chamber of Commerce.

Sabato, Larry J. 1975. *Aftermath of Armageddon: An Analysis of the 1973 Virginia Gubernatorial Election.* Charlottesville: The University Press of Virginia.

Sabato, Larry J. 1996. *Virginia Votes: 1991–1994.* Charlottesville: The University Press of Virginia.

Stonecash, Jeffrey M. 1995. *American State and Local Politics.* New York: Harcourt Brace College Publishers.

Younger, Edward and James Tice Moore, eds. 1982. *The Governors of Virginia: 1860–1978.* Charlottesville: The University Press of Virginia.

CHAPTER THREE

The General Assembly: Coping with Change and Tradition

Quentin Kidd
Christopher Newport University

Connie Jorgensen
Piedmont Virginia Community College

Since the 1960s, state legislatures across the country have undergone great change both in the amount of time they spend in session and the amount of work they do out of session. Thirty years ago the "typical" state legislature was made up of part-time legislators whose real jobs were not at the state capital but rather at home. Today, however, many state legislatures are more professional policy-making institutions composed of a diverse set of career-minded politicians with large well-paid legislative staffs at their disposal. This transformation from part-time representative of the people to professional legislator, along with the expanded policy-making role being passed down to the states from the federal government, has caused state legislatures across the country to become very powerful actors in the public policy arena.

In Virginia, the oldest representative body in the New World, the General Assembly has managed to grow and modernize in a unique way, consistent in many ways with the history and tradition of Virginia politics. House Delegates and State Senators continue to represent Virginians in a "part-time" capacity, with most holding down "full-time" jobs as attorneys, private business owners or educators. The Virginia General Assembly meets annually, but sessions are relatively short and vary from between thirty days to ninety days depending whether the year is even or odd. In extraordinary situations, the General Assembly can meet for a longer time period.

Despite the "part-time" nature of its membership however, in many other ways the General Assembly has evolved in a manner consistent with national trends and moved toward modernization. For instance, both the House of Delegates and the Senate have professional and support staff, and Delegates are even allowed year-round personal and district staff support. Senators are allowed personal and district staff support only during the legislative session. This growth in professional and support staffing has helped make the General Assembly more independent and effective as an institution, and is certain to be important to legislators as they continue to grapple with complex budget and policy issues. This chapter will provide some insight into the General Assembly by examining its history, membership, organization and procedures.

Historical Background

Virginians are proud of the fact that their General Assembly is the oldest elective legislative body in the New World. Indeed, the General Assembly, known as the House of Burgesses until 1775, can trace its roots all the way back to meetings in the choir of a church at the original settlement in Jamestown. When the first representative assembly convened in 1619, the territory was under the control of the Virginia Company, but when the company surrendered its charter in 1624, the Crown agreed to establish representative institutions on a regular basis (Greene 1963: 26–31).

In those early years, the representative body was in a subordinate position to the Crown-appointed governor and council. Around 1650, however, the legislature became bicameral. The representative branch (lower house) became known as the House of Burgesses and the appointed branch (upper house) kept its name as Council. This

Figure 3.1 Exterior shot of the Capitol building in Colonial Williamsburg. Courtesy of the Colonial Williamsburg Foundation.

configuration was consistent with the configuration of the British Parliament at the time. By the middle of the 1700s, the House of Burgesses had become, under the leadership of the landed gentry, a very powerful political body in Virginia, eclipsing in many ways the power of the council (Greene 1963: 26–31).

The basic structure of the General Assembly has not changed much since 1776, the year that the first Virginia Constitution was adopted. The first constitution was a short document, only about six pages long and was designed only to provide a frame of government. It gave the General Assembly vast powers (Pate 1932: 29–30). That first constitution stipulated that the legislature would be composed of "two distinct branches." The legislature would meet once every year "or oftener," and would be called the "GENERAL ASSEMBLY OF VIRGINIA." In addition to stipulating the number of branches the legislature would have, how often it would meet, and what it would be called, the constitution also named one branch the House of Delegates and the other the Senate. Each branch was given the authority to establish its own "speaker, appoint its own officers, settle its own rules of proceeding, and direct writs of election for supplying intermediate vacancies" (Morris and Sabato 1990: 6–7).

While the basic structure has not changed much, some of the important operating principles have changed. For instance, the original constitution gave the House of Delegates the authority to originate all laws, denying this right to the Senate. The Senate was given the authority to approve, reject, or amend (with the consent of the House) those laws passed by the House. The only exception was with money bills, which the Senate was required to either approve or reject, but could not alter. In addition, the original constitution gave the General Assembly the authority to choose the Governor. The constitution called for both houses to annually choose whom, by joint ballot, the governor would be, and to pay him an adequate, but modest salary.

The current constitution, ratified in 1971, calls for the same structure as that outlined in the original constitution. However, the current constitution is much more specific about how the legislature should organize itself, when the legislative session should begin, and what the limitations on the legislature's power are. In addition, the current constitution allows laws to be originated in either of the two houses.

Politically, while there have been periods of Republican ascendancy, since the end of the Civil War Virginia has been characterized as a solid one-party state, with monopoly control by the Democrats of the General Assembly and most statewide political offices. The dominance of the Democrats party has been particularly evident in the General Assembly, where Democrats held clear majority from Reconstruction until 1995.

By 1995, Republicans had made great gains in closing the gap between them and the Democrats in the General Assembly, the result of an increasingly competitive two party system dating to the early 1980s (McGlennon 1988: 56–58). The rise of the Republican party is at least partially the result of two simultaneous movements. On one side, conservative state Democrats began shifting to the Republican party in the late 1960s, while at the same and as a result of the fact that the Democratic party was shifting left. The Democratic shift to the left was caused at least partially by the influx of minority voters following the 1964 Voting Rights Act (Rozell 1998: 124–128). As a result of these movements, the composition of the Virginia General Assembly began

to change as well. In 1971, for example, Democrats held a 71 to 24 to 3 (three inde-
pendents) majority. In the Senate, Democrats held a 33 to 7 majority. Twenty years
later Democrats held a much slimmer 58 to 41 to 1 majority in the House and a 22 to
18 majority in the Senate (Rosell 1998: 130). In 1998, Republicans controlled the
Senate with a 21 to 19 majority, and there was an effective tie in the House with 50
Democrats, 49 Republicans, and 1 conservative independent who had joined the
Republican caucus. As a result of the rise of the Republican party, Virginia's General
Assembly is, for the first time in many years, home to a very competitive two-
party system.

Membership

Article IV of the Virginia Constitution stipulates the membership requirements of
the General Assembly. Members of the General Assembly must be at least 21 years
old at the time of election, must be residents of the district that they wish to represent, and must be qualified to vote. Since 1982, members have been elected from single member rather than multi-member districts. They cannot hold any other public
office in Virginia or in the United States government.

Such broad qualifications suggest that most citizens have an opportunity to serve
in the legislature and, technically they do. In reality, however, informal qualifications
constrain opportunities in many instances. We get an idea about how these
informal qualifications might constrain opportunities by looking at the "typical" state
legislator.

A typical member of the state legislature is a middle-aged, Protestant, white male
who has a college degree and probably practices law. In addition, he also possesses
enough resources (time and money) to devote himself to the task of campaigning for
a seat and then serving for a minimum of two years in that seat. In addition, he also
has enough time outside of the legislative session to attend to any state business in
Richmond that he is needed for, and to generally maintain a higher than normal public profile in his community.

The compensation for serving in the General Assembly is not enough such that a
member could live on it alone. Members of the House of Delegates earn $17,640 in
annual salary, with an additional per diem for food and expenses when they are in
Richmond. Senators earn $18,000 in annual salary, as well as a per diem while on
state business.

Such substantial investments in time and resources, as well as the minimal payment in return, makes the job of serving in the General Assembly prohibitive to most
"ordinary" Virginians. Very few Virginians can afford the personal investment that
campaigning for a seat in the House or Senate costs, and then leave their full-time jobs
(and salary) for months at a time attending to state business. Minorities, women, and
other "less-typical" legislative candidates face an uphill struggle if they hope to win a
legislative seat, even if they have substantial resources.

Nevertheless, despite these informal qualifications that do limit many Virginians
from pursing office, the legislature is slowly changing in its demographic profile. In
the 1998 session, nearly 16% of legislators were women and almost 11% were African

American. While these figures are nowhere near representative of the Virginia population as a whole, the legislature is becoming more representative of the Commonwealth's population. For instance, in 1990, the legislature was 12% women and nearly 10% African American.

Organization

The Virginia legislature is similar in organizational structure to most other state legislative bodies. Like all state legislatures except Nebraska, the Virginia General Assembly is a bicameral body. The Virginia legislature consists of a House of Delegates, typically called the "lower house," and a Senate, typically called the "upper house." The House of Delegates is required by the constitution to have no more than 100 members and no less than 90 members (currently there are 100). The Senate is required by the constitution to have no more than 40 members and no less than 33 members (currently there are 40). Senators serve four-year terms and Delegates serve two-year terms.

The Virginia constitution stipulates that the President of the Senate shall be the Lieutenant Governor, who must meet the same qualifications for office as the Governor but who is not limited to one term like the Governor is limited. The Lieutenant Governor, currently Republican John H. Hager, while "officially" presiding over the

Figure 3.2 The Senate Chamber. Courtesy of The Library of Virginia.

Figure 3.3 The House Chamber. Courtesy of The Library of Virginia.

Senate, does not have a vote except in the event of an equal split, in which case the Lieutenant Governor may cast the tie-breaking vote. Should the Governor leave office for any reason during his term, the Lieutenant Governor would step in as "Acting Governor."

While the President of the Senate is the "official" presiding officer, the presiding officer who actually conducts the Senate's day-to-day business is the President pro tempore. The rules of the Senate stipulate that the President pro tempore should be elected by the Senate and should be "a senior member in the Senate of the political party which comprises a majority of the membership of the Senate."

The current President pro tempore of the Senate is Stanley C. Walker, a Democrat from Norfolk, who was first elected to the Senate in 1972 and is currently the Senate's most senior member. Walker was re-elected President pro tempore in 1998 when neither Democrats nor Republicans held a majority in the Senate. Soon after being elected President pro tempore, however, a Democratic senator resigned to accept an administrative appointment from Governor Gilmore, and a Republican was selected in a special election to replace the departed Democrat. The result of this special election was a Republican majority of 21 to 19, with a Democratic President pro tempore.

At the beginning of each session following the election of Senators, members are elected to the eleven standing committees. Total membership of committees must reflect the composition of the membership of the two major political parties in the Senate. In addition, membership is also expected to reflect the several congressional districts of Virginia. In other words, Senate committee membership is supposed to reflect both the partisan distribution of the Senate itself as well as the demographic and geographical distribution of the Commonwealth. The eleven standing committees of the Senate are listed in Table 3.1.

Table 3.1: Standing Committees in the Senate

Commerce and Labor	General Laws
Courts of Justice	Local Government
Education and Health	Privileges and Elections
Finance	Rehabilitation and Social Services
Rules	Transportation
Agriculture, Conservation and Natural Resources	

The presiding officer of the House of Delegates is the Speaker, who is elected by the general membership of the House. The Virginia Constitution stipulates little about how the Speaker should be chosen or how often an election for Speaker should be held. However, the rules of the House call for the Speaker to be elected by the members in even-numbered years for a term of two years. The Speaker of the House is fourth in the line of succession to become Governor. However, if the Attorney General, who is third in line, is ineligible to serve as Governor, then the Speaker will do so.

With rare exception, the Speaker will be a member of the party controlling the majority of seats in the House. The 1998 legislative session was one of those rare exceptions however. In 1998, The State Board of Elections decided not to swear in the new members until their election results were officially certified. This meant that during the period in which the Speaker of the House was elected, Democrats held a majority of seats. Had newly elected members been sworn in at that time, however, there would have been an effective tie, with 50 Democrats, 49 Republicans, and one conservative Independent, Delegate Lacey E. Putney of Bedford County. A major battle ensued and the result was the election of Thomas W. Moss, Jr., to another term as House Speaker. House Democrats later agreed to a power sharing arrangement, which resulted in co-chairs of the House Standing Committees.

At the beginning of each session following the election of Delegates, the Speaker appoints members to the House's 20 standing committees. The rules of the House stipulate how many members shall serve on each committee and indicates that the chairman of the committee will be the first named member of that committee by the Speaker. Thus, the Speaker generally names committee chairs first, and then names the rest of the committee members after naming the chairs. The most powerful committees are those that deal with money and the budget, such as the Finance and Appropriations Committees. A list of the 20 standing committees is shown in Table 3.2.

Table 3.2: Standing Committees in the House

Agriculture	Appropriations
Chesapeake and Its Tributaries	Claims
Conservation and Natural Resources	Corporations, Insurance and Banking
Counties, Cities and Towns	Courts of Justice
Education	Finance
General Laws	Health, Welfare and Institutions
Interstate Cooperation	Labor and Commerce
Militia and Police	Mining and Mineral Resources
Privileges and Elections	Rules
Science & Technology	Transportation

The General Assembly has the power to legislate on all matters unless the Virginia or U.S. Constitution specifically prohibits or restricts this action. Its chief responsibilities are to make laws for the Commonwealth, to levy taxes, and to adopt the state budget. Aside from these "constitutional" responsibilities, the General Assembly has many informal responsibilities that come with representing the people and responding to the people's needs. These informal responsibilities are often referred to as "constituency service."

The length of the legislative session is constitutionally mandated. The legislature meets annually, beginning on the second Wednesday in January and continues for 60 days in even-numbered years and 30 days in odd-numbered years. If necessary, the "short session" can be extended for 45 days. As the amount of legislative activity increases in both size and complexity, this option is regularly exercised. In 1980, a constitutional amendment was passed to allow for an additional session outside of the normal "short session" specifically so that the legislature could deal with matters that the governor has vetoed or returned to the assembly with amendments. This "veto session" takes place the sixth Wednesday after adjournment for no more than three days, unless extended for an additional seven days by a majority vote of each house. Finally, the governor can call a special session if requested by two-thirds of each house or the governor deems it necessary.

Legislative Procedures

In January 1998, 2,654 bills and resolutions were introduced by the January 26 deadline, somewhat short of the record 2,904 set in 1993. The lowest number of introductions in the last 20 years was 1,790 in 1984. In addition to the 2,654 bills introduced, there were 412 bills carried over from the previous legislative session. Whatever the source, each of these bills must be reviewed, if not totally prepared, by the Division of Legislative Services. While very labor intensive, over the years this process has become much more efficient due to increased computer usage.

In order to become a law, a bill must make a perilous journey. Figure 3.4 provides a rough guideline for how a bill becomes a law in Virginia. In most cases, bills are the result of requests from constituents or other interested parties to deal with a real or perceived problem. For instance, if a constituent is upset about her inability to access public transportation, she may make a request to her Delegate to help her with the problem. Not every problem that a constituent has requires that the Delegate introduce legislation, however. When a Delegate receives a request from a constituent, the Delegate first must decide whether it is an appropriate issue for the legislature to deal with. For instance, in the example above, the Delegate might first contact the public transportation authority and ask if they would be able to extend a bus line into this constituent's neighborhood. If the transportation authority agrees to do this, then the constituent's problem is solved without requiring action by the legislature. In this case, the Delegate would have provided "constituency services."

However, if the transportation authority says that it cannot extend a line into that neighborhood due to a lack of funding, the Delegate may consider asking the state to provide more money. This request could be made in the form of a bill that the Delegate would introduce into the House. If the Delegate chooses to make the request for more money in the form of a bill, the first step would be to ask the Division of Legislative Services to draft (or write) the bill. Once the bill is written and approved by the Delegate it is then introduced into the House and referred to the appropriate committee by the Speaker of the House. In the Senate, the Clerk of the Senate refers all bills and resolutions to the appropriate committees.

Members of the committee familiarize themselves with the bill and schedule public meetings to discuss the bill. Committee meeting dates are announced in advance so that the public will have the opportunity to observe and offer comments. If the committee approves of the request, then the bill is transferred (reported) to the full House for debate. Each bill is read three times, and members can offer amendments to the bill on the second reading. After consideration by the full House during the second reading, the bill is voted on during the third reading. The votes are recorded immediately and are visible to all present in the respective chamber. Virginia was the first state to use an electronic vote-tallying system of this kind.

Figure 3.4 How a Bill Becomes a Law in Virginia

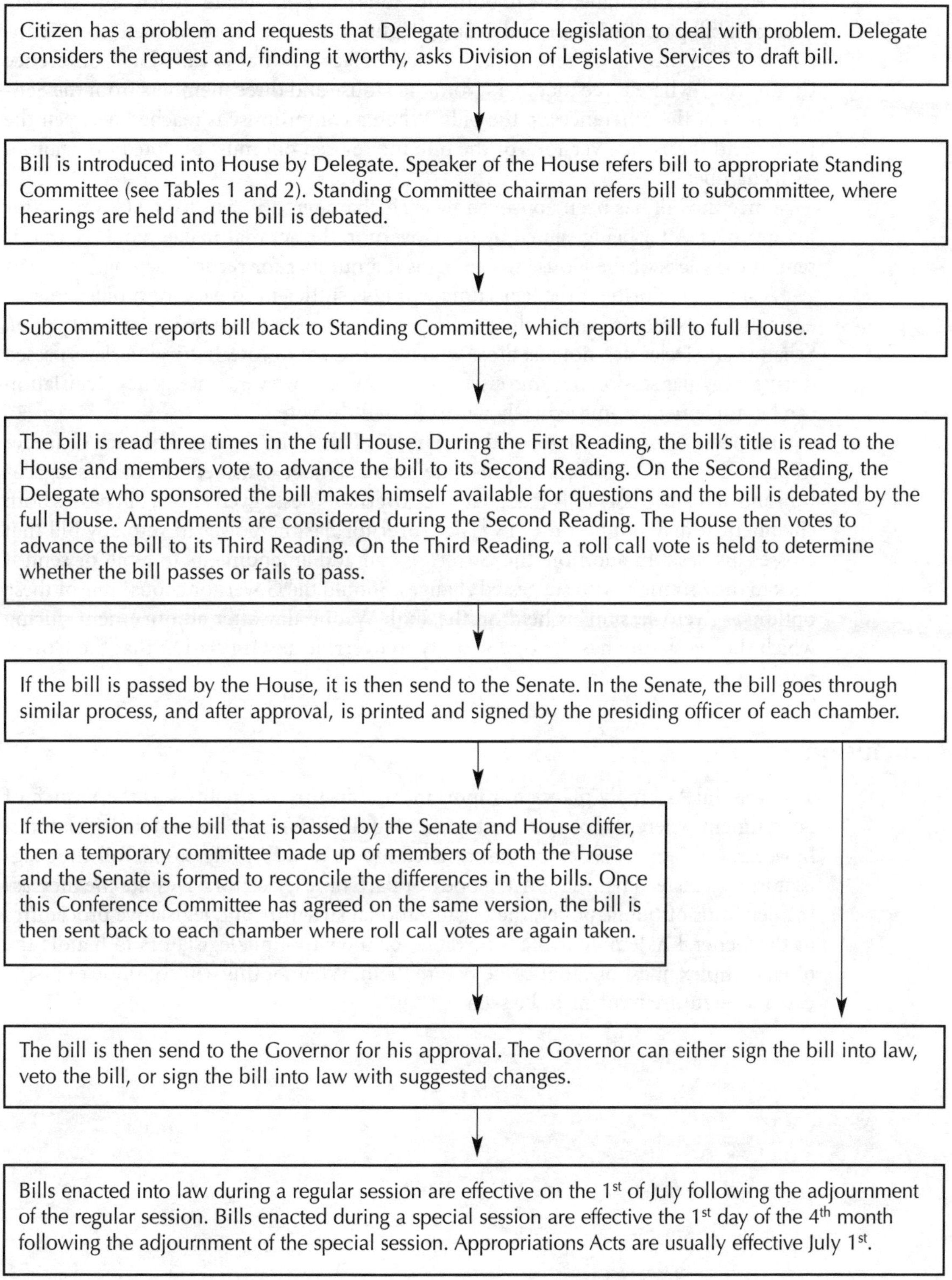

Citizen has a problem and requests that Delegate introduce legislation to deal with problem. Delegate considers the request and, finding it worthy, asks Division of Legislative Services to draft bill.

↓

Bill is introduced into House by Delegate. Speaker of the House refers bill to appropriate Standing Committee (see Tables 1 and 2). Standing Committee chairman refers bill to subcommittee, where hearings are held and the bill is debated.

↓

Subcommittee reports bill back to Standing Committee, which reports bill to full House.

↓

The bill is read three times in the full House. During the First Reading, the bill's title is read to the House and members vote to advance the bill to its Second Reading. On the Second Reading, the Delegate who sponsored the bill makes himself available for questions and the bill is debated by the full House. Amendments are considered during the Second Reading. The House then votes to advance the bill to its Third Reading. On the Third Reading, a roll call vote is held to determine whether the bill passes or fails to pass.

↓

If the bill is passed by the House, it is then send to the Senate. In the Senate, the bill goes through similar process, and after approval, is printed and signed by the presiding officer of each chamber.

↓

If the version of the bill that is passed by the Senate and House differ, then a temporary committee made up of members of both the House and the Senate is formed to reconcile the differences in the bills. Once this Conference Committee has agreed on the same version, the bill is then sent back to each chamber where roll call votes are again taken.

↓

The bill is then send to the Governor for his approval. The Governor can either sign the bill into law, veto the bill, or sign the bill into law with suggested changes.

↓

Bills enacted into law during a regular session are effective on the 1st of July following the adjournment of the regular session. Bills enacted during a special session are effective the 1st day of the 4th month following the adjournment of the special session. Appropriations Acts are usually effective July 1st.

Once the bill has passed the House, it is then sent to the Senate, where a request is made that the Senate give its approval of the bill also. It is often the case that bills are introduced simultaneously in both the House and the Senate. When different versions of a bill pass the House and Senate, the two bills must be reconciled (made consistent). This process of reconciliation takes place in what is called a "Conference Committee," where three members from the House and three members from the Senate work out the differences in the bills. When a compromise is reached between the House and the Senate versions of the bill, the revised bill must be voted on again in each chamber.

Once the bill has been approved by each chamber, it is sent to the Governor for his approval. After being signed by the Governor, the act that makes a bill a law, it is sent to the Clerk of the House who assigns it a number for record keeping.

A simple majority of the legislators voting is sufficient to pass most bills, however finance bills require an absolute majority. An absolute majority is a majority of *all* Senators and Delegates, not just those who were present to vote. In Virginia, laws passed during a regular session become effective on July 1. However, "emergency" legislation can be implemented immediately with a four-fifths vote.

In 1998, "Crossover Day" was February 17. This is the deadline for each chamber to pass all of its own bills. After this date each chamber considers the other's legislation and actually passes bills that go to the governor's desk. Even after a bill passes both chambers, it may not become law. The Governor has the power to veto any bill that crosses his desk. In addition, the Governor can add amendments to a bill or send it back to the Assembly with suggested changes. Should the Governor choose one of these options, a "veto session" is held on the sixth Wednesday after adjournment during which the legislature has the opportunity to override any legislation that the Governor's vetoed.

Conclusion

The General Assembly plays an important role in Virginia politics as the branch of government where the people are represented. Unlike many other state legislatures, however, the General Assembly has resisted moves toward professional full-time legislators and instead has remained a body of part-time legislators. Despite the increasing demands of public policy, the organizational structure and legislative procedures of the General Assembly make it possible for the part-time legislators to handle the often complex questions that come before them. Whether this will continue to be the case in the future remains to be seen.

Bibliography

Greene, Jack P. 1963. *The Quest for Power.* Chapel Hill: University of North Carolina Press.

McGlennon, John J. 1988. "Virginia's Changing Party Politics." In Robert H. Swansbrough and David M. Brodsky, eds., *The South's New Politics.* Columbia: University of South Carolina Press.

Pate, James E. 1932. *State Government in Virginia.* Richmond: Appeals Press.

Rozell, Mark J. 1998. "Virginia: The New Politics of the Old Dominion." In Charles S. Bullock III and Mark J. Rozell, eds., *The New Politics of the Old South.* Lanham, MD: Rowman & Littlefield Publishers.

Morris, Thomas R. and Larry J. Sabato. 1990. "First State Constitution." *Virginia Government and Politics: Readings and Comments*, 3rd revised edition. Charlottesville, VA University of Virginia and Virginia Chamber of Commerce.

CHAPTER FOUR

Virginia's Judicial Selection Process: Still Unique Though Its Partisan Stripes Are Changing

John T. Whelan
University of Richmond

Virginia's judicial selections, once the jealously guarded prerogative of Democrats in the General Assembly, have been anything but politics as usual since 1996. This was most evident in the 1997 legislative session as Democrats and Republicans deadlocked over the selection of a Supreme Court justice, highlighted near the end-of-the-session in a futile marathon set of deliberations, running over a 29 hour "legislative day."[1] That deadlock afforded Republican Governor George Allen an opportunity to make an interim appointment to the Court. Senate Republicans had insisted on naming a "known Republican"[2] and used their newly won parity status with Senate Democrats to block any nominee not to their liking. On May 2, 1997, approximately 10 weeks after the Assembly adjourned, Governor Allen appointed U.S. Magistrate Cynthia D. Kinser to the vacancy, making her only the second Republican on the Court and the first since 1988.

For Assembly Republicans, 1997 marked the first time they played a major role in the selection of a Supreme Court justice. More fundamentally, the case illustrates the partisan power changes that have occurred in the Assembly since Republicans gained parity with Democrats, first in the Senate in 1996 and then in the House of Delegates in 1998, forcing historic power sharing agreements between the parties in the respective chambers. It remains to be seen whether the old judicial selection process has been permanently displaced; for sure, party roles have changed, a noteworthy development in the nation's oldest legislature where traditions weigh heavily.

In this paper, the old Democrat-dominated judicial selection process, centered in the closed Democratic legislative caucuses, will be examined, as will the Republican induced changes that have occurred since 1996. As we shall see, power has become more diffused in the changed selection process, outcomes less predictable, and more prone to stalemate. The changes have also been accompanied by renewed calls for reforms to the selection process, posing an ironical test for Assembly Republicans—long term critics of the old process, yet seemingly poised to take over control of the Assembly and thus capable of reinstituting the old process under a Republican guise.

The Old Judicial Selection Process

The Formalities

The Virginia constitution, Article VI, Section 7, stipulates that the General Assembly shall elect the justices of the Supreme Court and the judges of the other courts of record, namely the Court of Appeals and the Circuit Courts. Successful judicial candidates must secure the votes of "a majority of the members elected to each house of the General Assembly. . . ," thus, an affirmative vote of 21 senators and 51 delegates is required. Additionally, the Assembly is authorized to prescribe the manner in which judges of courts not of record, principally General District Courts and Juvenile and Domestic Relations Courts, will be selected. Prior to the 1970s, such judges were usually appointed by the judge or judges of the Circuit Court District within which the vacancy occurred; since then, the General Assembly has reserved those selections to itself. Still, the Circuit Court judges retain a nominating role when vacancies occur in these judgeships within their circuits. By law they are required to nominate up to three candidates for such openings; however, the Assembly is not restricted itself to these lists of nominees when it elects District level judges (Morris and Sabato 1990, 269).

The Virginia judiciary had 386 authorized positions as of May 1, 1998; seven justices of the Supreme Court, 10 judges of the Court of Appeals, 147 judges for the Circuit Courts, 121 for the General District Courts, and 101 for the Juvenile and Domestic Relations Courts (Supreme Court of Virginia 1998). Supreme Court justices are elected for a 12-year term, Court of Appeals and Circuit Court judges for eight years, and the General District and Juvenile and Domestic Relations Court judges for six years.

Historically, Virginia has used the legislative election method for judicial selections, except for a 19-year period under the Constitution of 1851 when popular election was used (Howard 1974, 740). Only four states use a legislative selection process and Virginia is alone in selecting all full-time judges by this method (Council of State Governments 1996, 133–135).

Starting in the early 1970s, the Assembly, through its Courts of Justice Committees, began formally screening judicial candidates, including incumbent judges up for re-election, and certifying their eligibility for election (Morris 1976, 3). The Constitution, Article VI, Section 7, requires only that candidates for the Supreme Court, Court of Appeals, and the Circuit Courts be residents of the state and members of the state bar for at least five years prior to their selection. Additionally, Circuit Court judges must reside within the jurisdiction of their courts during their term of office. The Constitution leaves to the General Assembly the authority to determine qualifications for the General District Court and Juvenile and Domestic Relations judges and the Assembly has stipulated that such candidates must be members of the state bar at the time of their selection and reside within the jurisdiction of the courts on which they sit.[3]

Given the dearth of formal requirements, informal qualifications have proved more significant in affecting the makeup of the Virginia judiciary. Unfortunately, there is little research on the criteria legislators use in evaluating judicial candidates; however, some insights into the process can be discerned from the sorts of questions that the Courts of Justice Committees ask of judicial candidates as part of their certification process.[4] Candidates fill out a lengthy written questionnaire, asking them to provide confidential information on their personal background (e.g. age, place of birth, education, and marital status); the nature of their law practice, particularly court related, and if applicable, judicial experience; other possible business commitments and, if elected, what they intend to do about such commitments; bar association experiences, including any possible endorsements from such organizations; memberships in civic, social, and fraternal organizations and whether any might practice "invidious discrimination"; any civil, criminal, or professional-ethical problems they may have experienced; and the condition of their health. Additionally, the Committees solicit information from the Judicial Inquiry and Review Commission (the constitutional body that investigates possible judicial misconduct and disciplines judges) and the Virginia State Bar about possible complaints and proceedings involving the candidates. In summary, a review of the requested information by the Committees suggests an emphasis on discerning the nature of a candidate's legal experience and possible problems that might compromise the person's judicial capacity.

The Democratic Caucus

While judicial candidates were screened by the Courts of Justice Committees and then elected by a vote of the two houses, in practice judicial selections in a Democrat-dominated Assembly were decided in closed Democratic party caucuses. And in the caucuses, Democratic legislators usually deferred to the party members from the area in which the judge would sit. Former Delegate Richard R. G. Hobson (D-Alexandria) described how the system worked by urging his Democratic colleagues in a floor speech to respect "a principle that I learned when I first came down here. . . I won't mess with your judge and you don't mess with mine."[5] Openings on the Supreme Court and Court of Appeals, though less frequent, affected all the members, thus involving a broader array of forces within the caucuses, often pitting one region against the other in the support of candidates. For their part, judicial aspirants typically sought bar association endorsements and the support of prominent community figures, especially ones with Democratic party connections.

Once the House and Senate Democratic caucuses decided on their nominee, Democrats in the respective chambers were bound by party rules to vote for the caucus nominee on the floor, thus shutting Republicans out of the selection process.

Such disciplined party behavior was not typical for the Virginia General Assembly after the breakdown of the Byrd organization in the late 1960s, underscoring the importance Democratic legislators attached to judicial appointments—the most important Assembly-controlled patronage.

Before the 1971 Constitution went into effect, Assembly Democrats decided judicial selection in a combined caucus; since 1972, they have caucused separately (Howard 1974, 742). The separate caucusing practice parallels the new language in the 1971 Constitution which requires a candidate to receive the vote of a majority of the members elected to each house of the Assembly. This caucusing change enhanced the power of Senate Democrats, representing the smaller legislative body, but it also raised the possibility of a deadlock between House and Senate Democrats. For example, Democrats in the 1983 session couldn't agree on candidate for a Supreme Court vacancy, giving Governor Charles S. Robb an opportunity to appoint the first African-American, John Charles Thomas, to the Court.

Not surprisingly, the Virginia judiciary has had a decided Democratic Party orientation, including an identifiable contingent of former Democratic legislators and figures with close ties to them. For example, a 1995 *Richmond Times-Dispatch* series on judicial selections found a dozen former Democratic legislators serving as judges.[6] Such appointments often led Republicans and other critics to charge that the old selection process was prone to cronyism.[7]

Alternative Pathways

While the dominant role of the Democratic caucuses was the distinguishing feature of the old selection process, two variants need to be kept in mind for a fuller picture of the old process. One involved the governor's interim appointment role, a constitutional power long part of Virginia's constitutions and a reminder of the extensive appointment power Virginia governors enjoy. The other variant involved the practices of Fairfax county legislators over the last several decades in nominating candidates for judicial positions in their county. Though restricted to this county, it gave Republicans a say in judicial selections and would serve as a model for the judicial selection provision in the 1996 Senate power sharing agreement.

Article VI, Section 7, of the Constitution gives the governor the power to fill vacancies in the Supreme Court, the Court of Appeals, and the Circuit Courts that occur when the General Assembly is not in session, or because the Assembly couldn't agree on a candidate. Such vacancies on the courts not of record, the General District Courts and the Juvenile and Domestic Relations Courts, are filled by the Circuit Court judges having jurisdiction over the open position. Interim appointments, or "pro tempore" appointments as they are called, must be confirmed by the General Assembly in the next legislative session, regular or special, as the appointments expire 30 days after the commencement of that session.

Historically, the governor's interim appointment power has given the chief executive a major role in judicial selections. Indeed, Thomas R. Morris writes that "for 50 years prior to 1980, the original incumbency of all Supreme Court justices was determined by the governor, with the last such legislative rejection of an interim appointee being in 1901" (Morris and Sabato 1990, 270). He added that to a somewhat lesser extent, governors played a similar role for Circuit Court judges; for example, a 1975 survey of Virginia Circuit Court judges found slightly more than half had been appointed initially by the governor.

The General Assembly's part-time nature facilitated the governor's interim appointment role. Prior to the 1971 Constitution, which instituted annual sessions, the legislature met biennially and then only for 60 days. Of course, governors, knowing their interim appointments needed legislative confirmation in the next session, were not unmindful of legislative sentiment when exercising their appointment powers. In any case, the governor's interim selection role has become less prominent over the last several decades. For example, six of the ten justices who have gone onto the Supreme Court since 1980 were initially selected by the Assembly. Indeed for judges sitting on the Circuit Courts as of June 1998, at least 71% had been initially selected by the Assembly.[8]

Regardless of the frequency with which governors have exercised their interim appointment power, they have used this power to diversify the makeup of the Virginia judiciary, particularly that of the Supreme Court. Governor Linwood Holton, the first Republican governor in the twentieth-century, appointed in 1972 the first Republican to the Court, former Congressman Richard H. Poff. Fifteen years later, Governor Allen placed Cynthia Kinser, the second Republican, on the Court via an interim appointment. So, too, the black justices have taken this pathway to the Court; John Charles Thomas in 1983, a Robb appointee; and Leroy R. Hassell, appointed in 1989 by Governor Gerald Baliles to fill a seat vacated by Thomas' resignation. As of June 1998, the seven-person Supreme Court has three women and one African-American; surprising demographic diversity for a state not known for such patterns in its major political institutions. Two of the three women and the one black initially were selected as gubernatorial interim appointments. Overall, women and African-Americans constitute 17% and 11% respectively of the state's judgeships.[9]

In contrast to the high profile role the governor could play through the interim appointment process, Fairfax County legislators have developed since the mid 1970s a little noticed power-sharing practice for nominating candidates for judicial positions in the county.[10] Local bar associations would screen candidates and communicate their recommendations to the county's legislative delegation, though the legislators didn't restrict their consideration to the bar associations' recommendations. The legislators, Democrats and Republicans, would review applicant materials, interview candidates, and then by secret ballot decide who they would nominate for a position. Although the local deliberations were bipartisan, the ensuing judicial nominations still had to be routed through the Democratic caucuses; however, the caucuses always "honored" the Fairfax members' recommendations, according to Senator Joseph V. Gartlan (D-Fairfax). And, thus, more than two decades before power sharing would come to the Assembly, Fairfax County, the state's largest jurisdiction, had been developing a model for how such arrangements might work in judicial appointments.

The Process in Transition

The Senate Parties Strike a Deal

The Republican ascendancy to parity status doomed the old Democrat-dominated selection process, though not without a good deal of Democratic resistance. The Republican breakthrough occurred first in the Senate as a consequence of the 1995 elections. At first, Senate Democrats, despite having their ranks reduced to a 20–20 seat tie with Republicans, had planned on retaining control of the chamber by having the Democratic Lt. Governor Donald S. Beyer, Jr. cast tie-breaking votes on organizational matters. That plan was thwarted by maverick Democratic Senator Virgil Goode who threatened to vote with Republicans if power wasn't more equitably shared. After two days of organizational wrangling at the opening of the 1996 Assembly session, the two parties worked out a historic power sharing agreement which included a provision giving Republicans a role in judicial selections.

Senate rule 18c required first that the Courts of Justice Committee certify judicial candidates as "qualified for election" and then it specified that "Senators, all or part of whose Senate Districts are within the Circuit or District for which a judge is to be elected, shall *jointly nominate* a qualified person for said election" (emphasis added).[11] It then added that "if such senators are unable to agree on a nominee, any Senator may nominate a qualified person for such Circuit or District." The stipulation that all Senators, regardless of party, be involved in the nomination of candidates for judicial positions within their constituencies resembled the Fairfax model for judicial nominations, though the Fairfax arrangements also included House members of both

Figure 4.1 Virginia Supreme Court. Courtesy of The Supreme Court of Virginia.

parties and local bar associations in a non-partisan screening role. And while the new Senate rules in judicial selections clearly signaled the end of the dominant role of the Democratic caucus in that body, they were unclear on other matters. For example, left unsaid were nomination procedures for the Supreme Court and Court of Appeals, the courts at the pinnacle of the state's judiciary, with statewide jurisdictions affecting all the members.

In sharp contrast to the Senate, the Democrat-led House of Delegates continued to operate under the old judicial selection procedures in 1996 and 1997. The Democrats' comfortable majority status had eroded to a narrow, 52 to 47 to 1, margin in 1996; yet, if anything, the House Democratic leadership had become more adamant in protecting party prerogatives, including that of judicial selections. At the outset of the 1996 Assembly session, House Speaker Thomas W. Moss, Jr. (D-Norfolk) asserted: "What the Senate does is the Senate's business. . . . No, the Senate rules will have no effect on the way the House selects judges."[12] Thus, judicial candidates in 1996–97 had to negotiate a tricky bifurcated political process: win a Democratic majority in the House, namely in the Democratic caucus, and a bipartisan majority in the Senate— for a controversial nomination, a recipe for gridlock. Such was the case in 1997 when the Assembly was unable to fill the Supreme Court vacancy caused by the retirement of Justice Roscoe B. Stephenson, Jr. Ten candidates would be nominated in one or both houses for the position, with two gaining a majority vote in one house (on a straight party vote, Democratic candidate Margaret P. Spencer, an African-American Richmond General District Court judge, won a House majority; whereas Republican candidate Wiley F. Mitchell of Virginia Beach, a lawyer for Norfolk Southern Corporation and former state Senator, won a bipartisan Senate majority, when four Democrats broke ranks and supported his candidacy); however, neither candidate could win a majority in the other house.

The House Adopts Its Version of Power Sharing

Like the Senate in 1996, the House in 1998 had its opening days of the session dominated by an organizational struggle between the two parties. After the November 1997 elections and a series of special elections on the eve of the 1998 session, Republican strength had risen to 49 seats, and coupled with a Republican-leaning independent, gave the party for the first time parity with House Democrats. However, Republicans were unable to get three of their special election House victors certified and thus seated by the opening day of the session, allowing Democrats, over boisterous Republican protests, to ram through the re-election of Speaker Thomas W. Moss, Jr. The next day, Democratic leaders reversed course and struck a power sharing deal with Republicans. Unlike the 1996 Senate agreement, however, it contained no provision governing the election of judges.

The new found power of House Republicans in judicial selections and the problems posed by the absence of a House power sharing procedure in such situations were highlighted in a case involving Delegate Thelma Drake, a second term Republican from Norfolk. Drake, the only Republican representing Norfolk in the Assembly, blocked for six weeks a Norfolk Circuit Court nomination for Joseph A. Leafe, a former

Norfolk Mayor and Democratic House member, because the Norfolk Democratic delegation, which included the Speaker, had not consulted her about filling a newly created Juvenile and Domestic Relations judgeship for the city. "I don't have any personal problem with Joe Leafe," said Drake. "But I do think this is a new day. We have parity in the House of Delegates. We're sharing responsibility. We're in a whole new time, and things are different now. Republicans should have a voice."[13] Since judicial candidates need 51 votes in the House, a majority of the members elected to that body, either party could block the other's choices. Eventually, Drake was consulted, albeit informally, Leafe was elected, and the Juvenile and Domestic Relations judgeship filled. Still, the leverage wielded by a junior Republican highlighted the demise of the House Democratic Caucus, some two years after its Senate counterpart had experienced a similar fate.

Taking Stock

It remains to be seen how the judicial selection process will work with power sharing. Since the Senate has had only three sessions under these arrangements and the House one, any assessment will be preliminary in nature. Regardless, the changed selection process has drawn its share of critics. For example, Senator Bill Bolling (R-Hanover), writing soon after the Assembly's failure to fill the Supreme Court position in 1997, observed that "the Assembly's failure to fulfill its constitutional responsibility was a disappointment to all involved; more than that, it was perhaps the clearest indication we have to date that our current process for selecting judges in Virginia does not work."[14] He went on to note other lower court vacancies that went unfilled, declaring that the process would not earn a "passing grade in most Virginia classrooms, and it should not be acceptable in the Assembly either."

To assess such an indictment, it is helpful to look at the Assembly's judicial selection record before and since power sharing with respect to the type of court and action required of the Assembly. Accordingly, Table 4.1 depicts the Assembly's record for three sessions before and since power sharing for the four levels of the state court system, and for the four types of judicial actions facing the Assembly. Legislative elections may involve incumbent judges standing for re-election, interim (pro tempore) appointments requiring confirmation, or nominees seeking election to fill vacancies, or new judgeships added by the Assembly.

The General Assembly in any given session is faced with a large number of judicial elections, averaging 70 during the six sessions in question. As reflected inable 4.1, most involved judgeships at the Circuit and District Court levels, with sitting judges seeking re-election at all levels being the most prevalent selection situation facing the members, comprising 53% of all elections (221/420). Given the prominence of the interim appointment-confirmation process in an earlier period, it is striking how few interim–pro tempore confirmations occurred during the 1993–1998 period. Only 8% (33/420) of the elections involved this type of judicial selection. Since historically the Assembly has been reluctant to deny re-election to incumbent judges, and interim appointments were unlikely to be made that couldn't secure legislative confirmation, legislative attention tends to focus on the open judgeships, involving elections to vacancies and newly created positions.

Whatever the faults of the old Democrat-dominated, caucus-based selection process, it wasn't inefficient. As depicted in Table 4.1 for the 1993–95 sessions, the Assembly completed action on all incumbent judges seeking re-election and interim appointees requiring confirmation, as well as filling 95% (92 of 97) of the vacancies

Table 4.1 Virginia General Assembly's Judicial Selection Record: Pre-Power Sharing, 1993–1995 Sessions & Power Sharing, 1996–1998 Sessions

Type of Selection

Level Of Court	Re-Electing Incumbent Justices & Judges		Confirming Interim (Pro Tempore) Appointments		Filling Vacancies		Filling New Positions	
	93–95	96–98	93–95	96–98	93–95	96–98	93–95	96–98
Supreme Court	1/1	—	—	1/1	1/1	0/1	NA	NA
Court of Appeals	—	—	—	1/1	2/2	1/1	—	—
Circuit Courts	46/46	30/31	—	8/8	27/27	14/18	6/6	4/4
District Courts:								
General District	25/25	59/60	2/2	5/5	25/27	15/18	5/5	2/2
Juvenile & Domestic Relations	22/22	34/36	7/7	9/10	15/16	8/16	11/13	4/8
Totals	94/94	123/127	9/9	24/25	70/73	38/54	22/24	10/14

Sources: Journal of the Senate & House of Delegates of Virginia, 1993–1997; Judges & Their Terms, *State of the Judiciary*, Virginia Supreme Court, 1993–1998 (the latter year is forthcoming); and Division of Legislative Services, Virginia General Assembly.

and new positions. This occurred in a legislature operating under one of the shortest annual legislative schedules in the country, and while the Assembly overall was struggling to cope with a growing legislative workload.

Since power sharing, the Assembly still evidences a high overall batting average in processing judicial selections; however, the process also has become more contentious, less predictable, and more prone to stalemate.

The re-election of incumbent judges has become less automatic; one judge at least has been forced off the bench in each of the last three sessions. In 1997, for example, Republicans blocked the re-election of two judges: James F. Berry, a Clarke County Circuit Court judge, and David B. Summerfield, a Scott County Juvenile and Domestic Relations judge. The former was best known for denying Oliver North in 1994 a concealed-weapon permit while North was the Republican candidate for the U.S. Senate. Summerfield won a temporary reprieve after the 1997 session when his Circuit Court judges re-appointed him on an interim basis, only to be denied re-election again in the 1998 session. The re-election of incumbent judges may provide Republicans with added leverage in the selection process, since nearly all judges coming up for re-election in the near future were elected to the judiciary under the old Democrat-controlled process.

Selection problems were most evident in filling open seats, with the Assembly's inability to fill the Supreme Court position in 1997 being the most visible indication of the stalemate potential inherent in the power sharing arrangements. As reflected in Table 4.1, during the 1996–1998 sessions, the Assembly failed to fill 29% of the vacancies and new positions. Fifteen of the twenty unfilled positions occurred at the District Court level, with the Juvenile and Domestic Relations judgeships being most prone to this outcome.

To be sure, the Assembly's judicial selection process has had its problems in the new power sharing era. This has been most evident in filling openings associated with vacancies and newly created positions, and in the House of Delegates, with its failure to formalize judicial selection power sharing arrangements. To the extent the Assembly leaves positions to be filled by the Governor or Circuit Court judges then it has defaulted on its constitutional responsibilities. Yet the problems associated with power sharing also reflect the realities of accommodating a larger set of forces in the selection process. And for both parties, power sharing has been a novel governing arrangement; indeed, the Virginia General Assembly in 1998 is the only state legislature with both chambers operating under power sharing arrangements. Fortunately, when positions go unfilled the Constitution does provide for a back up appointment process, though when such situations are the result of partisan stalemates it doesn't reflect well on the Assembly.

Conclusion

Steeped in a rich, historical tradition, Virginia's brand of state government and politics has always had its distinctive features, and the judicial selection process is a case in point. The formal selection procedures—legislative election of all full-time judges—have long set Virginia apart from other states. That distinctiveness was heightened by a political process which allowed the Democrats, operating through their closed legislative caucuses, to largely monopolize judicial selections, long after Republicans had become a force in other arenas of state government.

While the formal judicial selection procedures are still intact, the Republican emergence to parity status in the General Assembly has ended the dominant role of the Democratic caucuses in those selections, laying to rest, at the state level, the last vestige of the old Democratic one-party system. Currently, both chambers of the Assembly are operating under power sharing agreements between the parties and struggling to make the judicial selection process work. As power has become more diffused in the selection process, outcomes are less predictable and are more prone to stalemate.

The changes have also been accompanied by renewed calls for reforming the selection process, with judicial nominations commissions leading the reform agenda. The nonpartisan commissions, made up of lawyers and lay persons, would screen judicial candidates and recommend lists of qualified candidates to the Assembly, or, in the case of interim vacancies, to the governor or circuit court judge(s). By potentially circumscribing the parties' role in the nomination of judicial candidates, such reforms pose an ironical test for Republicans, long time critics of the old judicial selection practices. The Party is just beginning to share in the selection of judges and perhaps is poised electorally to take control of the Assembly and thus be capable of instituting its own version of the old judicial selection process. In any case, since 1996, it has not been politics as usual in the selection of Virginia's judges. Nor seemingly will it be so in the foreseeable future, whether the Assembly continues to operate under power sharing arrangements, the Republicans institute their version of the judicial selection process, or both parties are required to share control with some other entity such as the judicial nominations commissions.

Bibliography

Council of State Governments. 1996. *The Book of the States, 1996–97 Edition.* Lexington, KY: Council of State Governments.

Howard, A.E. Dick. 1974. *Commentaries on the Constitution of Virginia,* Vol. II. Charlottesville: The University Press of Virginia.

Morris, Thomas R. 1976. "The Virginia Judiciary, 1776–1976." *The University of Virginia Newsletter* 53(1).

Morris, Thomas R. and Larry J. Sabato. 1990. *Virginia Government & Politics: Readings and Comments,* 3rd revised edition. Charlottesville: University of Virginian and Virginia Chamber of Commerce.

Supreme Court of Virginia. 1998. "Judges & Their Terms." In *State of the Judiciary.* Richmond: Supreme Court of Virginia.

Endnotes

1. According to the General Assembly's rules, a "legislative day" does not end until both houses adjourn. Thus, legislators can extend the legislative day by simply recessing instead of adjourning.
2. *Richmond Times-Dispatch,* February 19, 1997, p. A6.
3. Section 16.1-69.15-16, Code of Virginia.
4. For questionnaires, see Division of Legislative Services, Virginia General Assembly.
5. *Richmond Times-Dispatch,* January 15, 1995, p. A16.

6. *Richmond Times-Dispatch,* January 15, 1995, p. A1.

7. Ibid. For example, then-Governor George Allen, a former Republican delegate, characterized the process as "a purely political crony approach."

8. Journal of the Senate and House of Delegates of Virginia, 1969–1997, and data received from the Virginia Supreme Court. On 14 of the 146 sitting Circuit Court judges, it wasn't clear from the journals how the judges were selected.

9. Data from the Virginia Supreme Court.

10. This paragraph is based on an August 5, 1998 telephone interview with Senator Joseph V. Gartlan, Jr. (D-Fairfax), Co-Chairman of the Fairfax delegation, Chair of the Senate Courts of Justice Committee, and a 27-year member of the state Senate. According to Senator Gartlan, the Fairfax process has been aided by the fact that the Fairfax judicial circuit falls within one jurisdiction. In addition, it involves one set of bar associations, most notably, the Fairfax Bar Association, which is the state's largest local bar association and has an active and non-partisan membership. See, also, "How Judges Are Selected in Fairfax," The *Washington Post,* March 18, 1996, p. A16.

11. Manual of the Senate, General Assembly of Virginia, 1996–1997, pp. 102–103.

12. *The Virginian-Pilot,* January 15, 1996, p. A1.

13. *The Virginian-Pilot,* January 31, 1998, p. A1, and see also March 6, 1998, p. B1.

14. *Richmond Times-Dispatch,* February 26, 1997, p. A13; for a rebuttal by Senator Gartlan, see March 26, 1997, p. A18.

CHAPTER FIVE

Virginia Bureaucracy: The Corporate Model Applied to Government Administration

B. Douglas Skelley
James Madison University

Virginians, like most Americans, tend to think of the governor or the legislature when they consider their state government. Most of their encounters with state government occur, however, in consuming state services and responding to the demands of state agencies. In other words, the feature of state government Virginians deal with most is its bureaucracy. The Department of Motor Vehicles, the Virginia State Police, ABC stores, and James Madison University, are examples of the varied nature of state bureaucratic agencies. Some serve regulatory functions, some provide services, some deliver products, and some do all three.

Political scientists often call a state's bureaucracy the "fourth branch" of government despite the fact that most agencies are actually a part of the executive branch. Although created by the legislative branch and subordinate to the "real" branches of government, the bureaucracy gets this label because it often behaves as an institution unto itself, enjoying power, influence, and governmental discretion. The role that bureaucracies play in states today confers this governmental significance. Laws are meaningless if they cannot be implemented and enforced. State bureaucracy takes the laws, and often court decisions, and brings together people, money, and technology in an organized way to provide the services, goods, or regulations the laws require. Bureaucrats must have the resources, expertise, and the discretion to make the intent of the law a reality.

In order to apply and adapt laws to the "real world," bureaucratic agencies make decisions and rules about how the laws can be applied in practical situations. Administrators' training, experience, and professionalism produce bureaucratic expertise. State agencies not only apply the law, but other branches of government, when addressing public problems, often rely on them for expert advice. As a result, bureaucracies have considerable influence over public policies proposed by their apparent masters, the governor and state legislators. Bureaucratic activity reflects the political support of politicians, clients, and other indirect constituents of government programs. Administrative discretion allows agencies to reward and please some in society while denying and displeasing others. Bureaucratic activity reflects the political power of government agencies and generates significant political feedback, which the governor and the legislature may have to address.

In this chapter the "fourth branch" of Virginia government will be examined in terms of (1) its organizing principle: What principle has guided Virginia state organization? (2) structure and scope: How elaborate is its organizational structure and what quantity of resources do its activities require? (3) the regulation of its fiscal and human resources: How are fiscal and human resources acquired and allocated?

Organizing Principle

When Harry F. Byrd ran for governor in 1925, he envisioned state government as a commercial enterprise and promised to reorganize and run state government like a "great business corporation" (Lipson, as quoted in Morris and Whelan 1990, 220). In truth, the foundation of a *corporate model* for Virginia state government had already been established in the 1918 Budget Act which made the governor chiefly responsible for the budget. The introduction of the short ballot in 1928, a reform supported by Governor Harry F. Byrd and his Reed Commission, made the governor one of only three state-wide elected officials along with the Lieutenant Governor and the Attorney General (Leighty and Zoller 1994, 3). As a result the Virginia governor has not had

Image 5.1 Seal of the Commonwealth. Courtesy of
The Library of Virginia.

to share administrative power with other elected officials, as in some states; rather the Virginia governor establishes control over most of the state apparatus by appointing all heads of state departments, commissions, agencies, and institutions (Morris and Whelan 1990, 219). Governor Byrd also succeeded in further strengthening the power of the state's "chief executive officer" by gaining the abolition of some state boards and commissions and the consolidation of others into twelve departments (Morris and Whelan 1990, 221).

Consequently the Virginia governor operates more like a corporate CEO than a representative of the public. Constitutionally denied the opportunity to serve successive terms, the governor's power expands because public responsiveness cannot be rewarded. Since bureaucratic professionals represent the only sustainable expertise in the executive branch, agency influence over policy directives remains a powerful force. Governors, legislators, and reform commissions have sustained and elaborated this corporate model in the commonwealth's government.

All state bureaucracies tend to grow and divide as governors and legislators seek to satisfy diverse constituency demands. Further pressure for agency expansion arises as state administrators rationalize requests for new resources to address problems of organization, policy, and greater responsibility. Repeatedly during this century governors and legislators have taken reorganizing initiatives, some with effect, all aimed at creating more business-like coordination and efficiency. The 1942 Personnel Act, an example of this trend, enhanced the governor's powers by giving that office control over the classification and pay of state employees through the Department of Personnel and Training (Morris and Sabato 1990, 217).

The creation of a governor's cabinet in 1972 moved Virginia government even closer to the corporate ideal and left the most remarkable imprint on the state's bureaucratic structure since the Byrd reforms. A typical line-staff organizational concept was borrowed from the business world "to alleviate bottlenecks in the state's administrative structure and to develop a straight-forward reporting relationship with the governor" through "appointed executives, accountable for large functional units" (Leighty and Zoller 1994, 5–6). Executive branch agencies were organized into functional secretariats that are under the direction of a cabinet member who reports directly to the governor or the governor's chief of staff. As with the U.S. President's cabinet, the importance of the cabinet as an organ of communication, coordination, policy-making, and control depends on each governor's desire to rely on this structure.

Structure and Scope

Organizational Features

All three branches of government have bureaucratic elements, and there are a few organizations placed outside the three branches and labeled "independent" agencies or commissions.[1] By far, most of the state bureaucracy lies under the authority of the governor and is organized into eight secretariats. (Governor Gilmore is proposing an additional Secretariat of Technology.)

The twelve agencies of the Secretariat of Administration assist the governor in the managing state-owned property, human resources, and health benefits. They also investigate human rights complaints, allocate state funds to local constitutional officers, supervise elections, oversee charitable gaming, and assist veterans seeking federal benefits. Some of these agencies also provide other state agencies with laboratory, information technology, and telecommunications services.

The Secretariat of Commerce and Trade monitors and promotes the economic wellbeing of the state through its fifteen agencies. Some of these provide grants and loans for housing, businesses, and economic planning activities, while others regulate to insure the quality of products and services as well as safety and fairness in the workplace. The Secretariat of Education bears the responsibility for setting standards and providing financial support for local public schools, community colleges, and state-assisted colleges and universities. This secretariat directs cultural agencies, including the Library of Virginia and the Virginia Museum of Fine Arts, while underwriting many local cultural activities through the Virginia Commission for the Arts. Twenty-five agencies ranging from the Department of Education to Gunston Hall fall under this administrative umbrella.

The Secretariat of Finance has the smallest number of units, five, but these include agencies that are central to the governor's management of the bureaucracy such as the Department of Planning and Budget. This secretariat includes agencies that forecast and collect revenues (taxes), manage state funds and investments, sell bonds, hold internal audits, direct state planning as well as plan and execute the governor's budget.

The activities of the twelve agencies of the Secretariat of Health and Human Resources address the medical needs of the poor and other populations with special needs such as the physically handicapped and the mentally ill. In addition the secretariat oversees social services activities, which include various forms of assistance to financially needy populations.

The Secretariat of Natural Resources oversees eight agencies that protect the environment, regulate hunting and fishing, maintain state parks, and preserve historic sites.

Fire protection, law enforcement, corrections, and criminal justice services are provided by the eleven agencies of the Secretariat of Public Safety.

The Secretariat of Transportation is most directly associated with the building of roads by its Department of Transportation. In addition its four other agencies provide commuter rail, port services for oceangoing vessels, regulation of rail and air transportation as well as the sale and operation of automobiles and trucks.

The general assembly has created its own bureaucracy consisting of staffs that perform auditing, legislative support, and technological functions. In addition, a variety of specialized commissions advise the general assembly on policy and program matters. Two notable elements of this sixteen-agency bureaucracy are the Auditor of Public Accounts (APA) and the Joint Legislative Audit and Review Commission (JLARC). The APA reviews financial management activities of the executive and judicial branches and assists the general assembly in making sure that money is spent according to statutory mandate. This office also audits the financial affairs of local governments.

The APA is one of the vital "checks and balances" instruments employed by the legislative branch to oversee the other branches of state government. The APA actually reports through JLARC, which has a broader "checking" mandate. Besides financial management review, JLARC reviews, on an ongoing basis, the performance of state agencies and conducts special studies as directed by the general assembly. JLARC issues many reports for the benefit of legislators as well as the public (Virginia Auditor of Public Accounts 1998; Virginia Joint Audit and Legislative Review Commission 1998a).

The bureaucracy of the judicial branch consists of agencies that provide administrative support for the state court system as well as the staffs of several commissions, which aid and advise the court system regarding management, procedures, and policy. The state constitution charges the Chief Justice of the Supreme Court of Virginia with supervising the administration of the entire court system of the Commonwealth. The chief justice's responsibilities include presiding over various committees charged with improving the administration of justice. The Executive Secretary of the Supreme Court is an administrator who aids in carrying out the duties of the Chief Justice. Among other activities, the Executive Secretary prepares the budget for the judicial branch, manages the finances of the system, and gathers statistics on the operations of the courts for reporting and policy purposes (Virginia's Judicial System 1998).

Legislatures create independent agencies and commissions in order to de-politicize, or appear to de-politicize, a policy area or governmental activity. Independent agencies or commissions might also be established because an activity is of a highly specialized nature that doesn't appear to fit into any one of the three branches of government. By reducing the direct influence of the general assembly and the governor, the agencies in this category are thought to carry out their duties more objectively or in a more business-like manner. The seven independent agencies are a mixed lot. They range from the regulatory State Corporation Commission with its quasi-legislative and quasi-judicial functions to the financial activities of the Virginia Higher Education Tuition Trust Fund to the business management of the Chesapeake Bay Bridge and Tunnel Commission.

Fiscal and Human Resources

An inspection of the budget for the 1999–2000 biennium (Virginia Department of Planning and Budgeting 1998b, 1998c) indicates the scope of the operations of the major subdivisions of state government. Since most of the bureaucracy of the state lies in the executive branch under the governor's direction, it isn't surprising that most of the resources of the state will be consumed by the agencies of the eight secretariats. In the current biennium, the Secretariat of Education will dispose of more resources than any other major division of government. Education will expend nearly $8 billion per year and support the activities of some 43,600 college professors, schoolteachers, staff, and administrators. The Secretariat of Public Safety, which has grown rapidly in recent years with the implementation of new anti-crime policies, will employ some 25,000 people and use about $1.5 billion. Another major consumer of resources is Health and Human Services, which is expected to spend a yearly sum of almost $5 billion and employ 17,000 people. Fourth in spending and personnel will be the Secretariat of Transportation, which will dispose of $2.6 billion through the activities of 12,268 individuals. The executive offices of the executive branch—the offices of the governor, lieutenant governor, attorney general, etc.—will account for some $23 million dollars of expenditures and hire the services of some 335 employees. In total, the executive branch will employ approximately 100,000 people and spend about $18.5 billion in each year of the 1999–2000 biennium.

Outside of the executive branch the independent agencies together hire more people and spend more money than the legislature or the judiciary. Of the $150 million dollars independent agencies will spend in each year of the biennium, the State Corporation Commission will benefit from about $56 million and the state Lottery Department about $69 million. The Medical College of Virginia Hospitals Authority receives approximately 3,700 of the 4,940 positions in this category of agencies, while the State Corporation Commission and the Lottery Department account for most of the rest.

The operation of the judicial branch is expected to require nearly $223 million and 2,650 positions per year in the 1999–2000 biennium. The combined activities of the local District Courts—Combined, General, Juvenile and Domestic Relations—account for the largest share of these resources, $104.7 million and 1,592 employees. The Circuit Courts command the next largest sum, $60.5 million, supporting judicial activities employing some 150 people. It is interesting to observe that more money is spent by the Public Defenders Commission ($15.1 million) on the defense of indigent criminals than on the operation of the Virginia Supreme Court and the administration of the court system in general ($11.4 million). The former employs more than twice (272) the personnel of the highest court (109).

The smallest share of state resources goes to the organizations of the legislative branch. By far the support structure of the general assembly requires the most fiscal and human resources in this category, $21 million and 213 staff personnel. These numbers do not include the people and funds of the Division of Legislative Services, which are $3.9 million and 54 positions. Not only is it relatively cheap to make the laws, but it is also relatively inexpensive to monitor the expenditure of public funds and assess the prospects and performance of public policy. The Auditor of Public Accounts operates with $9.4 million per year employing 180 in staff, whereas JLARC costs $2.8 million and retains about 35 people.

Management of Fiscal and Human Resources

Revenues, Budgets and Budgeting

Nothing holds greater administrative significance than a government's budget. Nothing, moreover, repeatedly commands more political attention of the legislature. A budget is many things. It isn't just a spending plan. A budget serves as a planning tool, a management tool, a device for prioritizing state spending in accord with the values of the government's leadership and its constituencies. For a state bureaucracy, the budget determines how well agencies can implement legislation, how many and whom it can afford to hire, how important the policies are its programs seek to effect, and how successful its leadership is in dealing with both politicians and constituents. Proposing an agency budget and having the legislature sustain it through allocations demands skillful performance by both bureaucrats as well as politicians. There is no greater example of the politics of the administrative process than that of budgeting.

Where does the money come from that the state allocates in a budget? State monies are classified into two categories: the non-general fund and the general fund. The distinction here lies between revenue that is collected for some specific purpose defined by the law and tax monies collected for general purposes. Slightly more than half the financial resources of the state are non-general funds, consisting mostly of federal grants, institutional revenue such as tuition and fees paid by students, and transportation taxes such as fuel taxes and vehicle license fees. General fund revenues come from sources such as the state income tax, corporate income tax, sales tax, insurance premium tax, and the public service gross receipts tax. In the budget process, the governor and the general assembly exercise the most discretion over the general fund (Virginia Department of Planning and Budgeting 1997a).

What kind of budget process does Virginia employ? Like the federal government and most other state governments, Virginia uses an "executive budget" process—to be distinguished from a legislative budget process. Before 1918, state agencies reported their budget requests directly to the appropriations committees of the general assembly. The governor, the nominal head of the administrative apparatus of the state, had no specific role to play in the process until its end when he approved or vetoed the appropriation legislation. Turn-of-the-century reformers posed the question: How can the governor be held responsible for government operations while playing so minor a role in determining the resources needed for them? They touted the executive budget as the answer to this question. The executive budget stands as one of this century's important administrative innovations. Virginia government adopted this budgetary innovation in 1918, earlier than most states. The executive budget places in the hands of the governor, the responsibility to coordinate, formulate, and propose the state's budget.

In governments with executive budgets, there are generally three phases of budgetary activity: the executive preparation phase, the legislative allocation phase, and the budget execution, or administration, phase. The bureaucracy plays a significant role in all of these, but it is especially involved in the preparation and administrative phases. In even numbered years the Virginia governor prepares a two-year, or biennial, budget with the assistance of the Department of Planning and Budget (DPB), today an agency with more than sixty staff members (Virginia Department of Planning and Budgeting 1998a). State agencies receive guidance from the governor on the administration's priorities and spending targets. A strategic planning process in each agency assesses its programs and needs. Based on this assessment, each agency generates a budget proposal that it submits to the DPB in the late summer or early fall.

The economic recession of the early nineties brought renewed pressure on governments to demonstrate greater efficiency and effectiveness. As a result, the budging process within the executive branch underwent considerable revision under the Allen administration. Traditionally governments have relied heavily on budgetary line items and object-of-expenditure budgets to control inputs into government agencies. While controlling fiscal inputs, these approaches do nothing to connect an agency's resources to the programmatic activities it is mandated to carry out. A performance budget, in contrast, focuses on the activities performed by an agency and allows the budgeter to connect what monies an agency receives with the services it is to deliver. In other words, a measurement of the costs of units of service can be made with a performance budget.

The Allen administration sought, in the style of reinventing government, to integrate the state's earlier efforts at strategic planning and performance measurement into the budget process (Virginia Department of Planning and Budget 1997b). The anticipated results of these changes include accurately assessed future needs, accurately budgeted program objectives, and accountability for the efficient achievement of measurable objectives. In keeping with contemporary public management ideas, agencies are to see both their internal and external clients as "customers," and customer expectations are expected to guide their strategic planning.

Before submitting a budget request, Virginia executive agencies must conduct an issues assessment to determine their strengths, weaknesses, opportunities, and threats (SWOT)? To identify the critical issues faced in the upcoming budget period, an agency surveys customers' expectations. The governor's policy office, the cabinet secretary's office, and the DPB, each receive an agency's assessment and works with the agency to develop goals, objectives, and strategies that are intended to reflect the governor's policy positions and the needs of the customers of the agency. The agency ultimately submits an activity-based budget that offers packages of service levels and measures of anticipated agency performance. The measures provide a basis for tracking agency performance, which become available to the public each December with the governor's budget document.

During the fall of the budget year, it is DPB's job to review each agency's budget proposal for accuracy, need, funding alternatives, and policy conformity. During the late fall the governor and the cabinet secretaries, supported by DPB and the secretaries' staffs, put together a budget that reflects the governor's priorities. This is the essence of the executive budget process: it is the chief executive's priorities that are presented in the budget, not an individual agency's or the legislature's. The governor submits the proposed budget to the general assembly on or before December 20 in the form of a bill (a proposed law) along with documents providing rationales for the proposed expenditure.

Virginia maintains the tradition of a short, winter legislative session. The budget-year session is a little longer because of the demands of the budget process. The general assembly convenes on the first Wednesday of January, and the governor's proposed budget bill is introduced to both houses, finding its way to the House Appropriations Committee and the Senate Finance Committee. The governor's bill may be amended by these committees or by their respective chambers, once the bill is returned to their floors for debate. Ultimately the two houses of the general assembly, represented in a conference committee meeting, will arrive at a common version of the amended bill. After final approval by both houses, the amended bill returns to the governor for signature.

The Virginia governor has four options regarding the returned appropriations bill: (1) sign it into law, (2) veto the whole bill, (3) veto certain items in the bill, or (4) recommend more amendments. If the governor takes any of these options other than signing the bill into law, the general assembly is reconvened in the spring for a special budget session to consider the governor's actions and to resolve them. The budget that is ultimately passed into law goes into effect on July 1 of the even numbered year. Because planning expenditures for a two-year period is difficult, it is common for budget amendments to be introduced in the legislature during the following session of the odd numbered year.

The budget execution phase involves monitoring the spending behavior of state agencies. Agencies are not permitted to spend their funds whenever they please; rather, portions of their allocations are released periodically. Agencies also must spend their funds as prescribed by law. Accountants in every agency, the DPB, and the General Assembly's Auditor of Public Accounts office are responsible for seeing to it that resources are used appropriately and legally.

Employees, Classification, and Compensation

Government is a "service industry"; therefore, it tends to be labor intensive. More than 100,000 Virginians are employed by the state. They represent a broad range of jobs and professions. If any organization is to function well it must hire people with the knowledge, skills, and abilities to do the tasks required by its mission. Turn of the century reformers believed that "good" government required personnel systems that greatly limited unwarranted and corrupting political influences on administrative employees. Throughout the twentieth century, state personnel systems have evolved toward principles of merit hiring, job security and, to varying degrees, political neutrality.

In Virginia, the Personnel Act of 1942 placed the classification and compensation of employees under the control of the governor (Morris and Sabato 1990). Virginia does not employ the independent, civil service commission model promoted by reformers at the beginning of the century. Rather, the staff personnel office model provides the basis for personnel administration in the state. The director of personnel and training is appointed by the governor, and the Department of Personnel and Training (DPT), an executive branch entity, supervises and assists government agencies with human resource practices. In truth, the Virginia practice was ahead of its time in that modern management theory has become increasingly critical of the inflexibility of managing human resources through independent civil service commissions. As with fiscal resources, the question of responsibility was raised: Should not the chief executive, who bears responsibility for executive branch performance, be able to hire, fire, and assign human resources for efficiency and effectiveness, something independent commissions don't allow? Although personnel authority is centralized in the governor, in application Virginia's personnel system is a very decentralized one with agencies establishing their own employment practices under general policies and regulations promulgated by the DPT.

Virginia government identifies three categories of public employees: covered, excepted, and wage employees (Virginia Department of Personnel and Training n.d./1998). At a state university a "covered employee" might be a "classified," full-time air conditioning and heating repair person, a warehouse supervisor, or department secretary. The professors at a university would be "excepted employees," whose terms of employment have been established by the university and stated in a contract. An employee in the university's dining hall might be a "wage employee," who is essentially a part-time employee working no more than 1,500 hours in any 365-day period.

Covered positions are the ones that we think of as "typical" government jobs. These positions have specific job descriptions that dictate certain qualifications jobholders must meet. Each of these positions is placed in one of twenty-three grades in a compensation schedule (Virginia Department of Personnel and Training 1997). Each grade has twenty-one steps, which span the smallest and greatest salaries a classified employee can be paid in a job in that grade. As of November 1997 a job in grade one, with compensation at step one paid $11,932, the equivalent of minimum wage. The maximum pay in the schedule, grade 23 at step 21, is $132,262, about eleven times that of the lowest pay. Covered employees must go though a probationary period of six months before becoming a "continuing" employee with full rights as a state employee under the law.

Public employee unions have not found Virginia's political culture hospitable. In a right-to-work state, it is not surprising that public employees are not effectively organized. Although state employees in Virginia can organize, there is little incentive to do so because under Virginia law employees cannot bargain collectively or "meet and confer" with agency management for wages or working conditions. During the Allen administration, for example, corrections officers organized their first successful union in Virginia (American Federation of State, County, and Municipal Employees 1996). The activities of their Virginia Alliance of State Employees (VASE), associated with the American Federation of State, County and Municipal Employees, illustrates the kinds of actions public employee unions must resort to without the right to bargain. Recently VASE used "Corrections Officers Appreciation Day," established by the legislature, as an opportunity to gain the attention of legislators and the public regarding their concerns. Pursuing legislators' votes on issues that directly and indirectly affect members becomes the focus of public union action, not bargaining for a contract.

Extending the Corporate Model

The recent tenure of Governor Allen witnessed efforts to reform Virginia government in many ways including its bureaucracy (Atkinson 1996). Allen's first executive order in January 1994 was to create the Governor's Commission on Government Reform, better known as the Blue Ribbon Strike Force. The commission, dominated by conservative business and political appointees, generated more than 400 recommendations that questioned what government should be doing as well as how government goes about its business. Although many of the recommendations were not implemented, the Allen administration made changes in the planning and budget process, as described above, and sought to reduce the state workforce through terminations, early retirement programs, and attrition while putting a freeze on hiring. Governor Allen managed to reduce the number of career employees by about 9,000 (Atkinson 1996, 2). Governor Gilmore, installed in office in January 1998, now seeks to overcome a decline in morale among state employees by initiating a "reaching out to state employees" program. This is an effort aimed at getting lower level employees involved in productivity improvement (Virginia Governor Jim Gilmore 1998).

The Allen administration's reforms reflected a mix of current business ideas, such as "rightsizing" the workforce, widening supervisors' span of control, and flattening organizational hierarchies, as well as current "reinventing government" notions, including labeling citizens as "customers" and privatizing some services and activities. These changes complement, rather than detract, from the organizational culture of Virginia government. Their conservatism and business origins provide a further elaboration of the corporate model of government administration as it evolves in Virginia and strengthens the governor as the central administrative actor in the state. Governor Gilmore, also a conservative Republican, can be expected to sustain and extend many of the Allen administration's initiatives, but in a more incremental way. The return of economic good times in the second half of this decade of the nineties has reduced the pressure for radical changes in Virginia bureaucracy.

Bibliography

American Federation of State, County, and Municipal Employees 1996. *Co. Appreciation Day Success in Virginia* [WWW Document]. URL http://www.igc.org/afscme/press/acu29603.htm

Atkinson, Frank B. 1996. "George Allen's 1,000 Days Have Changed Virginia" *University of Virginia News Letter* 72 (September).

Leighty, W. H. and T. D. Zoller. 1994. "Virginia's Reorganization Experience: Lessons from the Past for the Future" *University of Virginia News Letter* 70 (March).

Morris, T. R. and L. J. Sabato 1990. *Virginia Government and Politics: Readings and Comments,* 3rd Revised Ed. Charlottesville: University of Virginia and Virginia Chamber of Commerce.

Morris, T. R. and J. T. Whelan 1990. "Gubernatorial Management of State Government in Virginia." In T. R. Morris and L. J. Sabato, eds., *Virginia Government and Politics: Readings and Comments,* 3rd. Revised Ed. Charlottesville: University of Virginia and Virginia Chamber of Commerce.

Virginia Auditor of Public Accounts 1998. *About APA* [WWW document]. URL http://legis.state.va.us/apa/aapage.htm

Virginia Department of Planning and Budgeting 1997a. *Frequently Asked Questions About Virginia's Budget* [WWW document]. URL http://www.state.va.us/dpb/budget/faq.htm

Virginia Department of Planning and Budgeting 1997b. *Virginia's Performance Budgeting Process* [WWW document].
URL http://www.state.va.us/dpb/pm/aboutpm.htm

Virginia Department of Planning and Budgeting 1998a. *About DPB* [WWW document]. URL http://www.state.va.us/dpb/about/aboutdpb.htm

Virginia Department of Planning and Budgeting 1998b. *Governor Gilmore's Executive Amendments to the Introduced 1998–2000 Budget* [WWW document].
URL http://www.state.va.us/dpb/budget/execamnd.htm

Virginia Department of Planning and Budgeting 1998c. *Introduced 1998–2000 Budget* [WWW document]. URL http://www.state.va.us/dpb/budget/proposed.htm

Virginia Department of Personnel and Training 1997. *Schedule of Standard Rates of Pay* [WWW document].
URL http://www.cns.state.va.us/dpt/services/compens/schedule.htm

Virginia Department of Personnel and Training n.d./1998. *Human Resource Policy* [WWW document]. URL http://www.cns.state.va.us/dpt/

Virginia Governor Jim Gilmore 1998. *The First 100 Days: Preparing Virginia for the 21st Century* [WWW document].
URL http://www.state.va.us/governor/100days.htm

Virginia Joint Audit and Legislative Review Commission 1998a. *General Authority* [WWW document]. URL http://jlarc.state.va.us/

Virginia Joint Audit and Legislative Review Commission 1998b. *JLARC Goals and Objectives* [WWW document]. URL http://jlarc.state.va.us/

Virginia's Judicial System 1998. *The Supreme Court of Virginia* [WWW document].
URL http://www.courts.state.va.us/scov/scov.htm

Endnotes

1. A copy of the Organizational Chart of Virginia State Government is available free from the Office of the Secretary of the Commonwealth, P.O. Box 2454, Richmond, VA 23218. It also can be found at the Secretary of the Commonwealth homepage, http://www.soc.state.va.us/stateg.htm.

SECTION TWO:

Instruments of Political Power

CHAPTER SIX

Budgeting in Virginia: Power, Politics, and Policy

John T. Whelan and Daniel J. Palazzolo
University of Richmond

As he stood before a packed house at the Richmond Marriot hotel on election night, November 4, 1997, Republican Governor-elect Jim Gilmore confidently predicted: "We will, in this administration, immediately move to eliminate the personal property tax on cars and trucks." Echoing a populist tone that defined his campaign, Gilmore summoned legislators to carry out the people's will: "The General Assembly of this state has a responsibility to eliminate this car tax and respond to the people of Virginia."[1] A few months later, as Gilmore struggled to push his campaign pledge through the General Assembly, he again resorted to a public relations campaign to regain the momentum that had faded after legislators weighed the value of repealing the car tax against competing budget priorities. Ultimately, a trimmed down version of Gilmore's proposal to repeal the car tax passed the General Assembly, yet Democrats also succeeded in enacting a state-funded initiative to repair and build local schools. According to many politicians and journalists, the car tax repeal and the school construction initiatives were 'historic" achievements.[2] Yet, the 1998 Session of the General Assembly also featured a continuation of partisanship, executive-legislative competition over the agenda, and increased participation by rank-and-file members.

In this chapter, we will first sketch out how budget making has evolved from an executive-centered, Democratic dominated process to one in which the executive and the legislature, Democrats and Republicans, share power. Secondly, the makeup of the budget will be analyzed, the major revenue sources and spending programs identified, as well as the trends in those realms. In doing so, we will highlight the constraints and opportunities facing the participants in the budget process. Finally, we will discuss how budgeting during the 1998 session illustrated several institutional and partisan features that had been in place before the session began.

The Evolving Institutional and Political Context

Executive Dominance

Historically, Virginia has had an executive-centered budget process, led by the governor, who, for much of the century, operated in a political system in which the Democratic Party controlled the executive and legislative branches (Palazzolo and Whelan 1993). Virginia was one of the first states to establish an executive oriented budget process with the passage of the Executive Budget Act in 1918. The Act made the governor the state's chief budget officer, responsible for overseeing the formulation of a budget for submission to the Assembly and the execution of the legislatively adopted budget. The office of governor is strong in Virginia, and significantly, legislators in a 1969 study ranked the budget powers as the governor's most important powers.

While governors had responsibility for formulating the budget, they customarily included key legislators in that process. Then, too, the Democratic Byrd organization's dominance of Virginia government from the mid-1920s to the mid-1960s normally assured a similar outlook among governors and legislative leaders on major issues. Still, the Assembly was poorly equipped to make independent evaluations of program alternatives. In fact, the Governor's budget staff assisted the House Appropriations and Senate Finance Committees when they reviewed the executive budget.

Yet the executive budget process was not without its own flaws. As part of an overall executive branch modernization process, the executive budget process was restructured in the 1970s. A Department of Planning and Budget was established, professional staffing upgraded, program budgeting introduced, and budgeting and accounting systems automated. The new 1971 Constitution had liberalized the state's capacity to borrow, a marked departure from the Byrd era, pay-as-you-go fiscal tenet. Thus, heading into the 1980s the state's executive-centered budget process was modernized to meet the enlarged governing mission facing Virginia governors and other key executive officials.

Legislative Emergence

In the 1960s, the Democratically-dominated General Assembly, reflecting a national state legislative reform movement, had begun to modernize its operations. The election in 1969 of the state's first Republican governor in the twentieth century, Linwood A. Holton, Jr., helped spur the reform process. Over the next decade, the Assembly moved to annual sessions, permitted under the new Constitution, and added professional staff, office facilities for members and staff, automated information and bill drafting systems, and a nationally recognized oversight unit, the Joint Legislative Audit and Review Commission (JLARC).

Spearheaded by the House Appropriations Committee (HAC), the legislative budget process also underwent change. The HAC had long enjoyed a privileged position in the legislative budget process, compared with its counterpart, the Senate Finance Committee (SFC). Until the early 1980s, the Executive Budget Bill was first introduced in the House and only late in the session after the HAC and its parent chamber finished their review would the SFC and then the Senate begin their deliberations. The 1970s saw the HAC move to strengthen its position. Full-time, year-around, professional staff were hired, monthly meetings of the committee between sessions became a routine, and subcommittees were established, enhancing member specialization. In the late 1970s, the SFC followed suit, hiring their first permanent professional staff in 1979, and four years later, in a tradition breaking move, introducing their own budget bill at the outset of the session. The SFC had some institutional features that made it a formidable counterpart to the HAC. The SFC had jurisdiction over both taxing and spending matters; the HAC shared those responsibilities with the House Finance Committee. Additionally, the SFC had a more inclusive chamber membership, especially among the key power figures.[3] Both Committees, dominated by senior Democrats, were accustomed to a good deal of autonomy in their respective chambers, deliberating in private on important issues and enjoying considerable deference when they brought their budget proposals to the floor.

While the executive now confronted a more challenging bicameral review process than had been the case a decade earlier, a good deal of cooperation persisted among the governors and the budget committee leaders. As political scientist Alan Rosenthal

Figure 6.1 The capitol building in Richmond. Courtesy of PhotoDisc, Inc.

pointed out in his description of gubernatorial-legislative relations in Virginia during the late-1980s:

> In Virginia . . . the legislature works from the governor's budget bill. But the budgetary process is "wired" in the sense that the governor will not send over a budget that will make key legislators unhappy. The budget is worked out beforehand. Governor Baliles has an open process in developing the executive budget. Legislators come to the governor with their wish lists. The leaders, more often than not, have their priorities included in the governor's budget. If they do not, the governor will usually figure out an alternative way of funding their priorities. Throughout the budgetary process, Baliles maintains contact with legislative leaders and committee chairs, so that they are familiar with the recommendations he will make. Therefore, few public confrontations take place (Rosenthal 1990, 137–138).

Thus, though the legislative committees became less dependent on the executive for information and analysis, Democratic legislators worked together with governors of both parties to formulate the budget.

The New Budget Politics

The last phase of legislative budget developments has been unfolding since the late-1980s and is characterized by three important trends. First, the budget committees' autonomy has been challenged by more frequent participation of non-budget committee members in the process. Second, the level of partisanship increased, culminating in Republicans gaining power sharing status with Democrats by 1996 in the Senate and 1998 in the House. Finally, by comparison to traditional norms, we have seen an unusual degree of conflict between the governor and the Assembly.

As we have noted, participation in the budget process expanded with the emergence of the HAC in the 1970s and the SFC in the 1980s. Yet by the late 1980s, and especially in the 1990s, non-budget committee members began to participate more actively in the budget process, posing a direct challenge to the committees' autonomy. For instance, budget committee bills became subject to floor amendments. While it was unusual for the challenges to succeed, they signaled an increased restiveness in non-budget committee ranks.

For their part, the budget committees have become more responsive to outsiders, both in and out of the Assembly. Since 1992 the committees have solicited public input on the budget by holding pre-session hearings around the state. The committees also have conducted budget briefings for non-budget committee members during this period. Indeed, since the 1992 session the Senate Finance Committee has held a two-day "retreat" for the entire Senate shortly before the annual session. And in 1992, Delegate Robert Ball (D-Henrico), the HAC chair, sponsored legislation which required the governor to submit the executive budget by December 20, adding approximately a month of pre-session review time for interested parties.

Underlying the restiveness in non-budget committee ranks was a growing partisanship, especially in the House of Delegates. Republican strength had grown considerably in the Assembly, more than doubling from 1974 to 1994, with the Party increasing its seats in the Senate from seven to eighteen and in the House from twenty to forty-seven. Despite those gains, Republicans remained underrepresented on the budget committees. For example, if the majority-minority party ratio of seats in the budget committees had been proportional to the chamber as a whole in 1994, the Republicans would have had nine seats instead of five on the twenty-member HAC and seven seats instead of three on the fifteen-member SFC.

The Republicans' status would change abruptly in the Senate in 1996 and in the House in 1998, as the party gained parity with the Democrats in the respective chambers, forcing historic power sharing agreements. As part of the 1996 Senate agreement, Republicans gained co-chairmanship of the SFC and eight of the seventeen seats in the expanded committee. On the House side, Democratic leaders, protecting a slim and eroding majority (52 Democrats, 47 Republicans, and 1 Independent), were, if anything, more adamant in protecting party prerogatives, including control of the budget process. Republican strength in the HAC, already underrepresented, was reduced from five to four seats. Two years later, however, House Democrats were forced into a similar power sharing agreement, which in the budget realm gave House Republicans co-chairmanship of the HAC and fifteen of the thirty seats on the expanded committee.

Still, House Democrats retained some procedural advantages. By re-electing the Speaker, Thomas W. Moss, Jr. (D-Norfolk), in a controversial opening-day power move,[4] House Democrats maintained control of the chamber's presiding officer, capable of making important floor rulings. The Speaker, under the House version of power sharing, also retained the important committee assignment role. Still, Republicans for the first time in this century share in running the Assembly and the legislative budget process in particular. Currently, Virginia has the only state legislature where both chambers function under power sharing agreements.

Finally, while executive-legislative relations will be marked by episodes of both co-operation and conflict in any separation of powers system, Virginia experienced uncharacteristic episodes of conflict in the 1990s. First, Governor L. Douglas Wilder precipitated a showdown with his Democratic colleagues in the Assembly by cutting programs they favored without consulting with budget committee chairs. After the Assembly altered his budget bill, Wilder amended the bill with 86 additional items. Then, in an unprecedented maneuver, the Assembly defeated 59 of Wilder's amendments.

Four years later, Republican Governor George Allen's budget proposals, coming in the second year of his administration, ignited another high profile clash between the Governor and the Assembly. In 1995, Allen proposed a $2.1 billion, five-year tax cut for businesses and individuals, and $403 million in spending cuts, more than half of which would come from health and human services, and education. The plan, crafted with little input from Assembly leaders of either party and unveiled shortly before the 1995 session, spurred considerable opposition, cutting across both parties. In particular, the higher education measures, coming on the heels of the Wilder-era budget cuts, counter-mobilized a powerful business-higher education lobby. The lobbying effort culminated on the eve of a critical legislative budget vote with a well-publicized letter from three former Virginia governors, most prominently Mills Godwin, deploring Allen's budget proposals. The Assembly rejected Allen's budget package. Later, during the veto session, the Assembly rebuffed the Governor again by rejecting his proposal to return $300 million in lottery profits to local governments. Allen's defeats raised questions in statehouse circles about whether the Governor's proposals were political measures rather than governing documents, aimed at drawing clear distinctions between Democrats and Republicans for the forthcoming Assembly elections.

To be sure, the Allen-Assembly clash, coming in a divided party government context, had a stronger partisan element than the earlier Wilder case. Still, both clashes highlighted the increased contentiousness in gubernatorial-legislative relations during the 1990s. Ironically, both Governors Wilder and Allen would end their terms assuming a more conciliatory stance with the Assembly. Still, their experiences with the legislature marked a final phase in the development of the Virginia budget process. Since the late-1960s, the process has evolved from an executive-centered, Democratic-dominated process to one in which the executive and the legislature, Democrats and Republicans, share power.

Makeup of the Virginia Budget

The budget of Virginia is a complex document containing data on various sources of revenues and spending for thousands of programs. Yet, at a fundamental level, the budget reflects important choices about who gets what, when, and how from state government, and who pays for it. A brief overview of the budget provides a basic understanding of the key choices confronting Governor Gilmore and Members of the General Assembly during the 1998 session.[5] As we shall see, the spending and tax choices available to legislators in any given year are constrained by the structure of the budget

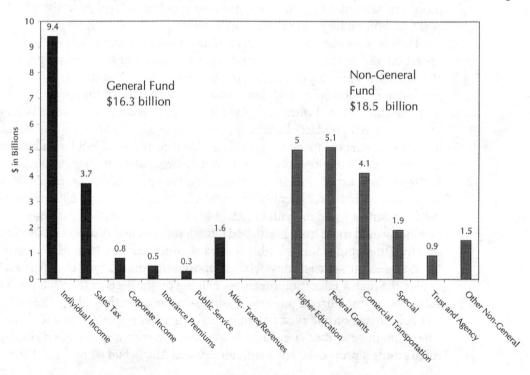

Figure 6.2 Sources of General and Non-General Funds

and existing commitments to state agencies and programs. Under the Virginia Constitution (Art. X, § vii), the Governor and the General Assembly are required to balance the state budget.[6] Nevertheless, budget priorities do change in response to economic conditions, federal grants, the costs of state services, and the deliberate actions of policymakers.

We begin with a few facts about where state revenues come from and how the money is spent. As Figure 6.2 illustrates, the state budget is generally divided into two parts: general funds and non-general funds. Revenues for the general fund come from various sources, but most revenues are collected from the individual income taxes and sales taxes. As Figure 6.3 illustrates, just over 50% of general funds go toward education, and much of the remainder finances ongoing services. Non-general funds consist of federal grants and fees earmarked for specific purposes. For example, federal grants pay for a portion of the state's costs for Medicaid, a state-run health program for the poor, and university operations are financed partly by tuition fees paid by students. Altogether, transportation, college and university operations, and health-related programs, like Medicaid, comprise two-thirds of non-general funds.

The structure of the budget does not allow legislators to make dramatic changes in spending and tax policy in a single legislative session. All of the non-general funds are earmarked for specific purposes and most of the general funds are dedicated to ongoing state programs. The Governor and state legislators cut spending from some services and allocate it to others, but those are typically small changes.[7] They can also increase taxes or fees to pay for additional services, but those too are likely to be small; after all, raising taxes is never a popular course of action.

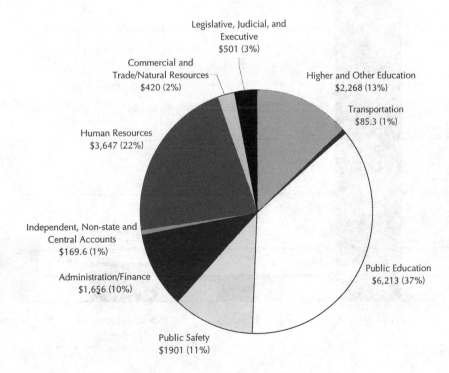

Figure 6.3 General Fund Operating Expenses

Nevertheless, over a period of time, even without any new major program initiatives, all states experience shifts in budget priorities in response to societal changes, legislative developments, and public needs. In Virginia, although taxes have not increased, overall spending has grown by 46% since 1990. Moreover, as Figure 6.4 illustrates, four major programs or activities—public education (grades K–12), adult and juvenile corrections, Medicaid, and debt service—have accounted for 75% of spending growth. Medicaid grew from $300 million in 1985 to $1.1 billion in 1996, largely because of Federal laws that increased eligibility for health services, general health care inflation, and the increasing costs of long-term care for Medicaid-eligible elderly and disabled persons. Corrections costs went up with increases in the number of state inmates and the accompanying rise in operating expenses. Education spending increases resulted from additional enrollments of about 108,000 new primary and secondary school students since 1990 and the implementation of new Standards of Quality. Finally, increased debt service, by far the fastest growing driving force in the budget, stems from bonds issued during the early 1990s to pay for capital outlays when general revenues were in short supply.[8]

As legislators prepared for the 1998 General Assembly Session, the four programs/activities that have been driving spending over the past eight or ten years were

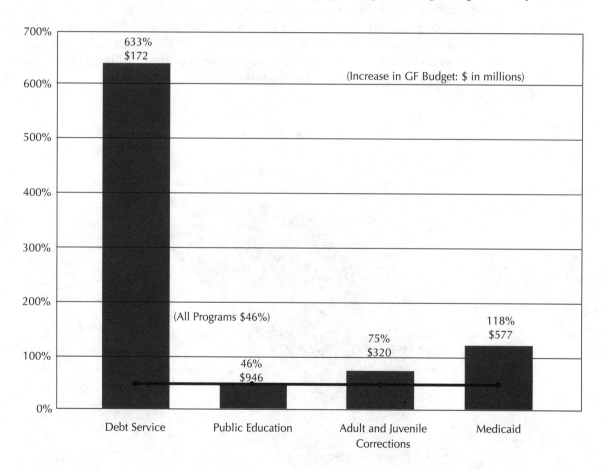

Figure 6.4 Budget Drivers Since 1990
(Four Programs Accounted for 75% of General Fund Budget Growth from 1990 to 1998)

expected to remain the most costly programs, and the economy was projected to grow at a moderate pace. The revenues derived from expected economic growth would cover the cost growth of the budget drivers, maintain salaries of government employees, and slightly increase capital outlays. Expected revenues were not large enough to cover certain other priority items, such as the Year 2000 computer problem, increases in higher education priorities recommended by the Commission on Higher Education, or funding any new initiatives.[9] Against this backdrop, the General Assembly would be charged with initiating a federally funded children's health insurance program administered by the state, deal with the priorities recommended by outgoing Governor George Allen, and address Governor Gilmore's election campaign proposal to repeal the car tax.

The 1998 General Assembly Session

How did the legislature respond to the budget situation in 1998? In light of previous trends in budgeting, one might expect some degree of legislative-executive competition, partisan tensions, and wider participation that has characterized the process since the late-1980s. Despite Gilmore's convincing electoral victory and mandate to repeal the car tax, he had more of a "policy mandate" than a "governing mandate," since House Republicans lacked the majority needed to rubberstamp his campaign pledge.

Then, too, Gilmore was a newly elected governor, facing the formidable challenge of putting together an administration, with all the personnel, organizational, policy and budget tasks entailed in that short ten week transition from election to inauguration. Since the 1998 session would be the even-year, biennial budget adoption session, the proposed 1998–2000 executive budget, under formulation since the previous Spring, would largely be the creation of the outgoing Republican Governor George Allen. Indeed, despite all the Virginia governor's powers, the fact is that a new governor is always hamstrung by the priorities laid out by his predecessor. Fortunately, Governor Gilmore was succeeding a fellow Republican who had set aside $260 million in the proposed 1998–2000 budget to help fund the first two years of the car tax initiative. Unfortunately, though, after his budget analysts re-estimated the cost of repealing the car tax, Gilmore had to ask the legislature for nearly twice the amount Allen had set aside to finance the car tax plan.

Executive-Legislative Competition

Within weeks of 1997 election, Governor Gilmore experienced the complications of transforming his campaign pledge into a legislative reality. While Gilmore skillfully tapped into popular resentment by proposing to repeal the car tax during the campaign, once the legislative process began, the strategic situation had changed. The capacity of the legislature to conduct fiscal analysis provided the basis for an executive-legislative struggle that had become commonplace over the years. A Senate Finance Committee report released shortly after the election found that Gilmore's proposal to cut the car tax would cost twice as much as the Governor-elect estimated during the campaign and could not be reliably financed with additional revenues generated solely from economic growth.[10] The fiscal realities sparked a clash between the Governor and the General Assembly that was evidenced by two points: (1) a conflict over budget priorities, and (2) Gilmore's strategy of trying to intimidate Delegates and Senators with a public relations style campaign to build support for the car tax initiative.

After the Senate Finance Committee report was released, Stanley C. Walker (D-Norfolk), co-chairman of the Senate Finance Committee, asked: "What do you do about a request in higher education, in public education, in social services, in health? Do you say, 'Well, yes, use all of that surplus on the car tax,' and then start going backward on the other areas? To my mind, this leaves some tough choices to make."[11] House Democratic Floor Leader Delegate Richard Cranwell, the leading Democrat in that chamber, seized the opportunity to pursue an issue that was equally appealing to voters—school construction.[12] Democrats also raised the issue of tax fairness, alleging that the largest tax breaks would go to individuals with the most expensive vehicles who happened to live in counties that depended heavily on the car tax for local revenue. Thus, they countered the car tax with a proposal to eliminate the 4.5% tax on food, something all Virginians would equally benefit from. Though Gilmore still had a strong base of support in the General Assembly, the legislature was not about to roll over and deliver his populist idea, and eventually both issues took the steam out of Gilmore's plan to repeal the car tax.

By mid-February, Gilmore responded to the waning enthusiasm for the car tax repeal in the legislature and launched his public relations campaign to build support for the proposal. He flew around the state promoting the tax cut, and his staff organized telephone banks and sent out mass mailings to encourage constituents to contact their delegates and senators. Gilmore's strategy to go public, was as much a sign of weakness as strength; an indication that Gilmore needed public support to fortify his bargaining leverage with legislators. Gilmore admitted to reporters, "I'm feeling the heat; I'm applying the heat."[13]

Party Politics Within the Assembly

The partisan divisions that emerged over the years in the General Assembly continued in 1998, but they were muted somewhat by the bipartisan appeal of the three main budget issues and by the need for both parties to compromise in a power-sharing situation. As the session unfolded, the partisan divisions over tax and spending priorities were clear enough on several votes in the budget committees and in both chambers, and the partisan rhetoric was heated at times. The main partisan divisions on the Senate Finance Committee were over Democratic plans to increase funds for school construction, and in the Senate chamber over a bill to eliminate the food tax. On the House side, the parties divided over the food tax cut—with Democrats voting in favor and Republicans voting against when they were forced to decide between the car tax initiative and food tax cut.

The school construction issue posed a more complicated problem on the House side. Republicans ultimately joined with Democrats to support school construction, and several moderate Republicans spearheaded the initiative. However, it is not clear how much of the agreement across party lines stemmed from a genuine bipartisan concern to help localities, or a Republican reaction to Cranwell's strategy to force a popular, mom and apple issue on the agenda. Cranwell linked Gilmore's tax plan with aid to schools, arguing that repealing the car tax would make the situation worse by sapping localities of a major revenue source.[14] Certainly moderate Republicans, like Anne G. "Panny" Rhodes (Richmond) and James H. Dillard (Fairfax), supported school construction funds as a budget priority, but it is not clear how many Republicans got on board as a result of political danger of opposing a popular idea.

Interestingly, though, the key issues in the budget debate did not cut purely along party lines. Repealing the car tax was as much a regional issue as a partisan issue, school construction was a statewide problem, and many Republicans who favored cutting taxes did not wish to vote against the Democrat-sponsored tax cut on food. As Table 6.1 shows, the parties in both chambers ranked the three major budget priorities differently. Thus, in the House, while Democrats wanted *more* aid for school construction and Republicans a *bigger* tax cut, plenty of Republicans favored allocating some money for local school projects, and many Democrats supported repealing the car tax. On the Senate side, Republicans wanted as much of a car tax as they could get, but several fiscally conservative Republicans worried about the long-term effects on revenues. Thus, unlike their House colleagues, Senate Republicans opposed school construction in order to finance the tax cut. So, it was hard to tell how much the debate reflected partisan posturing or genuine differences over priorities.[15]

Table 6.1 Distribution of Ranked Preferences by Party and Chamber

	Car Tax Cuts	Food Tax Cuts	School Construction
House Democrats	3rd	2nd	1st
House Republicans	1st	3rd	2nd
Senate Republicans	1st	2nd	None
Senate Democrats	3rd	1st	2nd

Source: Compiled by authors and based on evaluations of roll call votes and budget proposals.

In the end, neither the Governor nor the Assembly, neither Republicans nor Democrats, could hope to advance their priorities without the other. Thus, the process gravitated toward compromise, with both parties gaining a smaller share of their original goals. Governor Gilmore won passage of a car tax cut amounting to $435 million in the 1998–2000 budget and about $2.6 billion over five years, if carried out as planned. However, the amount was $60 million less than Gilmore originally requested for the first two years, and the car tax cut was incorporated in the biennial budget, rather than adopted as separate legislation. Thus, only two years were covered, allowing future legislators to review the program. Additionally, the bill included a number of fiscal safeguards designed to slow the tax cut if state revenues fell short of current projections.

For their part, Assembly Democrats won passage of a $110 million, two-year program to provide state grants to local school divisions for school construction, repair, and debt service. School divisions would receive at least $200,000 the first year, with the rest of the money allocated on the basis of the number of pupils per school division. However, the $110 million was only one-quarter of what the Democrats hoped for originally and it paled in comparison to an estimated $6 billion localities would need to repair and construct schools.

Participation: Opportunities and Constraints

The trend in wider participation in the legislative budget process accelerated in the 1998 session, further undercutting the budget committees' traditional autonomy. In one sense, the budget became part of a broader partisan-electoral struggle, with each party advancing initiatives, hoping to enhance or regain strength in the Assembly. Perhaps the best example occurred where Delegate Cranwell effectively marshaled support within the House Democratic Caucus to hold Governor Gilmore's car tax initiative hostage to school construction funding. Given Gilmore's impressive election campaign, it is no surprise that the Assembly passed some sort of car tax repeal. On the other hand, given the demoralizing electoral defeats Democrats experienced before the session, it was quite surprising for them to achieve a state-funded local school construction initiative.

At the same time, the realities of power sharing dictated compromise, muted the partisan differences as the process evolved, and ushered in an unprecedented diffusion of power. The diffusion of power made the resolution of issues, at times, more difficult, but it also created opportunities for wider participation. To accommodate power sharing, for example, the budget conference committee was expanded from eight to twelve members, making the process more unwieldy. The details of the school construction financing plan and the distribution formula were not resolved until a later special session held in conjunction with the annual veto session. Yet Republicans, for the first time in both chambers, shared responsibility for crafting a budget and neither party was strong enough to do it alone. To be sure, traditional budget committee figures retained a prominent role, vividly illustrated at the end of the session when both houses waited on the twelve member conference committee to finalize compromises between the House and Senate. Yet their discretion was constrained by prior agreements struck between the coalitions in which non-senior members played important roles. For example, Rhodes, a moderate Republican teamed up with Thomas M. Jackson (D-Galax), to advance funding for school construction.

Conclusion

Today, the legislative budget process in Virginia is a venue for elected officials and parties to pursue their policy goals and political interests amidst the ebb and flow of fiscal opportunities and constraints. In 1997 and 1998, large influxes of revenues made it possible for a populist governor of an emerging Republican party and a feisty, seasoned legislator of a waning Democratic party to share the benefits of an expanding budget pie. Each won a policy victory and a political victory in a contentious struggle over budget priorities and partisan advantage.

In the future, budget battles in Virginia are likely to continue to feature conflicts over policy, while each party duels for political advantage in a competitive electoral context. Students of Virginia politics should take note of the trends we have described in this chapter, for they raise important questions about how the budget process works, how our politics are evolving, and how elected officials decide to allocate state resources for public services. We might want to consider the implications of making long-term commitments to tax cuts or costly programs in an uncertain fiscal environment. For the moment, certain check points in the system seem to prevent elected representatives from over-extending state resources. The budget must be balanced, the state has a rainy day fund available in case of a recession, and fiscally conservative members will resist liberal uses of borrowing to finance capital spending projects. Still, the pressure to cut taxes and spend more is not likely to be diminished in an era when the budget process has become as much a political instrument as a planning device and a means to resolve conflicts over competing priorities.

Bibliography

Gibson, Tucker. 1969. "The Governor of Virginia as Legislative Leader." *University of Virginia Newsletter* 45 (5): 20

Palazzolo, Daniel J. and John T. Whelan. 1993. "Budgeting in Virginia: Assessing Institutional Developments and Change in a State Legislature." *Southeastern Political Review* 23 (4): 705–731.

Rosenthal, Alan. 1990. *Governors and Legislatures: Contending Powers.* Washington, D.C.: CQ Press.

Schack, Lawrence L. 1998. "Governor George Allen: Virginia's 'Riverboat' Gambler," in Thomas R. Morris and Larry J. Sabato, eds., *Virginia Government and Politics: Reading and Comments,* 4th revised edition. Charlottesville: University of Virginia and Virginia Chamber of Commerce.

Schapiro, Jeff E. 1998. "Too Damned Many Republicans." *State Legislatures* 24(7): 45.

Endnotes

1. Quoted in Spencer S. Hsu and Ellen Nakashima, "Gilmore Leads GOP to Victory in Virginia; Race for Governor Powers Sweep of Statewide Offices," *Washington Post*, 5 November 1997, sec. A.

2. See, for example, Michael Hardy and Tyler Whitley, "A 'Historic' Session," *Richmond Times-Dispatch*, 26 April 1998, sec. A.

3. The SFC's 15 members constituted 40% of the Senate; the HAC's 20 members represented 20% of the House. Among the SFC's membership in 1992, for example, were chairs of eight other Senate committees, including Rules, Privileges and Elections, and Courts of Justice, which with SFC were thought to be the Senate's most prestigious committees.

4. Republicans were unable to get three of their special election House victors certified and thus seated by the opening of the 1998 Session, allowing Democrats, over boisterous Republican protests, to ram through re-election of the Speaker.

5. Indeed, our principle source of information is a brief document prepared for legislators by the staff of the Senate Finance and House Appropriations Committees. See, Senate Finance and House Appropriations Staff, "An Overview of the Commonwealth's Budget," October 31, 1997, pp. 1–24.

6. While the State operates under a biennial budget, the adoption of which occurs during the Assembly's even-numbered year session, the legislative budget process has evolved into an annual process with the biennial budget routinely subject to amendment in the odd-year session.

7. In one sense, the small changes mean a great deal to Delegates and Senators who seek funds for projects in their districts. However, this chapter deals mainly with the high profile issues that drive the budget.

8. Virginia is traditionally a fiscally conservative state, a legacy of the Byrd era. The state normally budgeted about 1.5 to 2.0 percent of the General Fund for capital outlays. Those funds were not available during the recession of the early 1990s. Democrat Governor Doug Wilder and the General Assembly restrained spending during that time, but Wilder refused to increase taxes. In order to pay for capital projects and stay within the balanced budget requirement, the voters approved a series of bond initiatives which resulted in the large debt service.

9. The Year 2000 problem was expected to cost $55 million. The Commission on Higher Education recommended a $181 billion package of priorities, including: continued tuition freeze, enrollment growth, and increased student financial aid.

10. See Ellen Nakashima, "Cost of Cutting Car Tax in Va. Could Double; Gilmore's Estimates Challenged by Report," *Washington Post*, 21 November 1997, sec. A.

11. Quoted in Ellen Nakashima, "Cost of Cutting Car Tax in Va. Could Double; Gilmore's Estimates Challenged by Report," *Washington Post*, 21 November, sec. A.

12. See R. H. Melton, "Deal Maker Shifts Strategy as House Power Changes," *Washington Post*, 17 February 1998, sec. B.

13. Quoted in R. H. Melton, "Gilmore Answers Foes With Car-Tax Publicity Campaign," *Washington Post*, 13 February 1998, sec. B.

14. Though local governments traditionally have been responsible for school construction and repair, they did not have the resources to absorb the expected costs. Local governments were about $2.1 billion shy of the projected $6.2 billion needed to repair and build school over the next five years. See Spencer S. Hsu and Ellen Nakashima, "Va. Assembly Approves Budget, Adjourns," *Washington Post*, 18 March 1998, sec. A.

15. Columnist Tyler Whitley suggests that there were clear partisan differences on the issues, but the evidence is thin. See Tyler Whitley, "Vote Hides Dealings on Car Tax, School Building Issues," *Richmond Times-Dispatch*, 24 July 1998, sec. B.

CHAPTER SEVEN

Forging 'Debatable Ground': The Transformation of Party Politics in Virginia

Stephen K. Medvic
Old Dominion University

In a famous phrase, written to Francis Hopkinson in a letter from Paris dated March 13, 1789, Thomas Jefferson declared, "If I could not go to heaven but with a party, I would not go there at all" (Jefferson, 1984, 941). Despite such a claim, Jefferson would eventually help create the first modern political party. This seemingly contradictory behavior points to the indispensability of political parties and to the important role they have played in the political history of the United States and the Commonwealth of Virginia.

The political party system of Virginia looks very different today than it did in Jefferson's day. Indeed, it looks different than it did half a century ago, when Robert and Carter Glass could write, "If Virginia is to be debatable ground between republicans [sic] and democrats [sic] there are no signs of it yet" (Glass and Glass 1937, 391–92). This chapter examines party politics in Virginia. It will trace the Old Dominion's path to a competitive two-party system, detail the current state of party competition, and consider the future of that competition. In other words, this chapter will explore the "debatable ground" that has been forged in Virginia and on which its parties now stand.

Parties and Party Systems

Before discussing the history of Virginia's political parties, two key concepts should be defined. First, a "political party," in the modern sense of the term, is one which seeks to win elections for its candidates. As Giovanni Sartori (1976) notes, "A Party is any political group that presents at elections, and is capable of placing through elections, candidates for public office" (64; see also Aldrich 1995). Though many other elements would go into a comprehensive definition, competing in elections is clearly what distinguishes parties from other political organizations such as interest groups (see Maisel 1993, 9–10 for a variety of definitions of "political party").

One of the more important ways of conceptualizing parties was formulated by the eminent political scientist V. O. Key, Jr. (1964). He held that parties consist of three parts—party-in-the-electorate, party-in-government, and party-as-organization. The first part refers to rank-and-file members of the party, or those individuals who identify themselves as being Democrats or Republicans (or some third party). The party-in-government is the partisan make-up and behavior of elected officials. The organization of legislatures by the majority party is one example of how the party-in-government operates. Finally, the party-as-organization is what many think of as the "political party." This is the structure of the party both in terms of geography (there are national, state and local party committees), leadership and membership, and resources.

The second key concept used in this chapter is "party system." According to Maurice Duverger (1963), whose work on political parties is classic, a party system is defined by "the forms and modes of [parties'] coexistence" (203). L. Sandy Maisel (1993) adds that party systems can be analyzed according to two characteristics—the number of competitive parties and the level (or intensity) of competition between

Figure 7.1 Thomas Jefferson. Courtesy of The Library of Congress.

the parties (11). Thus, while the two major parties compete in different degrees in the various state systems, the national scene is a fully competitive two-party system.

The Virginia party system has undergone enormous changes in the second half of the Twentieth Century. Before discussing the current state of party competition in the Old Dominion, we will turn our attention to the transformation of the state's party system from a one-party (or, more precisely, single factional) system to a competitive two-party system. Doing so will require some historical background.

Political Parties in Virginia Since the Civil War

"Of all American states," proclaimed V. O. Key, Jr. (1949), "Virginia can lay claim to the most thorough control by an oligarchy. Political power has been closely held by a small group of leaders who, themselves and their predecessors, have subverted democratic institutions and deprived most Virginians of a voice in their government" (19). This oligarchic tendency, according to Key, "is firmly rooted in the social structure of Virginia whose history is rich with political organizations" (19).

What we now pejoratively call "machine politics" has a long history in the state. After the commonwealth's re-admittance to the Union in 1870, the Readjuster (or Coalitionist-Republican) party played a powerful role in Virginia politics (Moger 1942, 183–85). In the late 1870s, William Mahone organized the Readjuster-Republicans into a successful political machine that took control of the legislature in 1879 and then won the governorship in 1881 (Moger 1942, 185). Soon, however, the Mahone machine became so corrupt that the term "Mahoneism" became synonymous with "'everything disreputable in Virginia politics'" (Moger 1942, 185).

When John S. Barbour was selected as chair of the Democratic party in 1883, which until then had been known as the Conservative party, Republicans had a formidable opponent on their hands. That year Democrats and Republicans campaigned against each other in each district in the state and two years later "the two parties fought vigorously and fiercely" (Moger 1942, 195). By century's end, however, Barbour had established a Democratic organization that had virtually eliminated the Republican party from Virginia politics.[1]

Thomas S. Martin succeeded Barbour as boss of the "Organization" shortly after the latter's death in 1892 (Moger 1968, 111–112) and quickly built on his predecessor's success. Though the Anderson-McCormick election law of 1884 had given Democrats "complete control of the election machinery," the Organization wanted even greater control over the outcome of elections (Moger 1942, 193; 209). Consequently, a constitutional convention was convened in 1902 at which eighty-eight of the one hundred members (one from each House of Delegates district) were Democrats (Moger 1968, 187). The new constitution disenfranchised the vast majority of Virginia's black population through arduous registration restrictions and the poll tax. The new laws also diminished political activity among white Republicans, since many of them were illiterate and poor.[2] With the addition of mandatory direct primaries for statewide offices, which were implemented in 1905, Virginia's election laws helped guarantee the Democrats' dominance in state politics for at least the next sixty years. As Larry Sabato maintains, "The direct primary and the suffrage clauses of the new

Constitution combined to forge a new political order for the Commonwealth—which was simply a more firmly entrenched version of the old political order" (1977, 28).

The preeminence of the Democratic Party meant that its primary, rather than the general election, would be the future site of political conflict (Sabato 1977, 26). Of course, by the time Harry Flood Byrd took over the Organization machine, shortly after the death of Senator Martin in 1919, serious competition did not even exist in the Democratic primary. Indeed, Virginia had become "almost a one-party system within a one-party system" (Key 1949, 18).

Harry Byrd "had made the Democratic organization a well-oiled machine built upon unquestioning loyalty, political success, and aggressive and dynamic leadership by a hard core of the inner circle of which Byrd himself was the most influential member" (Moger 1968, 341). Though Byrd would eventually lose some major political battles, he would reign as the Commonwealth's most powerful man for more than forty years (Bass and DeVries 1976, 339–68).

Strangely enough, the Byrd Organization would lay the foundation for an eventual Republican resurgence. In 1928, a majority of Virginia voters backed Republican Herbert Hoover. This caused problems for the Democrats because the state's "loyalty" law required Democratic primary voters to have supported the Democratic ticket in the previous election (Sabato 1977, 32). If the Democrats refused to allow Hoover voters to participate in their next primary, they would be forced to turn away many of their otherwise loyal supporters. The Byrd solution was to distinguish between the state and national Democratic parties (Sabato 1977, 43). According to Sabato,

> By both blurring the distinction between the Democrats and the Republicans on the state level and emphasizing the distinction between national Democrats and Virginia Democrats, the Byrd Organization encouraged the development of ticket-splitting and independent voting habits which were to become even more predominant in later years (Sabato 1977, 43).

The fact that voters do not register by party in Virginia and that state elections are held in odd years, between national elections, further separates the national and state parties.[3]

Further estrangement occurred between the state and national party when Byrd opposed the nomination of Harry Truman for president in 1948. Because rank-and-file Democrats were supportive of Truman, who eventually won the state's electoral votes in November, Byrd decided to remain silent during the general election. His close associates, however, publicly supported Dixiecrat Strom Thurmond.

Byrd Democrats were never particularly fond of national Democrats. A staunch conservative, Byrd opposed much of the New Deal legislation initiated by Franklin Roosevelt. He insisted on a "pay-as-you-go" system of government spending, which meant there was rarely enough money to spend on capital projects or social services, including welfare and education. In the mid-1950s, Byrd attempted to mount a "massive resistance" movement to school desegregation orders issued by the federal courts (see Bass and DeVries 1976, 346). Of course, this rigid stance against integration was (or at least would soon become) an embarrassment to the commonwealth. As victorious as the Organization was in state politics, the Byrd machine "showed a genius for taking the side on national issues that would be defeated" (Moger 1968, 361).

Yet, political change at the national level was recognized by some in the Organization rather quickly. By the early 1960s, a moderating wind could already be felt blowing through the Old Dominion. Lieutenant Governor Mills E. Godwin, Jr., a conservative Byrd loyalist, moved to the center and "was able to construct an amazing coalition of liberals, moderates, and conservatives to give the Byrd Organization one last great victory when he sought the governorship of 1965" (Sabato 1977, 69). That election, however, would be the beginning-of-the end for the Organization. As if dissension within the Organization over the new moderate tack was not enough, Harry Byrd, Sr. resigned from U.S. Senate within days of Godwin's 1965 victory (Sabato 1977, 72).

The Organization had shown signs of weakness in the past, though they were few and far between. In 1949, anti-Organization candidate Francis P. Miller had run a close second in the party's gubernatorial primary to Organization candidate John Stewart Battle. Battle's 42.8 percent of the vote would be the worst showing for a Byrd Organization candidate until 1966 (see Sabato 1977, 61–62). That year, the Byrd Organization witnessed the death of its namesake and its own political death as machine candidates lost in primaries for one U.S. House seat and the U.S. Senate seat. Indeed, "After 1966 Virginia politics were described in new terms" (Sabato 1977, 76).

Sabato (1977) maintains that "the roots of [the Organization's] decline can be found in the three major legal alterations in the suffrage and the structure of representation" put in place in the 1960s. The first of these was the prohibition of the poll tax by the Twenty-fourth Amendment to the U.S. Constitution. Next was a series of court decisions that required states to apportion representation according to equal population, or the "one person, one vote" principle.[4] Finally, the Voting Rights Act of 1965 barred the use of literacy tests and other such measures designed to deny suffrage to individuals (Sabato 1977, 73–75). "In rapid-fire fashion, . . ." writes Sabato, "the restricted electorate which had been made-to-order for a political machine by the 1901–02 [Virginia] Constitutional Convention was transformed" (1977, 76). The changing political dynamics of the 1960s, therefore, meant that the Organization would not only have to adapt, but that it might be destroyed altogether. The influx of African-American voters into the system forced the Democratic party to take into account, if not act upon, black interests and demands and the party's liberal wing began to gain power. As the party changed, many of its most conservative members became Independents or Republicans, given the GOP's concomitant move to the right nationally. The conflict within the party reached a climax in 1969 when "the Godwin coalition fell apart as Democrats divided bitterly into conservative, moderate, and liberal factions" (Bass and DeVries 1976, 353). The result was the first Republican gubernatorial victory in almost a century as Linwood Holton garnered 52.5 percent of the vote. Holton would be the first of three consecutive Republican governors. Mills Godwin, the former Democratic governor who became a party "switcher," and John Dalton won both of the gubernatorial elections in the 1970s for the Republican party.

"For the first time in the post-Civil War history of the Commonwealth, the state parties were comfortable and aligned with their national counterparts" as liberals took control of the Democratic party while conservatives did the same in the GOP (Sabato 1977, 84). Two-party competition had arrived in Virginia. In fact, the 1970s looked like the beginning of Republican dominance in the state. The 1980s, however, brought the Democrats a number of key victories and gave Virginia a highly competitive two-party system.

Two Party Competition in Virginia

Through the 1970s, Virginia remained a "modified Democratic" state (see Maisel 1993, 16). Though Republican victories in statewide offices were the norm, rather than the exception, Democrats remained in firm control of the state legislature.[5] That control gave Democrats a slight nod according to most measures of state party strength. Nevertheless, "During the 1970s the strongest southern Republican party was in Virginia" (Jewell and Olson 1988, 35). In the 1980s, Republicans made significant gains in the General Assembly (as will be shown later) and Democrats compensated by winning key statewide elections. Thus, by the end of the 1980s, Jewell and Olson would classify Virginia as a "competitive two-party" system (1988, 29).

In the 1990s that two-party competition has intensified. While Republicans have taken control of the state Senate, have reached parity in the House of Delegates, and seem to have regained their "lock" on certain statewide seats, Democrats have won a few key statewide races and have taken back some U.S. House seats they lost in the 1980s. Though the party system remains competitive, it appears to be headed for "modified Republican" status.

We may better understand the Republican renaissance in Virginia if we take a closer look at election results and seat distributions from the last few decades. To begin at the top of the ticket, Virginians have been steadfastly voting for Republicans for president since the 1950s. In fact, since 1952 Virginia has given its electoral votes to Republicans in every election except 1964. Even in 1976, the Old Dominion turned its back on its southern neighbors and voted for Gerald Ford over the region's native son Jimmy Carter. "Virginia currently enjoys the distinction," notes John McGlennon, "of having supported Republican presidential candidates consecutively as long as any state in the nation. No state has denied its electors to a Democrat for a longer span of years," though ten other states have equally long streaks (1997, 209).

U.S. Senate seats have been a bit more competitive. Beginning in 1972, when Republican William Scott upset Senator William Spong, Jr. to capture the GOP's first Senate seat since 1889 (Sabato 1976, 59), Republicans have won six of the nine contests. Two of the three Senate races in the 1990s have been key battles for the parties and may be indicators of how competitive Virginia has become. In a 1994 race that gained considerable national attention (and was documented in the film A Perfect Candidate), Democratic Senator Charles Robb defeated the controversial Republican challenger Oliver North who spent over twenty and a half million dollars to Robb's five and a half million. In 1996, Republican Senator John Warner held onto his seat by defeating former State Democratic Party chair Mark Warner in a hotly contested race that again had the loser spending far more than the winner (Mark Warner spent over eleven and a half million dollars to John Warner's nearly six million).

Gubernatorial races have been electoral seesaw rides. Republicans controlled the governor's mansion in the 1970s, winning races in 1969, 1973 and 1977. Democrats took back the office in the 1980s with wins in 1981, 1985 and 1989. The governorship changed hands yet again as Republicans won convincing victories in 1993 and 1997.

Table 7.1 Republican Performance (as a percentage of the total vote) in Presidential, Senatorial, and Gubernatorial Elections, 1940–1997

Year	President	U.S. Senate	Governor
1940	31.6	--	
1941			--
1942		--	
1944	37.4		
1945			31.0
1946		30.5 (29.0)	
1948	41.0	30.8	
1949			27.4
1952	56.3	--	
1953			44.3
1954		--	
1956	55.4		
1957			36.4
1958		--	
1960	52.4	--	
1961			36.1
1964	46.2	19.0	
1965			37.7
1966		33.5 (37.4)	
1968	43.4		
1969			52.5
1970		15.3	
1972	67.8	51.5	
1973			50.7
1976	49.3	--	
1977			55.9
1978		50.2	
1980	53.0		
1981			46.4
1982		51.2	
1984	62.3	70.0	
1985			44.8
1988	59.7	28.7	
1989			49.8

1990		80.9
1992	45.0	
1993		58.3
1994		42.9[a]
1996	47.1[b]	52.5[b]
1997		56.2[c]

Notes: Double dashes (--) mean there was no Republican candidate in the general election. Percentages in parentheses refer to the results of special elections.

Sources: For all but a, b, and c, *Congressional Quarterly, Guide to U.S. Elections,* 3rd edition (Washington, DC: Congressional Quarterly, 1994).

[a] Richard M. Scammon and Alice V. McGillivray (eds.), *America Votes 21* (Washington, DC: Congressional Quarterly, 1995).

[b] Richard M. Scammon, Alice V. McGillivray, and Rhodes Cook (eds.), *America Votes 22* (Washington, DC: Congressional Quarterly, 1998).

[c] *Virginian-Pilot's* election archive on PilotOnline at http://data.pilotonline.com/election97/governor.htm

---

Republican strength in races for these three key offices is reported in Table 7.1. In all three columns, Republican candidates move from roughly a third of the vote (or less) to garnering majorities or pluralities. This occurred earliest at the presidential level as Dwight Eisenhower picked up the first majority for a Republican presidential candidate since Herbert Hoover did so in 1928. Republican gubernatorial and Senate candidates crossed a similar threshold for the first time in 1969 and 1972, respectively. That executive level candidates reached the majority mark first is not a coincidence. With Virginia governors prohibited from serving consecutive terms and U.S. president's limited to two such terms, incumbency plays a less significant role in executive branch elections than it does in legislative races. Still, William Scott was able to overcome the disadvantage of being a challenger when he defeated incumbent Senator William Spong in 1972. Republicans have picked up majorities in every Senate race they have contested since then, save 1988 and 1994 (both of which were victories for Senator Robb).

Table 7.2: Mean Number of Republican Seats in the U.S. House of Representatives, the Virginia House of Delegates, and the Virginia Senate, 1920s–1990s.

Decade	U.S. House	VA House	VA Senate
1920s	.4	6.60	3.00
1930s	.8	5.60	2.00
1940s	.0	5.20	2.20
1950s	1.4	5.80	3.00
1960s	2.4	9.00	3.40
1970s	5.8*	20.78*	5.89
1980s	6.4	31.90*	8.80
1990s	4.6	44.00*	17.00*

Notes: An asterisk represents a significant ($p < .01$) increase in the mean number of seats from the previous decade, as determined by the Scheffé test for pairwise comparisons of means. The data include the results of the 1997 Virginia legislative elections.

Sources: Means were calculated by the author. Partisan distribution of seats, by year, was provided by the following:

For U.S. House through the 1992 elections—*Congressional Quarterly, Guide to U.S. Elections*, 3rd edition (Washington, DC: Congressional Quarterly, 1994).

For U.S. House elections in 1994 and 1996—Richard M. Scammon, Alice V. McGillivray, and Rhodes Cook (eds.), *America Votes 22* (Washington, DC: Congressional Quarterly, 1998).

For VA House and Senate—Virginia House of Delegates, Information and Public Relations Office.

Table 7.2 reflects changes in party competition in terms of Virginia's U.S. House Delegation, and the General Assembly. Democrats, of course, maintained a stranglehold on virtually all of the state's U.S. House seats in the 1920s, 30s and 40s. In seventeen election cycles from 1918 to 1950, Democrats won all but six of the 160 seats that were up for election. No Republican served in Congress from Virginia in the 1940s and Democratic candidates often ran unopposed by Republicans in the general election. Republicans began winning at least a few seats in the 1950s, and have held no fewer than four seats since 1968. The decade of the 1970s, however, was a turning point in Republican representation in Congress. That decade saw a statistically significant increase over the 1960s in the number of seats held by Republicans. The 1972 elections, in particular, gave Republicans a boost as the GOP took seven of Virginia's ten seats. Though they continued to pick up seats in the 1980s, including a high-water mark of nine after the 1980 elections, the increase in the average number of seats held by Republicans was not significant. In fact, Republican representation has actually decreased in the 1990s. The additional seat given to Virginia after reapportionment in 1990 has essentially been Democratic. Democrats were even insulated from the Republican "revolution" of 1994, losing only one of the seven seats they held prior to that year's midterm elections. In the most recent Congress (the 105th), Democrats hold six of the eleven Virginia seats. "Only Virginia and Texas among the Southern states," notes McGlennon, "came out of the 1996 elections with Democratic house majorities" (1997, 218).

In the Virginia House of Delegates, Republicans have made slow progress toward reaching parity with the Democrats. After holding an average of less than seven seats (out of 100) for most of this century, Republicans began to gain ground in the 1960s. Republican gains have been significant, however, in every decade since the 1960s. Actually, grouping the data by decades overlooks some particularly important individual election cycles (see McClesky 1997,149–159). After the 1969 elections, the Republican delegation in the House of Delegates jumped from fourteen to twenty-four. Though it would drop back to seventeen in the middle of the decade (presumably due to the influence of Watergate), Republicans were back to their previous strength by 1980. The GOP gained nine seats in the 1981 election and by the end of the 1980s they held thirty-nine seats. In the 1993 cycle, Republicans picked up six more and today are in a position of virtual equality with forty-nine seats to the Democrats' fifty (with one Independent who caucuses with the Republicans).

On average, Republicans held fewer than four seats (out of forty) in the state Senate through the 1960s. Their gains in the upper chamber were far slower than in the House. The only decade in which significant gains were made from the previous decade has been the present one. Though the 1980s saw quite an increase in GOP representation, due in large part to a pick up of nine seats in 1979, it was the 1991 election that was a watershed for the Republicans (McCleskey 1997, 161). That year, they picked up eight seats, giving them a total of eighteen. Four years later they reached parity with Democrats and in 1997 they took control of the chamber for the first time. They now hold a 21 to 19 advantage in the Senate.

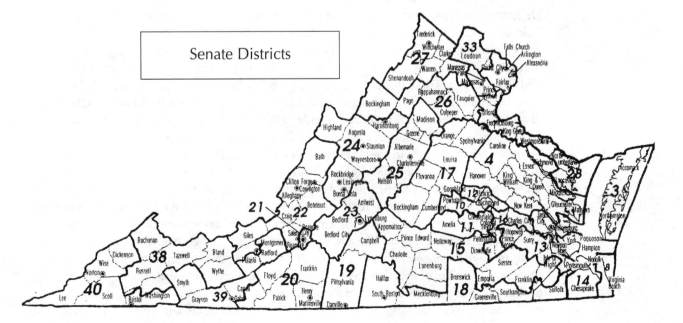

Figure 7.2 Senate Districts. Courtesy of The Library of Virginia.

Again, legislative incumbents hold so many advantages over their challengers that it is difficult for a party to pick up many of these seats. As such, Republicans have gained far more seats in the House of Delegates by picking up open seats (McCleskey 1997, 163). "In the senate," on the other hand, "Republicans have advanced about equally by defeating incumbents and by capturing open seats" (McCleskey 1997, 163). Still, most state legislative seats are safely in the hands of one party or the other. According to Clifton McCleskey, only twelve to fifteen seats in the House and six to eight Senate districts are up for grabs in any election year (1997, 163; see Barone et al. 1998, 369–376 for district voting patterns and demographics).

It is, of course, difficult to draw conclusions about the partisan make-up of an electorate based on partisan divisions among its elected officials. If we wish to generalize about party identification among voters, the easiest approach is simply to ask the voters which party they belong to. In a May 1998 survey of Virginia residents conducted by the Survey and Evaluation Research Laboratory at Virginia Commonwealth University, 27.5 percent of the respondents called themselves Democrats, an almost identical number identified as Republicans (27.4 percent) and 35.9 percent claimed to be Independents. When Independents were asked if they "lean" toward one party or the other, the percentage of Democrats rose to 39.8 percent while Republicans identifiers increased to 40.6 percent of the entire sample.[6]

Thus, the parties now maintain equal strength among citizens of the Old Dominion. Explanations for how Virginia Republicans gained identifiers cannot be explored here at any length except to note, as Scott Keeter has, that the GOP has benefitted from both conversion (voters switching party allegiance) and an influx of new voters to the state who are decidedly Republican (1992, 136–140).

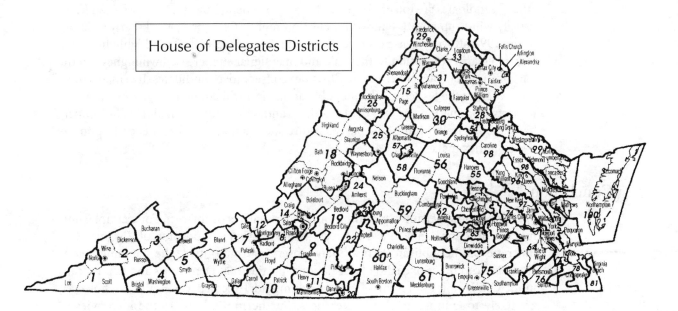

Figure 7.3 House of Delegates Districts. Courtesy of The Library of Virginia.

Brief mention of a key issue with regard to the party organizations should also be made. Given the historical dominance of a single party throughout the south, interparty conflict has long been a part of the region's party systems (McGlennon 1998, 150). The Organization and anti-Organization factions within Virginia's Democratic Party are well-known. Yet factions existed in the Virginia GOP as far back as the 1960s when conservative former-Democrats butted heads in their new party with moderate "Mountain" Republicans (McGlennon 1998, 151–152).

Today, Virginia's Democrats are more ideologically diverse than Republicans (McGlennon 1995, 98). This diversity produces ideological factions between conservative, moderate, and liberal party activists. More prominent, however, are the factions emanating from the interparty rivalry between Douglas Wilder and Chuck Robb (though there is reason to believe that these divisions are slowly disintigrating). Nevertheless, a regionwide survey of southern party activists in 1991 revealed that Virginia Democrats reported less factionalism than their counterparts in ten other southern states (McGlennon 1998, 154).

In the same study, Republicans placed near the middle of the pack in terms of factionalism (McGlennon 1998, 156). In all likelihood, the factional conflict in the GOP has increased in the last seven years. Mark Rozell and Clyde Wilcox (1996) find the source of this conflict is the Christian Right's transition from a social movement in the 1980s to a powerful wing of the Virginia Republican Party in the 1990s. That faction is so powerful, in fact, that a 1994 study of state parties by Campaigns & Elections magazine found Virginia to be one of eighteen states in which the Christian conservative presence in Republican party organizations "constitutes a working majority on major issues" (Persinos 1994, 22).

Rozell and Wilcox have argued that "the Christian Right fares best when it backs GOP candidates with broad-based electoral appeal," like former governor George Allen, who nonetheless keep Christian conservative interests in mind (1995, 130). When "their" candidates are too easily linked to the movement, however, the Christian Right usually winds up empty-handed on election night.[7] Of course, Mark Early's victory in the 1997 attorney general's race, despite his opponent's efforts to highlight such a link, is a glaring exception to that rule and may signal an increased willingness on the part of Virginia voters to consider Christian conservative candidates. It remains to be seen whether the leaders of this Republican faction will adopt a pragmatic approach to party nominations or will demand that candidates remain ideologically (or, perhaps, theologically) pure. The party's future success may very well depend upon the decision they make.

Conclusion

Space does note permit exploration into other matters of interest. For example, how much distinction can be made between the ideological composition of Virginia's Democratic and Republican Parties? Many observers from outside the state might conclude, as Lord Bryce once did of our national parties, that Democrats and Republicans in the Old Dominion resemble "Tweedledum and Tweedledee." Virginians, however, are likely to enumerate clear differences. Furthermore, how do the ideologies of

Virginia's Democrats and Republicans compare to those of the two parties in other states? One assumes, for instance, that Virginia's Democrats are more conservative than Republicans in some other states (though southern Democrats, at least in Congress, have become increasingly liberal; see Hoppe 1997). These and other issues must be left for another discussion.

Though it took decades to arrive, two-party competition seems firmly established in Virginia. State legislative elections in 1999 and Senator Robb's reelection bid in 2000 will be crucial in determining whether Republicans begin the next century in control of both chambers in the General Assembly, the Governor's mansion (as well as the lieutenant governor's and attorney general's office), and both U.S. Senate seats.[8] Only the U.S. House delegation will presumably remain in Democratic hands, though even that is by the slimmest of margins (six to five). While Virginia will not be central to any presidential campaigns in the near future, it should continue to be "debatable ground" between the two major parties at all other levels.

Bibliography

Aldrich, John H. 1995. *Why Parties? The Origin and Transformation of Political Parties*. Chicago: The University of Chicago Press.

Barone, Michael, William Lilley III, and Laurence J. DeFranco. 1998. *State Legislative Elections: Voting Patterns and Demographics*. Washington, DC: Congressional Quarterly.

Bass, Jack and Walter DeVries. 1976. *The Transformation of Southern Politics: Social Change and Political Consequence Since 1945*. New York: Meridian.

Duverger, Maurice. 1963. *Political Parties: Their Organization and Activity in the Modern State*. New York: John Wiley & Sons.

Glass, Robert C. and Carter Glass, Jr. 1937. *Virginia Democracy: A History of the Achievements of the Party and its Leaders in the Mother of Commonwealths, the Old Dominion*, Vol. 1. Springfield, IL: Democratic Historical Association.

Hoppe, Layne. 1997. "Increasing Liberalism Among Southern Members of Congress, 1970–1990, with an Analysis of the 1994 Congressional Elections." In *Southern Parties and Elections: Studies in Regional Political Change*. Eds. Robert P. Steed, Laurence W. Moreland, and Tod A. Baker. Tuscaloosa, AL: The University of Alabama Press.

Jefferson, Thomas. 1984. *Writings*. New York: The Library of America.

Jewell, Malcolm E. and David M. Olson. 1988. *Political Parties and Elections in American States*. 3rd ed. Chicago: The Dorsey Press.

Keeter, Scott. 1992. "Virginia's Party System: From 'Museum Piece' to Mainstream." In *Party Realignment and State Politics*. Ed. Maureen Moakley. Columbus, OH: Ohio State University Press.

Key, V. O., Jr. 1949. *Southern Politics in State and Nation*. New York: Vintage Books.

Key, V. O., Jr. 1964. *Politics, Parties, and Pressure Groups*. New York: Crowell.

Maisel, L. Sandy. 1993. *Parties and Elections in America: The Electoral Process.* 2nd ed. New York: McGraw-Hill.

McCleskey, Clifton. 1997. "Representation and Party in the Virginia General Assembly Since the Civil Rights and Reapportionment Revolutions." In *Southern Parties and Elections: Studies in Regional Political Change.* Eds. Robert P. Steed, Laurence W. Moreland, and Tod A. Baker. Tuscaloosa, AL: The University of Alabama Press.

McGlennon, John J. 1995. "Virginia: Experience with Democracy." In *Southern State Party Organizations and Activists.* Eds. Charles D. Hadley and Lewis Bowman. Westport, CT: Praeger.

McGlennon, John J. 1997. "Virginia: Old Habits Die Hard." In *The 1996 Presidential Election in the South: Southern Party Systems in the 1990s.* Eds. Laurence W. Moreland and Robert P. Steed. Westport, CT: Praeger.

McGlennon, John. 1998. "Factions in the Politics of the New South." In *Party Organization and Activism in the American South.* Eds. Robert P. Steed, John A. Clark, Lewis Bowman, and Charles D. Hadley. Tuscaloosa, AL: The University of Alabama Press.

Moger, Allen W. 1942. "The Origin of the Democratic Machine in Virginia." *The Journal of Southern History* 8 (2): 183–209.

Moger, Allen W. 1968. *Virginia: Bourbonism to Byrd, 1870–1925.* Charlottesville, VA: The University of Virginia Press.

Persinos, John F. 1994. "Has the Christian Right Taken Over the Republican Party?" *Campaigns & Elections,* September.

Rozell, Mark J. and Clyde Wilcox. 1995. "Virginia: God, Guns, and Oliver North." In *God at the Grass Roots: The Christian Right in the 1994 Elections.* Eds. Mark J. Rozell and Clyde Wilcox. Lanham, MD: Rowman & Littlefield.

Rozell, Mark J. and Clyde Wilcox. 1996. *Second Coming: The New Christian Right in Virginia Politics.* Baltimore: The Johns Hopkins University Press.

Sabato, Larry. 1977. *The Democratic Party Primary in Virginia: Tantamount to Election No Longer.* Charlottesville, VA: University Press of Virginia.

Sartori, Giovanni. 1976. *Parties and Party Systems: A Framework for Analysis.* Cambridge: Cambridge University Press.

Wilcox, Clyde, Mark J. Rozell, and J. Bradford Coker. 1995. "The Christian Right in the Old Dominion: Resurgent Republicans or Holy War?" *PS: Political Science & Politics* 28: 15–18.

Endnotes

1. Republicans did, however, remain a force in the southwestern part of the state and, later, in the Shenandoah Valley. Even at the height of Democratic dominance, V.O. Key (1949) could write, "In Virginia's southwestern congressional district Republicans and Democrats regularly fight over the congressional seat" (281).

2. For instance, "In the predominantly white ninth district, the stronghold of the Republicans, one out of every 4.2 voters could not read or write" (Moger 1968, 184).

3. While the separation of state and national parties would weaken the voters' attachment to the Democratic party in the long run, off-year elections actually helped Democratic candidates at the state level in the short run. That is, when Virginia voters began supporting Republican presidential nominees in 1952, off-year elections protected state Democrats against the "coattail" effect that surely would have benefitted down-ballot Republicans (Sabato 1977, 44).

4. The key Supreme Court decisions on representation from the 1960s are Baker v. Carr (1962), Wesberry v. Sanders (1964), Reynolds v. Sims (1964), and Kirkpatrick v. Preisler (1969).

5. As noted, Republicans won gubernatorial elections in 1973 and 1977. They also won two of the four U.S. Senate races; the other two were won by Harry F. Byrd, Jr. who ran as an Independent in the 1970s. In fact, no Democrat won a gubernatorial or U.S. Senate race from 1966 to 1981, something that occurred in no other state in the nation (Keeter 1992, 130). As for the two other statewide offices for which there are elections—lieutenant governor and attorney general— Republicans won one of three elections in the 1970s for lieutenant governor (a special election in 1971 was won by Independent Henry Howell) and the parties split the two races for attorney general. Thus, in the 1970s, Democrats won only two of the eleven statewide races, Republicans won six and Independents took the other three.

6. Data are from the Commonwealth Poll of May 6-14, 1998 and were provided to the author by Professor Scott Keeter of VCU. Sampling error on the survey was plus or minus four percentage points at the 95 percent confidence level. Percentages reported above are weighted according to sex, race, education, and region of residence so as to reflect Virginia's demographic composition (see statement of survey methodology at www.vcu.edu/srl/press/cpoll40.htm).

7. Rozell and Wilcox (1995) offer the following as examples of candidates who were linked too closely to the Christian Right and subsequently lost their elections: Guy Farley's bid for lieutenant governor in 1981 and Michael Farris's in 1993; the gubernatorial candidacies of Wyatt Durrette in 1985 and Marshall Coleman in 1989; and the 1994 congressional candidates in the Second, Fourth, Fifth, and Ninth districts. While they do not think Oliver North lost his senatorial bid in 1994 because of ties to Christian conservatives (but, instead, because of "personal liabilities"), Wilcox, Rozell and Coker (1995) recognize that those ties made linking North to the movement a great deal easier.

8. The U.S. Senate race in 2000 will probably pit Robb against popular former governor George Allen. It will surely be watched as closely as any race in the nation.

CHAPTER EIGHT

Issues, Horse Races, and Candidate Profiles: Press Coverage of Gubernatorial Campaigns*

Lawrence L. Schack
The University of Virginia

In 1991, Mark J. Rozell published an article entitled "Local v. National Press Assessments of Virginia's 1989 Gubernatorial Campaign" (Rozell 1991). Recognizing the lack of attention paid to the role of press coverage of statewide campaigns (Fico, Clogston, and Pizante 1984), Rozell looked to "enhance our understanding of how the press reports and interprets elections at the 'lower levels'" (Rozell 1991, 70). Relying on content analysis of print media articles about the campaign from both local and national news sources, Rozell offered the following three conclusions.[1]

First, certain events and issues, particularly those that lent themselves to "news values" that are ever-present in the news today—such as drama, novelty, timeliness, vividness, color, easily described stories with two distinct sides, terseness, good visuals, and pithy soundbites—received the bulk of the media's attention (Cook 1989 and 1998). To illustrate, though both the local and national media touched upon a wide array of issues, the one issue that received the lions share of attention throughout the 1989 gubernatorial campaign was abortion. In July of that year, the U.S. Supreme Court issued the landmark decision *Webster v. Reproductive Health Services, Inc.*, which gave states more authority to regulate abortion policy. Seized upon by both the candidates

---

* The author would like to thank University of Virginia student Nathan Miller for his help in the preparation of this chapter.

and the press, the controversial and intensely emotional issue of abortion became the central issue of the election, both on the campaign trail and in the pressroom.

Second, though the press might try to present themselves as coolly dispassionate in contrast to the intensity, color, and subjectivity of their subjects, "they do assign more weight to certain spokesmen and positions and hence tilt campaign coverage in a desired direction" (Rozell 1991, 70). Noting that 67% of the local press coverage of Democratic candidate L. Douglas Wilder was favorable, whereas only 44% of these same news outlets treated Republican gubernatorial candidate J. Marshall Coleman similarly, Rozell concluded that the liberal tilt of journalists as a group influenced the tenor of their coverage.

Third, media impact on the nature and development of election campaigns is pronounced. Far from simply holding up a mirror to external political actors and actions, the news media are directly involved in instigating them. By deciding which issues and events to emphasize and which ones to neglect, the news media—rather than passive receptors—are "precipitators of action," directly involved in the political process.

This chapter expands upon and complements Rozell's treatment. Focusing on the nature of the local coverage of the 1993 and 1997 Virginia gubernatorial elections, we look not only to identify patterns of press coverage, but also to shed some light on the causes of these patterns. The assumption, as with Rozell, is that press coverage is important to state-level campaigns and that it does influence both the nature of the campaign and voter perceptions. Therefore, examinations of press coverage of state-level campaigns are worthwhile.

The 1993 and 1997 Campaigns for Governor

Whereas the 1989 Virginia gubernatorial campaign was a historic, tumultuous affair, pitting Republican J. Marshall Coleman, a former state Attorney General, against Democrat L. Douglas Wilder, the incumbent Lieutenant Governor and first African-American elected to statewide office in Virginia, the 1993 and 1997 contests were relatively tame by comparison.

In 1993, Democrat Mary Sue Terry, the two-term Attorney General and first woman elected to statewide office in the Old Dominion, squared off against then little-known Republican George F. Allen, a former state legislator and one-term congressman. Having not won a single statewide office since 1977, Republicans—much like Virginia Democrats during their twelve year hiatus between 1969 and 1981—were admittedly starved for an electoral victory (Sabato 1996).

Though she enjoyed a wide early cushion in the polls—Allen's private tracking polls showed Terry enjoying a 27% lead in May of 1993—and was flush with cash at a time when the Allen campaign was struggling to compete, Terry's early advantage evaporated over the next few months. Looking to sit on her lead rather than go on the attack, Terry's complacency opened the door for the more aggressive Allen. After introducing himself to a statewide audience at the Republican's June convention, Allen then trumped Terry's signature proposal—a five-day waiting period before the purchase of a handgun—with a tough-on-crime message of his own that resonated with the electorate—the abolition of parole for violent offenders.

As the summer wore on, Allen began to eat into Terry's double-digit lead. By Labor Day, Allen's private tracking polls had Terry leading 47% to 40%, and by October, they showed the race tied at 41%. Thereafter, capitalizing on Democratic infighting, continually championing his anti-parole stance, and displaying an affability that helped to shield him from the extremist charges lobbed his way by opponents, Allen never lost his advantage (Sabato 1996).

In November, Allen received the support of 58% of Virginia's voters, winning nine of Virginia's eleven congressional districts and securing the highest winning percentage since Democrat Albertis Harrison captured 64% of the vote in 1961. In what was at that time the best Republican gubernatorial year of the century, the GOP also gained six House of Delegates seats, reducing the Democratic advantage to five (52 to 47). Because the state Senate was not up for election that year, the Republicans continued to endure a deficit of four (22 to 18).

Unlike 1993, in 1997 two well-known candidates vied for the electorate's support.[2] Neither Democrat Donald S. Beyer, the two-term incumbent Lieutenant Governor from Northern Virginia, nor Republican James S. Gilmore, III, the incumbent Attorney General, lacked name recognition. Gilmore, aiming to build on the gains posted in the mid-term 1995 state legislative elections (Republicans forged a tie in the state Senate that year) looked to ride the Commonwealth's surging Republican tide to victory. On the other hand Don Beyer, widely regarded as a media-genic candidate with a deft personal touch, hoped to buck the Republican trend. As the standard bearer for a party in danger of losing its century-old grip on the reigns of power in the Virginia General Assembly, and facing the possibility of dropping consecutive gubernatorial elections for only the second time this century, it was up to Don Beyer to renew and restore a party on the brink.

Though slow to heat up, the campaign received a boost in June when Gilmore announced his intention to effectively eliminate the local property taxes assessed on up to $20,000 of a car or truck's value. Skillfully seizing on this much-hated levy—a tax that was to be paid in many localities just prior to the November election, including the residents of the large suburbs in Beyer's vote rich home area of Northern Virginia—Gilmore pinned his hopes, those of his running mates, and those of his party squarely on his "No Car Tax" pledge.

Beyer, after initially denouncing Gilmore's plan as fiscally irresponsible, in July decided to enter the car tax elimination sweep stakes. Apparently swayed by arguments that he needed a counterproposal, Beyer introduced a less costly, but also less generous property tax relief plan. Though Beyer's strategy seemed at first to pay dividends—Gilmore's private campaign tracking polls showed their candidate's deficit increase slightly between June and July—by the end of August, these same polls showed the race to be a dead heat. Thereafter, as Beyer moved from issue to issue, searching for something to buttress his ebbing fortunes, Gilmore—largely on the strength of his "No Car Tax" pledge—began to pull away.

Gilmore won the 1997 Virginia gubernatorial election by a large margin, securing 56% of the vote, to Don Beyer's 43%. Marking the greatest GOP breakthrough this century, Republicans posted their first sweep of all three statewide offices, gained effective control of the Virginia Senate, and reduced the Democratic advantage in the Virginia House of Delegates to three.[3]

Media coverage of both the 1993 and 1997 Virginia gubernatorial campaigns exhibited certain identifiable patterns. First, similar to 1989, while the large majority of potential issues and talking points struggled for attention, two "news value" friendly issues—the abolition of parole in 1993, and property tax elimination in 1997—received an extraordinary amount of press emphasis. This emphasis was ever-present, and cut across the three media outlets examined here. Second, as the campaigns progressed, coverage of issues was displaced by stories which focused on the "horse-race," i.e. "who's winning, who is likely to win, and what the underdogs need to do to stage a comeback" (Rozell 1991, 74). This shift of attention also cut across media outlets. Third, there was a good deal of congruence between the news judgments of Virginia's big-three media outlets. This lends support to critics of the news industry who complain that media coverage tends to ignore the less exciting though no less important aspects of elections (Graber 1992 & 1996; Patterson 1993; Sabato 1993). After further examining these patterns, I will conclude with a discussion of the reasons for the identified trends.

Data Sources

This analysis is drawn from a survey of print media articles from the *Richmond Times-Dispatch, Washington Post,* and the *Norfolk-Virginian Pilot* about the 1993 and 1997 campaigns from June 1 of each election year through election day. A total of 578 stories appearing in these three newspapers were studied comprehensively. The

Figure 8.1 State Capitol, Richmond. Courtesy of The Virginia Chamber of Commerce.

coding of these stories is based on evaluations of the primary content of each news article.

The *Richmond Times-Dispatch (RTD)*—Virginia's Capitol newspaper—and the *Norfolk-Virginian Pilot (Pilot)*, which also owns and operates the *Roanoke Times*, are Virginia's most widely distributed newspapers. *The Washington Post (Post)*, though generally recognized as a national news daily, devotes approximately one-third of its "Metro" section to Virginia government and politics, and the occasional "A" section story. These three newspapers account for the vast majority of political reporting in Virginia and are therefore significant cue-givers for the rest of Virginia's press corps.

Analysis

In 1991, Rozell's analysis assessed local and national news coverage of the 1989 gubernatorial campaign in three general areas: (1) *Subject Matter*—articles categorized as issue, horse-race, character, profile, and others; (2) *Issue-Coverage*—abortion, crime and drugs, transportation and growth, among others; and (3) *Candidate-Coverage*—the amount of coverage given to each candidate as well as the type of coverage (positive, negative, or neutral).

The analysis conducted here, though largely similar, contains some important differences. First, "character" and "profile" stories have been collapsed into a single "profile" category. Relying on Rozell's definitions, a significant difference between character and profile coverage during the 1993 and 1997 Virginia gubernatorial campaigns was not discovered, i.e. the stories examined which included character elements, tended also to include profile elements, and vice versa. Rather than artificially create a difference when in fact none was observed, these two categories were simply combined.

Second, here candidate-coverage will not be discussed. In sum, news reporters have over time been primarily accused of carrying a liberal ideological bias into the news gathering process (Rusher 1988).[4] This argument has been supported by the release of various surveys showing that journalists are substantially Democratic in party affiliation and voting habits, progressive and antiestablishment in political orientation, and well to the left of the general public on many economic, foreign policy, and social issues.

Though these criticisms have some validity in different times and circumstances, in one media forum or another, critics of this view argue that the possession of an ideology does not necessarily effect news content. They contend that news professionals may be able to subordinate biases in pursuit of professionalism.[5] Further, this charge of political bias is said to ignore a host of non-ideological factors which are just as essential—if not more so—to an understanding of press bias (Cook 1989 & 1998).

Press bias of *all kinds*—partisan, agenda-setting, and ideological—can and does influence the day-to-day coverage of politics and government. Ideological bias then is not the silver-bullet that critics on both the right and left often insist that it is. Rather, it is just one piece in the media's news mosaic. Therefore, measures of, and conclusions based upon, the amount of favorable or unfavorable coverage extended to candidates are not discussed.

Third, Rozell's analysis covered only the period beginning on September 1, 1989, and ending on the day of the election, November 8. His decision to restrict his coverage to these dates was well grounded. Traditionally, Virginia gubernatorial campaigns really begin after the Labor Day holiday the first weekend in September. It is at this time that the campaigns tend to shift from a comparatively low to a high gear. This change of pace affects the candidates as well as the press corps. The action becomes more fast-paced, as each candidate searches for the edge that will propel them to victory come November. With this distinction in mind, it is hypothesized that press coverage of Virginia gubernatorial campaigns will differ over time. As such, press coverage is broken into two periods, June 1 through the end of August, and September 1 to November 8.

Finally, Rozell differentiated between local and national press coverage of the 1989 Virginia gubernatorial campaign. This determination was prudent given the historic nature of the 1989 election. The candidacy of Doug Wilder, who was seeking to become the first African-American governor in the United States, naturally garnered national media attention. The 1993 and 1997 Virginia gubernatorial elections, though historic in their own right, did not as readily lend themselves to national press coverage. As such, the role played by the national media in these elections is not examined.

Summer Coverage of the 1993 and 1997 Virginia Gubernatorial Campaigns

It is widely accepted today that voter's perceptions of candidates and the campaigns themselves are affected by the media's portrayal. When the voter seeks information about the campaign, the media's portrayal is the major—if not the sole—source of that information. Aware of the media's role in shaping voters' perceptions and lacking any other vehicle with the same reach, candidates look to use the media to craft a favorable image of themselves. Given this increasing reliance on the mass media both by voters and candidates, the role of the press as gatekeeper for news coverage in campaigns has grown (Davis 1996).

Acknowledging the elevated role of the media in contemporary campaigns both at the national and state levels, we should ask ourselves what kinds of coverage elections receive. Do the media evaluate candidates' qualifications and issue positions? Do they sufficiently cover the issues that will likely require the future attention of the eventual officeholder? Are adequate criteria supplied to enable voters to discern the merits of the competing policy options? Do voters receive enough information about each candidate's personality, experience, and ability to evaluate the candidate's likely performance if elected (Davis 1996)?

News media critics tend to answer the above questions in the negative. They complain that serious, in-depth campaign coverage at all levels of government is routinely set aside to make room for "profile" stories which focus on the personality, style, background and experience, and image characteristics of candidates. Another common criticism of the media is that they devote too much time and space to covering the "horse-race." The citizenry then does not learn a great deal about a campaign beyond who is winning and losing, as well as how candidates look, where they are from, how they speak, what experiences they bring to the table and the image they present.

By looking at press coverage of the 1993 gubernatorial election from June 1 through the end of August, it would seem that these criticisms are not wholly appropriate. As Table 8.1 shows, a healthy 37% of all news articles in the three papers surveyed focused on "issues," 40% for the *Post,* 37% for the RTD, and 32% for the *Pilot.* Not surprisingly—given the stress on criminal justice themes by both candidates—when this issue coverage is broken down, the topic that received the most attention was crime (33%). Other issues addressed include taxes and spending (15%), family issues (13%), education (11%), the economy (8%), transportation/regional development (8%), elderly/social services (6%), abortion (4%), and the environment (2%).

Table 8.1: Summer Press Coverage of the 1993 Gubernatorial Election by Source and Subject Matter

Subject	Washington Post		Richmond Times-Dispatch		Norfolk-Virginian Pilot		Totals	
	N	%	N	%	N	%	N	%
Issue	14	40.0	23	37.0	11	32.0	48	37.0
Horse-Race	10	29.0	21	34.0	8	24.0	39	30.0
Profile	4	11.0	8	23.0	7	20.0	19	14.0
Other	7	20.0	10	16.0	8	24.0	25	19.0
Totals	35	100	62	100	34	100	131	100

"Profile" stories accounted for 14% of total news coverage. While at times superficial, the lazy campaign pace of the summer months did afford the Virginia press corps time to pen a handful of in-depth analysis that offered voters a thorough view of the backgrounds both of Terry and Allen.

Media critics though would not be surprised to learn that "horse-race" articles constituted 30% of all campaign-related stories published during this period, 29% for the *Post,* 34% for the *RTD,* and 24% for the *Pilot.* Though only two officially released polls were conducted between the months of June and August—one June 8–10, and the other August 26–28, both by Mason-Dixon Opinion Research—all three papers devoted ample space to discussing who was ahead and who was behind, along with campaign strategies, and campaign fund-raising.

The final category of articles is labeled "other." Some stories did not fit into one of the three thematic categories, i.e. factual stories commenting on candidate endorsements, campaign advertising, and campaign events, among others. During the summer months of 1993, these stories accounted for 19% of all news reporting, 20% for the *Post,* 16% for the *RTD,* and 24% for the *Pilot.*

Turning now to press coverage of the 1997 Virginia gubernatorial campaign during this same period, what immediately jumps out is the greater emphasis on "issues" as a percentage of total news coverage, as Table 8.2 indicates. Driven largely by Gilmore's June announcement concerning the elimination of the personal property tax on cars and trucks, and Beyer's July decision to offer a similar tax-cut plan of his own, a full 54% of the stories printed during June, July, and August focused on issues. The *Pilot* led the way, devoting 75% of their coverage to issues. For the *Post* (47%), and the *RTD* (49%), coverage of issues accounted for almost one-half of all news stories.

Table 8.2: Summer Press Coverage of the 1997 Gubernatorial Election by Source and Subject Matter

Subject	Washington Post		Richmond Times-Dispatch		Norfolk-Virginian Pilot		Totals	
	N	%	N	%	N	%	N	%
Issue	9	47.0	24	49.0	15	75.0	48	54.0
Horse-Race	3	16.0	10	20.0	2	10.0	15	17.0
Profile	--	--	6	12.0	1	5.0	7	8.0
Other	7	37.0	9	19.0	2	10.0	18	21.0
Totals	19	100	49	100	20	100	88	100

Looking more closely at the issues, stories concerning taxes and spending—reports which included discussions of property tax elimination—received the most attention (33%). News reporters also chose to examine crime and drugs (21%), education (19%), the environment (10%), transportation/regional development (8%), agriculture (6%), and the economy (2%). For the number one issue—taxes and spending—44% of the *Post's* issue articles focused on taxes and spending, whereas for the *RTD* 29% of such articles did, and for the *Pilot* 33%.

Not surprisingly, this greater emphasis on the issues contributed to a marked decline in the number of "profile" and "horse-race" stories. Whereas 15% and 30% of the summer of 1993 coverage focused on candidate profiles and horse-race themes, respectively, in the summer of 1997 profile reports (8%) and horse-race coverage (17%) constituted 25% of *all* news stories.[6] Together then, profile and horse-race coverage of the Gilmore/Beyer campaign during this time period constituted less total news coverage than that afforded issues.

Finally, the one subject area where coverage remained static was the "other" category. In the summer of 1997, coverage of the day-to-day events of the campaign constituted 21% of the total news coverage, compared to 19% in 1993. Given the slow-moving nature of the 1997 campaign during these early months, this result was not unexpected.

Fall Coverage of the 1993 and 1997 Virginia Gubernatorial Campaigns

While in the summer months of 1993 and 1997 the news media bucked the expected trends, providing profile and horse-race coverage though at the same time offering an ample amount of issue coverage, press coverage of these same campaigns from September 1 through election day took on a decidedly different tone. As the pace of the campaigns quickened, and the polling organizations hit full stride, horse-race stories rather than issue coverage became the dominant focus of the press corps. Summer headlines such as *"Terry Wants 5-Day Wait to Buy Guns; Issue Could Influence Race for Virginia Governor"*,[7] and *"Beyer Tries to Change Subject from Taxes to Environment,"*[8] were oftentimes replaced by news story openings trumpeting poll results and the race for money, i.e. *"Allen Staying Ahead of Terry by Same Margin a Poll Suggests; The Democrat Would Need Almost All Undecided Voters' Support to Win,"*[9] *"Gilmore Surges to Lead Over Beyer, Poll Shows,"*[10] and *"Gilmore Leads in Poll, Money."*[11] Though not wholly horse-race oriented, fall coverage of these campaigns did more closely resemble that depicted by media critics.

Looking first at 1993, as we have already seen, from June 1 through the end of August, "issue" coverage accounted for 37% of total news coverage, while "horse-race" stories constituted 30% of all news stories. Conversely, as Table 8.3 reports, after September 1, issue coverage dipped to 25% (25% for the *Post*, 24% for the *RTD*, and 26% for the *Pilot*) of total news coverage. Reporting on the horse-race, however, jumped to 41%—41% for the *Post*, 40% for the *RTD*, and 43% for the *Pilot*. "Profile" stories, as well as those stories classified as "other," remained relatively static across time.

Table 8.3: Fall Press Coverage of the 1993 Gubernatorial Election by Source and Subject Matter

Subject	Washington Post		Richmond Times-Dispatch		Norfolk-Virginian Pilot		Totals	
	N	%	N	%	N	%	N	%
Issue	11	25.0	23	24.0	18	26.0	52	25.0
Horse-Race	18	41.0	38	40.0	30	43.0	86	41.0
Profile	8	18.0	12	13.0	7	10.0	27	13.0
Other	7	16.0	22	23.0	15	21.0	44	21.0
Totals	44	100	95	100	70	100	209	100

Breaking the issues down, similar to coverage during the summer months, in the fall crime garnered the majority of the media's attention (29%). Staying on-message for the duration of the campaign, Allen continually stressed and the media regularly discussed his tough-on-crime message. Beyond criminal justice issues, the press covered a broad range of topics, including taxes and spending (17%), education (14%), transportation/regional development (12%), abortion (6%), the Virginia Military Institute (2%), the environment (4%), race (2%), the economy (6%), family issues (2%), and the religious right (6%).

"Horse-race" coverage was undoubtedly influenced by the unprecedented number of political polls conducted during the months of September and October. In the 1985 election for governor in Virginia, a total of eight polls—two in the summer months, and six in the fall—were released by three polling organizations/sponsors. By 1989, this number jumped to a total of eleven polls—two in the summer, and nine in the fall—released by four polling organizations/sponsors. In 1993, this number rose yet again, resulting in thirteen polls—two in the summer, eleven in the fall—released by five polling organizations/sponsors. Interestingly, while some of these polls came within two percent of predicting the actual outcome of the 1993 governors race, others misjudged the eventual results by as much as ten percent. Echoing Sabato, given the oft-illustrated shortcomings of public opinion polls, rather than occupying the main ring of news coverage of election campaigns, perhaps in the future news organization will consider whether they should be relegated more to the sideshow (Sabato 1996, 70).

Looking now at press coverage of the 1997 governors race, similar to 1993, 1997 witnessed an increase in the percentage of "horse-race" stories during the latter months of the campaign, as reported in Table 8.4. Whereas 17% of the press's summer offerings focused on this, horse-race coverage accounted for 37% (31% for the *Post*, 38% for the R*TD*, and 43% for the *Pilot*) of all fall stories as shown in Table 8.4. This jump of 20% mirrors the more pronounced presence of public opinion polls in 1997. From April through August, four polls were conducted by two polling organizations/ sponsors. During September and October, fourteen polls were sponsored by eight different pollsters. Though some again came to within a whisker of predicting the campaign's outcome, others grossly misjudged the eventual result, proving once again the inexact nature of public opinion polling.

Table 8.4: Fall Press Coverage of the 1997 Gubernatorial Election by Source and Subject Matter

Subject	Washington Post		Richmond Times-Dispatch		Norfolk-Virginian Pilot		Totals	
	N	%	N	%	N	%	N	%
Issue	12	31.0	29	38.0	15	43.0	56	37.0
Horse-Race	15	39.0	31	41.0	10	29.0	56	37.0
Profile	3	8.0	3	4.0	3	9.0	9	6.0
Other	9	23.0	13	17.0	7	20.0	29	19.0
Totals	39	100	76	100	35	100	150	100

"Issue" coverage, which constituted 54% of the total news stories during the summer months of 1997, dropped to 37% (31% for the *Post*, 38% for the *RTD*, and 43% for the *Pilot*) of all fall coverage. Though this drop of seventeen percent was significant, issues did pull even with horse-race coverage throughout the fall, a finding that is a testimony to the potency of Gilmore's "No Car Tax" message. This slogan, plastered on thousands of signs across the Commonwealth and repeatedly referred to by each Republican statewide and Virginia House of Delegates candidate, became the clarion call of the 1997 election. A full one-third of all fall news stories focused on taxes and spending. Other issues considered include abortion (18%), crime (10%), education (10%), and the environment (10%), among others.

Discussion and Conclusion

We return now to the central purpose of this paper—to identify patterns of press coverage, and also to shed some light on the causes of these patterns. In looking at Table 8.5 and Table 8.6, and taking into account the earlier discussion, some notable patterns of local press coverage of the 1993 and 1997 Virginia elections for governor emerge. First, the evidence presented lends credence to the assertion that coverage of Virginia gubernatorial campaigns—specifically "issue" and "horse-race" coverage— does differ over time (see Table 8.5). During the slow summer months, discussions of issues dominated the print media. In the summer of 1993, 37% of all news stories focused squarely on the issues. From June through August 1997, this proportion jumped to 54%. However, when the clip of the campaign quickened from a slow waltz to a mad dash, coverage of these campaigns took on a different hue. In 1993, issue coverage accounted for 25% of the total news coverage during the fall—a 12% drop from the summer—while in 1997, the proportion of issue coverage from September through election day of the issues was 37%, a 17% decline.

Table 8.5: Comparison of Summer and Fall Press Coverage of the 1993 and 1997 Gubernatorial Elections by Subject Matter

Subject	Summer of 1993 Totals		Fall of 1993 Totals		Summer of 1997 Totals		Fall of 1997 Totals		All Coverage	
	N	%	N	%	N	%	N	%	N	%
Issue	48	37.0	52	25.0	48	54.0	56	37.0	204	35.0
Horse-Race	39	30.0	86	41.0	15	17.0	56	37.0	196	34.0
Profile	19	14.0	27	13.0	7	8.0	9	6.0	62	11.0
Other	25	20.0	10	16.0	8	24.0	25	19.0	116	20.0
Totals	35	100	62	100	34	100	131	100	578	100

Whereas issue and horse-race coverage exhibited a high degree of variability over time, those stories which fall under the "profile" and "other" themes remained markedly static. Profile stories accounted for 14% of the total news stories in the summer of 1993, 13% in the fall of that same year. In 1997, profile coverage in the summer and fall totaled 8% and 6%, respectively. Meanwhile, coverage classified as other totaled 19% (summer of 1993) , 21% (fall of 1993), 21% (summer of 1997), and 19% (fall of 1997).

Another constant pattern was the amount of attention paid to two specific issues—crime issues in 1993 and taxes and spending in 1997. In the fall of 1993, though issue coverage dipped as a percentage of total news coverage, print space devoted to crime remained steady—33% during the summer months, 29% during the fall. Similarly, coverage of tax and spending issues accounted for roughly one-third of all print stories catalogued here, both in the summer and fall of 1997.

Table 8.6: Comparison of Total Press Coverage of the 1993 and 1997 Gubernatorial Elections by Subject Matter

Subject	Total		Issues		Horse-Race		Profile		Other	
	N	%	N	%	N	%	N	%	N	%
Post	46	33.0	46	34.0	15	11.0	30	22.0	137	100
RTD	99	35.0	100	36.0	29	10.0	54	19.0	282	100
Pilot	59	37.0	50	32.0	18	11.0	32	20.0	159	100
Totals	204	35.0	196	34.0	62	11.0	116	200	578	1000

A final striking pattern is the similarity of news coverage across media outlets, as seen in Table 8.6. Looking first at the issues, the *Post, RTD,* and *Pilot* devoted 33%,

35%, and 37% of their total news stories, respectively, to issues. This same pattern emerges when we look at horse-race coverage—34% for the *Post*, 36% for the *RTD*, and 32% for the *Pilot*. The proportion of profile stories—11% for the *Post*, 10% for the *RTD*, and 11% for the *Pilot*—and coverage classified as other—22% for the *Post*, 19% for the *RTD*, and 20% for the *Pilot*—was also analogous across the sample.

Having identified these patterns, we should ask what factors contribute to their emergence. Looking first at the changing nature of the coverage devoted to issue and horse-race themes over time, it has been well documented that when given the choice, the news industry will report the interesting, unusual, dramatic, unpredictable, or controversial rather than the arcane, detailed, difficult to explain event or issue, regardless of the merits (Cook 1989; Rozell 1991, 87; Graber 1992; Davis 1996).[12] Accepting this as true, a corollary follows: horse-race coverage, with its emphasis on winning and losing, who's ahead and who's behind, and competing campaign strategy and tactics, enjoys a natural advantage over issue coverage. Given then the prevalence of polling organizations and sponsors who regularly gauged public opinion during the fall months of both gubernatorial election years and publicly released those results, the increased attention devoted to horse-race themes during this period is not surprising.

Turning to another identified pattern—the similarity of news coverage across media outlets—recently a great deal of attention has been paid to explanations of media coverage of politicians and campaigns that acknowledge the organizational pressures, and professional values and norms that extend across news organizations (Bennett 1996; Davis 1996; Cook 1998). Briefly summarizing, proponents of these explanations argue that the process of gathering and reporting the news is shaped by organizational strictures, i.e., the peculiarities of the beat system, the demand for regularized news, deadlines, among others, and professional pressures—referred to earlier as "news values"—present in all mainstream news organizations. These ubiquitous demands homogenize news gathering and reporting processes, resulting in individual news outlets mirroring and reinforcing each other's coverage.

While it is impossible at this point to say whether theories of organizational and professional pressures and norms wholly explain the type of news product the public receives, studies show that news professionals today who work for the mainstream press do endeavor to provide an unbiased news product (Cook 1989; Graber 1992; Davis 1996). But in an effort to achieve this goal, journalists and their editors are said to apply the dual standards of importance and interest, tending to judge stories by the seemingly objective measure of how well they fit news values rather than the blatantly subjective standard of how tightly they adhere to a particular political ideology. The evidence presented here supports this conclusion. Though tests of ideological bias were not conducted, a review of the press coverage of the 1993 and 1997 Virginia gubernatorial campaigns does provide insight into how the presumably unbiased choices of contemporary journalists may in fact contribute to a different kind of news bias, one that does not equally favor all campaign issues and events at all times. If this is in fact the case, then the goal of media objectivity in the Old Dominion remains still an elusive one.

Bibliography

Bennett, W. Lance. 1998. *News: The Politics of Illusion.* New York: Longman.

Cook, Timothy. 1989. *Making Laws & Making News: Media Strategies in the U.S. House of Representatives.* Washington, D.C.: The Brookings Institution.

Cook, Timothy. 1998. *Governing with the News: The News Media as a Political Institution.* Chicago: The University of Chicago Press.

Davis, Richard. 1996. *The Press and American Politics: The New Mediator,* 2nd ed. Upper Saddle River, NJ: Prentice Hall.

Fico, Frederick, John Clogston and Gary Pizante. 1988. "Influence of Party and Incumbency on 1984 Michigan Election Coverage." *Journalism Quarterly* 65.

Graber, Doris A. 1992. *Media Power in Politics,* 3rd ed. Washington, D.C.: CQ Press.

Graber, Doris A. 1996. *Mass Media and American Politics,* 5th ed. Washington, D.C.: CQ Press.

Patterson, Thomas E. 1993. *Out of Order.* New York: Vintage Books.

Rozell, Mark J. 1991. "Local v. National Press Assessments of Virginia's 1989 Gubernatorial Campaign." *Polity* Fall: 69–89.

Rusher, William A. 1988. *The Coming Battle for the Media.* New York: William Morrow.

Sabato, Larry J. 1993. *Feeding Frenzy: How Attack Journalism Has Transformed American Politics.* New York: MacMillan.

Sabato, Larry J. 1996. "The 1993 Statewide Elections: Virginia's Twelve Year Itch Returns," In *Virginia Votes,* 1991–1994. Charlottesville: Weldon Cooper Center for Public Service.

Endnotes

1. The "local" papers studied were the *Richmond Times Dispatch,* and the *Washington Post.* National sources included all news stories on the 1989 gubernatorial campaign from the *New York Times, Los Angeles Times, Christian Science Monitor,* and *Wall Street Journal,* as well as three national news weeklies— *Newsweek, Time,* and *U.S. News and World Report.*

2. For a detailed account of the 1997 gubernatorial election, see Larry J. Sabato, "The 1997 Virginia Election for Governor: The Republican Sweep," Weldon Cooper Center for Public Service, Charlottesville, Virginia, 1997.

3. Subsequent special legislative elections further reduced the Democratic advantage, resulting in a Virginia House of Delegates composed of 49 Republicans, 50 Democrats, and 1 Independent heading into the 1999 state legislative elections.

4. Also see Shirley Christian, "Covering the Sandinistas: The Foregone Conclusions of the Fourth Estate," *Washington Journalism Review,* March, 1982.

5. See Michael J. Robinson, "Just How Liberal Is the News?", *Public Opinion*, February/March, 1983.

6. While 1993 witnessed two pre-September election polls, 1997 saw three, an April Virginia Commonwealth University Commonwealth Poll, and two Mason-Dixon polls, one in May, and one in July.

7. *Washington Post*, June 9, 1993, p. A1.

8. *Virginian-Pilot*, August 11, 1997, p. B3.

9. *Virginian-Pilot*, October 29, 1993, p. A1.

10. *Washington Post*, October 23, 1997, p. A1.

11. *Virginian-Pilot*, October 31, 1997, p. A1.

12. This argument also helps to explain the popularity—as measured by the amount of copy space devoted to their coverage—of Allen's "abolition of parole" pledge and Gilmore's "No Car Tax" plan.

CHAPTER NINE

Intergovernmental Relations in Virginia: The Dillon Rule in Action

Stan Livengood
James Madison University

This chapter discusses the relationship of localities to the Commonwealth and the operation of local government in Virginia. The focus will be on forms of local government that are readily familiar—counties, towns, and cities. The chapter offers historical grounding in the subject and provides legal descriptions of local governments in relation to the General Assembly. Several case studies are also presented to explore complexities that are not readily obvious from a purely statutory description of the topic. As Deil S. Wright, one of the nation's leading authorities on intergovernmental relations has written, "state-local relations in the United States provide one of the most fascinating arenas for studying the interplay between law and politics" (1988, p. 312). Students will undoubtedly discover that the Commonwealth of Virginia proves to be no exception.

Legal Foundation: The Dillon Rule

The legal principle defining the status of local government in Virginia is oddly enough, traced to the Iowa Supreme Court. The doctrine has been named the Dillon Rule in deference to the Chief Justice of the Iowa Supreme Court, John Dillon, who delivered the majority opinions. The rationale for the Dillon Rule is drawn from two cases that were adjudicated during the June term of 1868—*City of Clinton v. Cedar Rapids and Missouri Railroad Company* (24 Iowa 455) and *Merriam v. Moody's Executors* (25 Iowa 163).

– 111 –

City of Clinton v. Cedar Rapids and Missouri Railroad Company was brought before the Court on appeal, in an effort to overturn an injunction imposed against the railroad company building track upon the streets of Clinton. The case dated to 1856, when the Iowa legislature, using a federal land grant, issued a contract to build railway line from the city of Lyons to the city of Cedar Rapids. The original company failed to construct the railway in the allotted time and the Iowa legislature canceled its contract. In the meantime, the Chicago, Iowa and Nebraska Railroad built a line from Cedar Rapids to a point two miles south of Lyons. This juncture became the city of Clinton, which ratified its municipal charter on April 5, 1859. That same year, the newly founded Cedar Rapids and Missouri Railroad petitioned for the opportunity to use the federal land grant wasted by the original company. The Iowa legislature responded by transferring a portion of the federal lands to the Cedar Rapids and Missouri to build a line from Lyons intersecting with the Chicago, Iowa and Nebraska in Clinton.

Clinton refused to allow the Cedar Rapids and Missouri to build rail inside its corporate limits. Claiming these thoroughfares as municipal property, the City Council had enacted an ordinance prohibiting placement of track upon its streets. The District Court awarded Clinton an injunction against the Cedar Rapids and Missouri, finding that "the right to construct a railway upon or over the streets of a city is dependent upon the consent of such city" (24 Iowa 455 at p. 462). Clinton's lawyer argued that the land had belonged to the state prior to establishment of a municipal corporation, but the act of incorporation passed jurisdictional control from the state to the municipality.

The Supreme Court disagreed that Iowa had repudiated legal authority over Clinton by creating a municipal corporation. The Court affirmed that the city was responsible for the streets within its jurisdictional boundaries, but explained that the streets are held "in trust for the public, not the people of the city alone, but the general public as well" (24 Iowa 455 at p. 470). The Court agreed that Iowa's constitution required compensation to be paid for public appropriation of property. However, Article I, Section 18, stated that "*Private* property shall not be taken for public use without just compensation to the owner" (24 Iowa 455 at p. 474). Since the streets are public, this clause did not apply.

The other core opinion that elaborates the Dillon Rule, *Merriam v. Moody's Executors,* concerns city streets as well. This time, the central issue was municipal improvement and proper methods for collecting payment. An amendment to the municipal charter was approved by referendum that provided for assessment and collection of a special tax used to construct street, alley, and wharf improvements in the city of Keokuk. The Tax Collector, under direction of the City Council, sold a vacant lot because the owners were delinquent in paying the special taxes. Owners of the lot contended that the charter amendment did not grant Keokuk power to convey real estate for nonpayment of the special taxes.

The Iowa Supreme Court agreed with the lot's owners. The city charter undeniably allowed for sale if the *general* taxes were delinquent. Yet, the charter amendment did not specifically declare that sale of property was authorized to collect the special taxes. Therefore, Keokuk officials were not entitled to assume this power. The Court grounded its opinion in precedent claiming that the power to "collect" did not authorize collection by sale. Rather, as outlined by Mr. Justice Wright in *Ham v. Miller* (20 Iowa 450) that the power to sell must be *expressly* given (25 Iowa 163, 173).

After inspecting all provisions concerning taxation in Keokuk's charter and its amendments, the Court concluded,

> "in respect to all other taxes, except those mentioned in sections 4, 5, 6 and 7 [of the charter amendment], the power to sell is expressly conferred upon the city. It is not conferred with respect to these. The fair and natural inference is, that the legislature purposely withheld it" (25 Iowa 163, 174).

The principle that should have guided the city in collecting the taxes owed was to exhaust any and all judicial remedies available, including attaching a lien to the property.

Two passages are traditionally used from these two cases to express the Dillon Rule. States, such as Virginia, that ascribe to the Dillon Rule have often quoted and cited these excerpts to explain state authority over localities. The first postulate, drawn from *City of Clinton v. Cedar Rapids and Missouri Railroad Company,* is often interpreted to exaggerate the state legislature's prerogative over localities.

> "The true view is this: Municipal corporations owe their origin to, and derive their powers and rights wholly from, the legislature. It breathes into them the breath of life, without which they cannot exist. As it creates, so it may destroy. If it may destroy, it may abridge and control. Unless there is some constitutional limitation on the right, the legislature might, by a single act, if we can suppose it capable of so great a folly and so great a wrong, sweep from existence all of the municipal corporations in the state, and the corporation could not prevent it. We know of no limitation on this right so far as the corporations themselves are concerned. They are, so to phrase it, the mere tenants at will of the legislature" (24 Iowa 455, 475).

A part of this passage has been underlined to call attention to its importance. These words are often obscured during discussions of the Dillon Rule. The scheme available to localities are defined by the state constitution. For example, Article VII, Section 8, of the Constitution of Virginia states:

> "No street railway, gas, water, steam or electric heating, electric light or power, cold storage, compressed air, viaduct, circuit, telephone, or bridge company, nor any corporation, association, person, or partnership, engaged in these or like enterprises shall be permitted to use the streets, alleys, or public grounds of a city or town without the previous consent of the corporate authorities of such city or town" (1971).

Whether a railroad could build track upon the streets of a Virginia municipality remains unclear. The constitution refers to a "street railway", which is not necessarily the same as an intrastate railway. Yet, the section proscribes with such sufficient force that municipal thoroughfares may not be used without express consent, that the question is at least open for discussion. Thus, the case that precipitated creation of the Dillon Rule, if it had been heard by Virginia courts, may have been decided differently.

Merriam v. Moody's Executors provides the second postulate of the Dillon Rule. This passage is much more specific and less frequently misinterpreted.

> "it must be taken for settled law, that a municipal corporation possesses and can exercise the following powers and no other: First, those granted in express words; second, those necessarily implied or necessarily incident to the powers expressly granted; third, those absolutely essential to the declared objects and purposes of the corporation—not simply convenient, but indispensable; fourth, any fair doubt as to the existence of a power is resolved by the courts against the corporation—against the existence of power" (25 Iowa 163, 170).

An underlying tension exists between governmental units in a federal democracy. Each stratum of government is prone to exercise demonstrable power over subordinate political units, expecting allegiance from those subordinate units in the implementation of policy. Each subordinate political unit is conversely attempting to stretch the boundaries of its political influence. A precise explication of authority is defined through continuous political engagement among the layers of government. These tensions are the essential ingredients that form the study of intergovernmental relations.

Statutory Definition of Localities

Vestiges of Virginia's original relationship to England are retained in the modern relationship between the Commonwealth and its localities. Much as King James granted legal charters that provided for installation of communities in the New World, Virginia's General Assembly constructs statutory provisions that regulate the formation and organization of local governmental units. Many Virginians fail to recognize that the localities in which they live are simply political subdivisions of the state government. The General Assembly constructs statutory provisions that regulate the formation and organization of localities. Counties, as direct representatives of state authority, provide local implementation of state policy. Municipalities are formal political structures established to provide urban public services for citizens in densely populated localities. Yet, as commercial and residential development spreads, the distinction is fading.

One difference between Virginia and other states is that cities are legally distinct from counties. Article VII, Section 1, of the Constitution of Virginia defines cities as "an independent incorporated community." The separation fosters conflict as cities and counties compete for taxing authority. Unlike citizens of towns, city residents are not subject to county ordinances or taxation authority. Legal separation even precludes county law enforcement officers from operating within the city's boundaries without prior authorization. Virginia towns are part of the county, but are lost as tax base if reincorporated as a city. Therefore, conversion and annexation are contentious issues in the framework of Virginia intergovernmental relations.

Virginia provides for popular election of five constitutional officers that operate at the local level. The constitutional officers include Commonwealth's Attorney, Sheriff, Clerk of the Circuit Court, Treasurer, and Commissioner of Revenue. These officers are representatives of state authority and are generally independent of the locality's governing body. All counties and cities are required to have some constitutional officers, depending upon factors such as population, type of governmental structure, or date of incorporation. Towns are served by constitutional officers elected at the county level.

The Commonwealth's Attorney prosecutes all criminal violations of Virginia law and represents the state in civil cases. The Board of Supervisors may opt to select a separate attorney to represent the county in civil proceedings and prosecute violations of county ordinances. The Sheriff's Department is responsible for protecting private property, maintaining order at court proceedings and at Board meetings, serving warrants and summonses, and supervising jail operations. The Sheriff is relieved of performing as the chief law enforcement officer if a county chooses to establish a police force.

The Clerk of the Circuit Court is the chief administrative officer for the Circuit Court. Responsibilities include recording court proceedings, administering oaths, filing land transfers, land tract maps and plats, collecting fines, selling licenses, and keeping disclosure statements. The Clerk might also be responsible for keeping minutes for Board of Supervisors meetings if there is no other assigned recorder.

Duties of the Treasurer include collecting revenue and disbursing funds for the county along with holding state funds that flow through the county office. The Commissioner of the Revenue conducts property valuations and tax assessments, maintains the tax books, and bills citizens for taxes due. Both officers are replaced by a Director of Finance under the County Manager, County Executive, and Urban County Executive governmental forms. The Director of Finance performs the duties of both offices and serves under the appointed managerial officer.

Counties

Counties are administrative subdivisions of Virginia's state government. Traditionally, all powers delegated to county governments were specifically delineated, leaving little room for deviation or creativity. This practice contrasted with municipal charters, which were constructed in broad terms to promote innovation and responsiveness.

All counties have an elected governing body called the Board of Supervisors. The Board is responsible for monitoring the conduct of government through its appointed officials, passing ordinances and establishing local policy, and raising revenue to support these programs. Specific powers and duties are delegated to the Board of Supervisors in the Code of Virginia. These include levying taxes and appropriating expenditures, preparing and approving the budget, auditing claims against the county and issuing warrants to settle accounts, constructing and maintaining county buildings, developing the Comprehensive Plan and enforcing land-use policy, ensuring the public's health, safety and welfare, and providing for the treatment and care of indigent or physically handicapped residents.

The number of Supervisors can vary from as few as three to as many as eleven. Supervisors may be elected from magisterial districts, or at-large by popular choice of all qualified voters. The Board chairperson is generally selected by members at the first yearly meeting, or elected at-large in some instances.

The Traditional Form of county government, with minor modifications, is still utilized by most of the ninety-five counties in Virginia. The Board of Supervisors retains responsibility for governmental operations, but nearly all counties employ a full-time professional to manage daily activities. Counties choosing the Traditional Form are required to install all five constitutional officers. It offers a decentralized authority structure and is especially adapted to rural environments.

Counties of historically rural character required urban delivery systems as population grew. In response, the General Assembly developed alternative forms of county government to meet these changing conditions. Each county selects its governmental structure through referendum.

The first option provided to county governments was the County Manager Plan. Created in 1930, it was restricted to counties having a population density of at least 500 citizens per square mile. Adopting the County Manager Plan prevents annexation of county territory by a city, unless the entire county is included and county residents approve the merger by referendum. Only Arlington County has adopted the County Manager Plan. It has subsequently been granted special consideration by the legislature, including an unrestricted ability to create new departments and establish a civil service commission.

The Operational Forms Act of 1932 provides for any county to select either the County Executive or County Manager Form. Both the County Executive and County Manager governmental forms establish a managerial officer to supervise public operations. The County Manager Form should not be confused with the optional County Manager Plan. It has no restrictions pertaining to population and is adopted by referendum.

Under the County Executive Form, a full-time professional is appointed by the Board of Supervisors to coordinate governmental activities. The County Executive is responsible for implementing Board decisions. All policy judgments are left up to the Board. The Director of Finance is usually recommended by the County Executive, but is officially appointed by, and serves at the discretion of, the Board of Supervisors. The counties of Albemarle and Prince William have adopted the County Executive Form.

The County Manager is officially vested with much greater authority and responsibility than the County Executive. The County Manager directly appoints all department heads and, by delegating this power to others, is indirectly responsible for appointing and assigning the salaries of all subordinates. In practice, the differences between the County Executive and County Manager governmental forms are minimal because the Board tends to approve all personnel decisions requested by the County Executive. Henrico County is the only locality to have adopted the County Manager Form.

In 1940, the General Assembly made available the County Board governmental form. This structure closely resembles the Traditional Form, except that it requires appointment of a County Administrator. Since most counties have appointed an administrative officer without adopting the County Board Form, the distinction is negligible. However, the County Board Form also requires election of one Supervisor at-large with all others elected by district. The counties of Carroll, Russell, and Scott have adopted the County Board Form.

In 1950, the General Assembly authorized the position of Executive Secretary to assist the Board of Supervisors. The Executive Secretary can recommend policy, but has no authority to implement decisions without express approval of the Board. This governmental option was considered especially useful to counties beginning the transition from a rural environment to provision of urban services.

In 1960, the General Assembly created the Urban County Manager and Urban County Executive governmental forms. The Urban County Manager Form has since been deleted as an option because no county adopted it. The Urban County Executive Form is available to counties with population greater than 90,000. Current provisions prohibit all new municipal incorporations. The Board is elected at-large and provided with an almost unrestricted authority to establish departments or assign new duties to existing departments. Fairfax County is the only locality to have adopted the Urban County Executive Form. In 1966, the General Assembly granted authority to replace sanitary districts with new configurations. These new sanitary districts serve as magisterial divisions for election of Supervisors. Each district is also represented by a citizen on the Planning Commission and the School Board.

The General Assembly strives to accommodate the contrasting circumstances that occur in Virginia. A variety of governmental forms are furnished, allowing counties maximum adaptability. In the past, counties petitioned the legislature to obtain special exceptions. In 1985, the General Assembly authorized counties to acquire charters, which may contain any powers available to municipalities. This legislation entitled counties to tailor government structure for meeting special requirements. Thus far, only the counties of Chesterfield, Roanoke, and James City have taken advantage of the provision.

Towns

Towns in Virginia are political subdivisions of counties and are subject to taxation and all ordinances passed by the Board of Supervisors. Since towns are legally subordinate political units, more freedom is allowed in annexing land from the county than is permitted to a city. Towns are generally not obligated to enforce state policies. For example, towns are not required to provide public education. This responsibility remains with the county. Thus, towns escape one very expensive duty associated with local government.

To become a town, an area must have a minimum population of 1,000 citizens and petition the Circuit Court for municipal incorporation. The Circuit Court certifies that the proposed advantages of incorporation cannot be provided through creation of a sanitary district or other special arrangement with county government. Once the Circuit Court approves the petition, the affected population must consent to incorporation through referendum.

If the voters ratify incorporation, the new town may select from either the Mayor-Council or Council-Manager governmental forms. The Mayor-Council Form is generally used by small localities. The Mayor is elected at-large and is provided with expanded administrative authority, such as the right to veto Council decisions and to appoint town officers.

The Council-Manager Form, first implemented in 1908 by the city of Staunton, appoints a full-time professional to manage daily operations. Council members select the Mayor from their ranks. The Mayor conducts Council meetings, but otherwise serves a largely ceremonial role.

When a town's population reaches 5,000 residents, it may choose to incorporate as a city. Reaching this density level does not require towns to become cities, the ultimate decision lies with the electorate. Conversion from town to city status requires judicial review. The Circuit Court investigates municipal fiscal capacity and examines projected impact on the county. If the Circuit Court approves the petition, then the electorate must ratify the conversion through referendum. Once the plan is ratified, the General Assembly confers a city charter by special act.

The low threshold for conversion to a city may contribute to the difficulty in coordinating governmental action in Virginia's metropolitan areas. The Virginia Metropolitan Areas Study Commission identified the issue in its report *Governing the Virginia Metropolitan Areas: An Assessment*:

> "Governmental fragmentation has been encouraged by the low population required for transition from town to city status. The number of cities has increased from 23 to 35 in the past two decades. The result is decreased county tax bases, the creation of small and inefficient primary units of government, and costly duplication of functions" (1967, 19).

The consequences are seen in the numerous cities currently exploring reversion to town status. Even though independence was gained from county government, many municipalities were not adequately prepared for the costs associated with expanded provision of public services. Equipping police departments and operating educational systems were often larger responsibilities than the municipalities anticipated.

Cities

All municipalities that have been incorporated as cities have chosen to operate under the Council-Manager governmental form. Although individual charters may differ, cities are obligated to perform many functions by general law. All cities must establish a Juvenile and Domestic Relations Court and a Municipal Court. Cities are permitted revenue authority, such as taxing property and charging a sales tax, and are allowed to incur indebtedness up to 10% of assessed property value. Cities are granted police power to protect public health and the general welfare. City Council exercises the power to pass ordinances and retains the right of eminent domain.

As autonomous governmental units, cities are required to install all five constitutional officers. Yet, some cities are allowed to share constitutional officers with the county. Usually, these officers are Clerk of the Circuit Court, Commonwealth's Attorney, and Sheriff, who serves as the City Sergeant. This arrangement is primarily continued because of the category of second class cities that existed prior to adoption of the 1971 Constitution of Virginia. The distinction between first and second class cities is now eliminated, but the practice has been retained.

Legal separation between cities and counties can contribute to lack of intergovernmental coordination. The difficulty flows from an escalation of communities involved in regional communications and negotiations. Yet, the net impact of governmental fragmentation remains impossible to evaluate because another factor that must be weighed is expansion of the democratic process. A difficult choice always confronting democratic institutions is the balance between policy coordination and local inclusion in the decision making process. (Code of Virginia 1998; Constitution of Virginia 1971; Virginia Metropolitan Areas Study Commission, 1967; *Virginia Government In Brief,* 1998; Wilkinson, 1998).

Case Studies

Historical insight and statutory examination are instrumental in comprehending intergovernmental relations. Yet, concentrated presentation of statutes and precedents risks leaving the topic devoid of human experience. The problems of Virginia intergovernmental relations are frequently perplexing. Elegant legal frameworks are difficult to translate into practice because life often escapes easy predictability. To make the practice of intergovernmental relations more tangible, two instances are drawn from the experience of the Commonwealth to introduce the sometimes complex practice of Virginia intergovernmental relations.

Orange County Conflict

Difficulty in coordinating action between different jurisdictions can be expected. Yet, disagreements concerning governmental coordination within a single jurisdiction also occur. The independence of Virginia's five constitutional officers engenders opportunity for conflict with the locality in which they serve.

Orange County, in conformance with state requirements, created an E-911 center in 1992. The county and the state share costs for operating the facility. Four dispatchers, responsible for fire and emergency calls, are paid by the county. Five dispatchers, responsible for law enforcement calls, are paid by the state. The dispatch center operated from a building that also contained the Sheriff's Department. The Sheriff assumed nearly undisputed authority over the dispatch center.

In May 1996, the Board of Supervisors hired a full-time coordinator to manage the dispatch center. It entered into agreement with the Sheriff creating a five-member committee that monitored dispatch operations. The Sheriff and one Deputy are established members of the committee.

During the fall of 1997, underlying tensions regarding dispatch operations spilled into open conflict. Sheriff William Spence suspended a county-paid dispatcher for ostensibly violating regulations and subsequently dismissed the individual. The Board of Supervisors took issue with Sheriff Spence's unilateral action, maintaining that the power to discipline dispatchers lies solely with the E-911 coordinator, especially if the dispatcher worked directly for the county. The Sheriff remains certain that his action was justifiable.

In order to prevent any future interference from the Sheriff in operating the E-911 center, the Board undertook moving the Sheriff's Department from its location with the dispatch center. The Board served notice to the Sheriff on October 1, 1997 that stipulated a January 1, 1998 deadline for vacating the premises and relocating to a renovated school building. The deadline was later extended to January 31 and then to mid-February because the necessary renovations were not completed.

The Sheriff refused to accept the board's ultimatum. Sheriff Spence was quoted in the *Richmond Times-Dispatch:*

> "I wouldn't agree to step back 20 years and go into that dilapidated building. It's a dump . . . [This event] has significant ramifications if a county board can interfere with a constitutional officer and move him without just cause anywhere they want to . . . This move is clearly punitive. I consider it a slap in the face."[1]

County officials threatened legal action to force the Sheriff to relocate, but by February of 1998 had reconsidered. The county initially ruled out moving the dispatch center because of cost, originally estimated at $100,000. The figure was later reduced substantially, partly because of equipment donations. The Board decided that moving the county dispatchers would avoid an expensive court battle with the Sheriff's Department.

Today, Orange County has two separate dispatch facilities. Calls are received by the county facility, which is located in the renovated school building. The county facility directly dispatches the call if it pertains to fire or emergency services. If the call pertains to law enforcement, it is routed to the state facility that remains in the same building as the sheriff.

Manchester Civil Suits

Annexation is understandably fraught with conflict because of lost tax base. When two localities willingly merge into a single governmental unit, the event is presumed to avoid conflict. Yet, a recurrent factor in political activity is protection of personal benefit. One problem with intergovernmental action is the inability to predict future consequences and motivations.

A portion of Richmond that lies south of the James River used to be a separate city. In 1910, the city of Manchester merged with Richmond to form a single municipal corporation. The merger agreement contained provisions securing for Manchester residents some prerogatives they had come to expect, including retention of the Circuit Court. Conditions of the merger agreement explain why Richmond is the only city in Virginia to maintain two courthouses, the Manchester and the John Marshall.

The two courts functioned as separate systems until 1984 when the General Assembly merged their operations. By tradition, the Manchester Court heard criminal cases almost exclusively. The retirement in 1987 of Judge Frank A. S. Wright and the appointment of Judge James B. Wilkinson to the Manchester bench began to alter this pattern. Judge Wilkinson became recognized for scheduling civil suits promptly and expediting their resolution. When juries awarded settlements of $1 million and

$10 million in 1995, Manchester became the preferred location for having a personal injury case decided.

During the 1998 session of the General Assembly, the City Council of Richmond asked that its city charter be streamlined to eliminate outmoded provisions. Two of Richmond's representatives to the House of Delegates, Franklin P. Hall and A. Donald McEachin, seized this opportunity to propose a charter amendment preventing transference of civil cases from the Manchester Courthouse without consent of the litigants. The John Marshall Courthouse had seven of the eight judges assigned to the Richmond Circuit Court and suits were being moved because of docket overcrowding and the importance associated with criminal cases. About one-third of civil suits were being moved from the Manchester Courthouse to the John Marshall Courthouse.

The proposed amendment was added in committee by Delegate Hall without consulting members of the Richmond government, including the City Council, Commonwealth's Attorney, Clerk of the Circuit Court, or Circuit Court judges. These officials were nearly unanimous in opposition to the amendment. They were quite infuriated at being excluded from consultation and by inclusion of the amendment in a bill designed to streamline the city charter.

Delegate Hall proclaimed he was simply restoring a promise made to citizens of Manchester concerning retention of their courthouse after merger with Richmond. Delegate McEachin is a personal injury lawyer who often files cases at the Manchester Courthouse. He admitted that Judge Wilkinson runs a fast court and that parking is easier to find at the Manchester Courthouse. The Hall Amendment was deleted from the charter bill on the floor of the House of Delegates and it was subsequently passed by the General Assembly.[2]

Conclusion

This chapter is by no means an exhaustive survey of Virginia intergovernmental relations. The presentation was designed to pique interest in the subject and to prompt further investigation. Many pertinent topics were excluded from consideration. For example, other forms of local government—planning district commissions, public service authorities, and special districts concerned with transportation, industrial development, or resource conservation were not addressed. Mandates from the state level to localities were excluded, an investigation that would encompass compulsory orders, regulatory oversight, and requirements for the receipt of grant funding. Grants-in-aid were not explored, including the sources and procedural conditions for external funding. Public debt was barely mentioned and one major factor excluded from consideration was the role of the federal government. Yet, this chapter makes clear that government structures is more complex in scope and procedure than many citizens appreciate. The Commonwealth of Virginia is a fertile location to study governmental interaction.

Bibliography

City of Clinton v. Cedar Rapids & Missouri Railroad Company, 24 Iowa 455 (1868).

Code of Virginia, Title 15.2 d 3603.

Constitution of Virginia, 1971.

Governing the Virginia Metropolitan Areas: An Assessment. 1967. Richmond: Virginia Metropolitan Areas Study Commission.

Jennings, George W. 1982. *Virginia's Government.* Richmond: Dietz Press.

Merriam v. Moody's Executors, 25 Iowa 163 (1868).

Virginia Government in Brief. 1988. Richmond: Commonwealth of Virginia Senate and House of Delegates Clerk's Office.

Wright, Diel S. 1988. *Understanding Intergovernmental Relations,* 3rd ed. Belmont, CA: Wadsworth Publishing Company.

Endnotes

1. See Christine Neuberger, "Orange Supervisors Order Sheriff Out of Building," *Richmond Times-Dispatch,* 29 January 1998, sec. B, and Christine Neuberger, "Government Feud in Orange Resumes," *Richmond Time-Dispatch* 19 February 1998, sec. B.

2. See Alan Cooper, "Bill Would Bar Transfer of Court Cases," *Richmond Times-Dispatch,* 11 February 1998, sec. B., Tyler Whitley, "Richmond Charter Approved," *Richmond Times-Dispatch,* 17 February 1998, sec. B., and Alan Cooper, "Manchester Courthouse Added to Historic Register," *Richmond Times-Dispatch,* 20 July 1998, sec. B.

CHAPTER TEN

The Internet as a Governmental and Political Resource

Alan J. Rosenblatt

George Mason University

The convergence of computer and telecommunication technology has ushered in a new era in democratic politics. The product of this convergence, the Internet, offers citizens far greater opportunity to access the government as well as offers the government greater opportunity to reach the people. More than just an exchange of information, the Internet offers the potential for true and timely citizen/government interaction.

Like other states, the Commonwealth of Virginia offers its citizens various Internet resources. Citizens can find their congressional delegation "online." They can access vast state government resources. They can even find many of their hometowns online. In addition to these official resources, Virginians can find a wealth of private sector resources offered by businesses and private citizens.

Since we are still at the beginning of this new era, the majority of citizens still do not have access to these new resources. This, however, is steadily changing as more and more people get online. To gain access, citizens must either purchase a computer with a modem or acquire access through work, school, or a publicly accessible computer at a library, "cyber-café," or commercial computer center.

Politics on the Internet

The Internet offers enormous potential for integration into the political system. It allows any user to broadcast and narrowcast information and services. More importantly, it can integrate two-way communication into any of these presentations (Gilder 1994).

All around us we hear people talking about the Internet and the Information Revolution. The words and phrases they use are often unfamiliar. This is because the Internet is so new; we are still discovering new ways to use it and describe what we do. Many of these new words refer to function; others refer to popular brand names of market dominant software. For now, this vocabulary is more limited than the technology.

One example of the shortcoming of this vocabulary involves our use of the expression the "Information Revolution." People tend to think in terms of the dominant media of the day (Postman 1985; McLuhan 1994). Today it is television, but tomorrow it will be the networked multimedia computer. Television, telephone, and computer technology are being integrated into a single hardware package. Because we are still largely thinking in the television mode, we are fixated on the concept of broadcast in expectations of the new age. This new age will be as much the Communication Age, as it will be the Information Age. McLuhan called it the Electronic Age. Often, today, you will hear it called the Cyber Age.

"Cyber" is a good word in this instance because it makes reference to the science of automating the exchange of information. In the Cyber Age, governments will be able to provide citizens with complete information regarding all aspects of civic life in a completely searchable electronic, digital environment. They will be able to process any transaction over this network and they will be able to provide direct interpersonal communication when necessary to resolve any problems not manageable by the automated system (Grossman 1995; Toffler and Toffler 1994).

Politicians will have these same abilities, though the purpose and form of their use will differ. While government will use the technology to facilitate its authority, politicians will use it for influence (Diamond and Silverman 1995; Selnow 1998). We should note that many politicians have been elected to public office, which makes them part of the government. While it is difficult to always separate politics from governing, we still try. For example, campaign laws prohibit Members of Congress from using any public resources for campaigning (these include their congressional staff, office phones, computers, or money from their office budget). They must demonstrate wholly separate accounting for their expenses and activities in each of these two activities. Of course this is difficult, especially when the Member is both a government official and a politician, but it is expected nevertheless (Casey 1996).

While government use of cyberspace should be constrained by the due process of the law, politicians will use cyberspace to win votes, sell candidacies, and promulgate their ideas about how things should work in this country. These activities are relatively unconstrained. Free speech guarantees provide wide latitude for the political use of cyberspace.

Citizens who extend themselves into cyberspace need to be aware of the differences between the types of information and services available. They should demand accuracy from those who govern and they should beware of being misled by those who seek to persuade. When citizens access public affairs information on the World Wide Web, the current dominant form of accessing cyberspace, they should note whether they are referencing an official source, or not. They should also take careful note of the content, no matter what the source; for even official sources may contain some political information that has slipped through the thin lines that form its border.

The Potential of the Web

Since the current dominant form of accessing cyberspace is the World Wide Web, we should establish some criteria for evaluating the quality of a political Web site. These criteria will help us avoid simply cataloguing the content of political Web sites only to "oooh and aaah" what we see. To truly appreciate our online political resources requires that we not only know how they add to what we had without them, but that we also know how much better they can already be. A Web site should be evaluated for the following characteristics: 1) aesthetics, 2) functionality, 3) communicability, 4) credibility, and 5) the quantity and quality of its information.

Aesthetics

A Web site should be pleasing to look at. Because we view the Web on a computer or video monitor, what we are viewing is bombarding us with light. This is very different from reading something printed on paper. Different combinations of color may treat our eyes or make them bleary. The way a Web page looks to the eye often determines whether or not the user will stay or move on. No matter how useful or important the content may be, if nobody takes the time to see it, it will have no impact.

When you first access a Web site, the first Web page you see should fill your screen with a well balanced, eye-pleasing presentation. If most people are using a 15-inch monitor, the page should not be designed to fit on a 17-inch monitor. This opening screen should contain all of the hyperlinks necessary to navigate through the Web site.

Functionality

A Web site should be functional. This is a broad concept, but extremely important. As you move through a Web site, there will be times when some information on the site elicits a response from the user to query for more information, submit a request for action, or some other normal response. Web sites are functional to the extent that they can handle these responses. For example, suppose you are reading about the requirements for registering your car because you have just moved to a new state. While reading the Web page, you learn that you must submit an application the Department of Motor Vehicles. At a minimum, you would like to be able to immediately get the address and phone number of the DMV. It would be even better if you could download and print the necessary forms so that you could fill them out before you go to the DMV. Even better still, if you could submit the forms electronically, you could avoid spending a long time waiting in line there. Further, it would be nice if you could ask questions to clear up your confusions while you are online.

This example demonstrates that there are many levels of functionality. You may also notice that the higher levels of functionality may carry increased risk of user fraud.

This is a trade-off that should be considered when evaluating the functionality of a Web site. Some services are best provided in person. For example, before we get our driver's license we must take an eye exam. This is best done in person. So, when you assess the functionality of a site, you should be sure that you balance what is possible to do with what is reasonable to do.

There are further functionality considerations. Moving between pages at the site should be quick. This requires that the Web site provide users with enough bandwidth to handle the demand for information. Hyperlinks on the Web site should connect to pages with content. Sometimes the links go nowhere, other times they connect to a transition page. Neither of these is functional. They leave the user unsatisfied and frustrated with the delay. The more delays built into a Web site, the less likely users will stay and use the resources in the site.

Communicability

The true power of the internet is its ability to allow communication between and among persons anywhere in the world for virtually no cost. The most basic means for this communication is E-mail, which allows the exchange of text messages and files through a electronic delivery system that takes as little as a couple of minutes to deposit the message into the other person's e-mail account. In addition to the basic text, a user can attach any sort of file (text, image, audio, or video) to the message. Provided that the recipient has the appropriate software, he can open and use the attached file after downloading it. Since there are relatively standardized formats for each of these file types, and since there are free viewers for almost any of these files available on the Internet, the recipient should have little or no trouble viewing or listening to the attached file. At a minimum, a good Web site should provide an email address to allow users to contact the authors of the site. It would be even better if the E-mail address on the page is hyperlinked to the E-mail application of the user's Web browser, thus allowing the user to simply click on the address, write the message, and send it with relatively little effort.

A more sophisticated method of electronic correspondence uses the *forms* feature. The newer versions of Web browsers allow Web developers to create a page on their site that looks like a template from a database application. Visitors to the site fill in the various fields on the screen with their name, address, E-mail address, phone number, topic of message, and the body of their message. Then they press a button on the screen to submit the communiqué. When submitted in this manner, the information can be sorted and stored automatically in a database at the Web site's facility. In a congressional office, for example, the name and address information can automatically be entered into a constituent database and the message can be forwarded to the staff member responsible for answering letters on that topic. By streamlining the operation in this way, congressional staff can answer more letters in less time. If all mail coming to the office is in this form, then resources used to pay a mail sorter could be used to pay the salary of another person to answer the mail.

Another method of communication found on the Web is the chat room. This is an application that runs on a Web site that allows many users to log in and become part of an ongoing, real-time discussion with other users and possibly a person who works at the Web site. On occasion, a chat room could be used at a government site to allow citizens to discuss policy with an elected official. At other times, the staff person who is responsible for a particular topic may host a discussion on that topic. Because this is a real-time discussion, caution is warranted. If a disruptive participant chimes in, he can destroy the quality of the chat. Fortunately, the host can block such a person if necessary.

A new generation of chat facilities is emerging that operate outside of the World Wide Web. Chat client software allows users to log into a host site and use the host's network server to conduct one on one communication with anyone else connected to the host's site. These clients allow users to build their own customized list or electronic roll-o-dex that will inform them whenever one of their friends or colleagues is online. When both are simultaneously online, the client software allows them to conduct real-time conversations. These can be text only, they can include file transfers, and now they can allow real-time audio and video exchange. Some of the most popular of these are Mirabilis's ICQ (www.icq.com) and Microsoft's NetMeeting (www.microsoft.com). NetMeeting allows for text, audio, and video exchange. ICQ is primarily text-based, but it integrates other clients, like NetMeeting, so users can use these other applications from within ICQ. Both allow the user to choose between one-on-one or multiple-person chat formats. These applications run simultaneously with any other software, allowing users to work on any other file and still be able to send and receive messages.

Credibility of Information

One of the biggest concerns about using the Internet for government and political purposes is the credibility of the information available. Because any user can become an Internet publisher, there is nothing to prevent someone from posting bogus information online. As such, the Internet user must be on guard lest they fall prey to misinformation and disinformation. Given the prevalence of both of these in normal politics, citizens going online must be doubly cautious to guard against being duped.

To evaluate the credibility of information found on the Web, users should ask the following questions regarding the Web site before accepting the information as true: 1) who pays for the site; 2) what is the political agenda of the site's owner; 3) what methods are used by the site to determine their facts; and 4) can the information on the site be independently corroborated? These are demanding questions. The bottom line is that a truly informed citizen does not believe everything he reads, hears, or sees without some assurances that the information is accurate.

Unfortunately, citizens rarely take the time to be thorough when gathering information (Zaller 1992). Political rumors too often carry the weight of fact. The Internet may make the dissemination of rumors easier and more likely. It also makes it easier to cross-reference information and find corroborating evidence to a claim. The key concern is that users carefully determine that the corroboration is from an independent source. It is no corroboration to find two sources that got their information from the same well.

Quantity and Quality of Information

Above all, a good Web site contains as much high quality information as it needs to perform its purpose. As long as storage space is available at a premium, it is not feasible for every Web site to provide exhaustive information. Rather, a good Web site will identify its purpose and provide as much information as is necessary. Sometimes a Web site will be small, sometimes large. A member of congress's site will not be as large as the Library of Congress's *Thomas* system. On the other hand, some public officials provide much more information about what they are doing and what they believe than others. Since the Web is so new, it is to be expected that many hard-working, respect-deserving public officials do not have good Web sites. But as we grow accustomed to these new technologies, we can expect a greater demand for quality electronic access to government and public officials.

Getting Information and Services on the Internet

The most common method for accessing the Internet is through the World Wide Web (WWW). Users explore the Web using a Web Browser. While there are many Web Browsers, the most commonly used are Netscape's Navigator and Microsoft's Internet Explorer. Many users also access the Web through America Online (AOL), but still use one of these two browsers when they do.

A Web Browser provides a graphic interface to the Internet. The browser's window allows users to see text, still images, animation, video, and hear audio, provided all of the necessary plugins are installed. Plugins are enhancements to the browser, some of which are free and some of which are available for a modest cost. These pulgins are generally necessary to view and listen to audio/video information. The most commonly used are RealMeadia, QuickTime, VivoActive, and NetShow. Each of these is available in a stripped down version for free, and many sell "plus" versions with enhanced resolution and features.

Each Web site is identified by a URL address. The most common form of this address is www.name.com. Not all sites begin with "www," but most do. The "name" usually is suggestive of the owner of the Web site. In www.netscape.com, the middle part of the address specifies Netscape as the site owner. While this is generally the pattern, users should be wary of misleading addresses. During the 1996 presidential campaign, for example, several parody sites paralleled official candidate sites. Some of these sites were attacks on the candidate, for example, www.dole96.com poked fun at Robert Dole, while his official site was www.dole96.org. This leads us to the final portion of the URL address. This part indicates the nature of the organization owning the site. Commercial sites generally end with ".com." Non-profits organizations, like political campaigns, often end in ".org." Universities end in ".edu." Government sites have the ".gov" designation. Military sites end in ".mil." A less specific designation is ".net." The assignment of these "domain names" is currently centralized through one source, but a suit has been recently filed to challenge this monopoly, and if successful would likely lead to the creation of new designations. Meanwhile, other countries have their own systems, and they also add a country code. So, for example, in the United Kingdom, commercial sites are designated ".co.uk."

Once connected to the Web, users can navigate their way through millions of Web sites by using any of several means. These include search engines, indexes, and Web sites filled with hyperlinks.

Search Engines

Search engines allow users to conduct a full text search of the Web. These services use automated search programs, often called Web crawlers, that regularly scan the Web for newly added Web sites. The contents of these are added to the site's database and made available through its search program. These search programs generally allow users to type in keywords, phrases, names, or any text that may help identify the information they seek. Oftentimes advanced searches are possible that allow users to specify several terms and even exclude terms from their search. Sites that offer these services include HotBot, Lycos, and AltaVista. Several of these engines can be accessed through one site called www.search.com.

Web Indexes

Web Indexes are similar to search engines because they allow broad based keyword searches of the Web. They differ because they are edited and organized by category. The most popular of these indexes is YAHOO! (www.yahoo.com). The advantage of an index is that the links are regularly tested and chosen because of their relevance to their category.

Hyperlink

While search engines and Web indexes allow the user to focus their search using key words and phrases, users may also choose the serendipitous approach of following links from one Web site to another. If a user finds a good Web site to start their research efforts, they may be able to jump to several other Web sites by clicking on the links found on each of the Web pages they encounter. This is a free-form type of exploration that may often yield high quality results in short order. This is especially true if one of the sites the user encounters is filled with useful links to related sites.

Virginia Government on the Internet

The Commonwealth of Virginia has an extensive official Web site. The homepage can be found at http://www.state.va.us/. From this homepage, visitors can access official government information and services, as well as access links to a variety of other useful Virginia resources. These include tourist information, links to educational institutions, local and regional Virginia sites, and weather conditions in the Commonwealth. The Virginia delegation to the United States Senate is also on the Web. Senators are generally available through the Senate's homepage (http://www.senate.gov/), or you can go directly to the Senator's page by adding "~Senator's Name" after the last "/" in the Senate address. The current Senators can be reached by adding "~robb" or "~warner" (http://www.senate.gov/~robb/ and http://www.senate.gov/~warner/). Members of the delegation to the United States House of Representatives can be found on the House's Web site at http://us.house.gov/. Again, by adding "Representative's Name" (no ~ necessary for the House) you can directly access the member's site. These sites provide information about each member of the Virginia delegation, as well as policy and legislative information the member wishes to provide. Individual delegates to the Virginia Legislature are also available, but only for some members. A partial listing is available from YAHOO!, at http://www.yahoo.com/Regional/U_S__States/Virginia/Government/Elected_Officials/. Lastly, there are many unofficial Web sites providing much information regarding the Commonwealth of Virginia.

Commonwealth of Virginia Resources

The official Virginia government homepage (http://www.state.va.us/home/governmt.html) provides links to several official state government resources, both on the main Web site and on the Web sites of various agencies and departments with their own Web server computer system. These resources offer citizens useful information about the formation of public policy and about the people and institutions that make public policy. They also provide information and interactive services to citizens of Virginia.

Citizens wishing to learn about any policy being debated in Virginia can access useful information from the official government site. Using this Web site, we can find out if the Governor has made a speech on the issue and read the text. We can read the text of the bill. We can also read the opinions of recent court cases that may relate to the issue. The opportunity to become more fully informed allows us the opportunity to become more effective citizens.

In particular, users can access the governor's homepage. This page has undergone recent changes and is likely to be changed often, as we should expect with all well-maintained Web sites. The site has been updated with a more aesthetically pleasing presentation, but the content remains similar to the older design. For example, the Speech page continues to provide links to the texts of all of the governor's speeches, but it still does not provide information on the content of the speech without actually scanning the speech. The News Release page provides more useful titles to help identify the topic of the communication. Further, it subdivides the links by issue and provides a hyperlinked list of these topics at the bottom of the page. This makes this page more useful than the Speeches page. The site also offers a Calendar so citizens can know what the governor is doing day to day. Overall, the governor's Web site offers a great deal of information about his policies and activities. The site, however, does not take full advantage of Web technology. There are no search engines to help users find what the governor's position may be on a particular topic. The information may be on the site, but users must page through much text in order to find it. This is an example of how the mindset created by the print media still dominates the presentation on the World Wide Web.

The Virginia General Assembly can also be accessed through the Virginia Government homepage (http://legis.state.va.us/). In this part of the Virginia Web site, visitors can learn more about what is happening in the legislature. The Legislative Information System (LIS) provides users with the ability to track bills as they progress through the legislative process. Bill texts, minutes of floor meetings, and information on individual members' legislative activities are all available. More impressive, the LIS offers citizens the ability to search the Virginia Code, the Virginia Administrative Code, and the text of bills and resolutions under consideration. These are full text search engines that allow citizens to type in words and phrases they wish to find in each of the respective databases. This is a great example of the power of the Internet. More than just an electronic brochure, this is a fully interactive database of citizen resources. From the LIS, users can learn about the full scope of a policy, from laws already on record to modifications proposed in current bills before the chamber. Some individual delegates have homepages as well. Yahoo! (http://www.yahoo.com/Regional/U_S__States/Virginia/Government/Elected_Officials/) has a partial listing of these Web sites.

If we follow the link on the Virginia Government homepage to "Virginia state agencies, boards, commissions, and councils on the Internet," we will find a long list of various executive branch offices devoted to the administration of the various laws and regulations in effect in Virginia. On this page, we can also find a link to the Virginia Judicial System. It is unclear why the judiciary has been buried in a list of executive branch links. Further, the link to the court system is labeled "Appeals, Court of, of Virginia." Yet when the link is accessed the user is taken to the homepage of the Virginia Judicial System (http://www.courts.state.va.us/), a site with links to all levels of the Virginia judiciary. This site allows citizens to read recent court opinions. It links to the Virginia State Law Library, publications of the Judicial System, and to the homepages of each of the various courts in the state. The page also links to a survey users can fill out regarding their experiences in the court system. This site is pleasant to look at, extremely functional, and takes advantage of many of the abilities offered by the Web.

Many other government links are included on the "Virginia state agencies, boards, commissions, and councils on the Internet" page. Some of them are simple brochures for an agency or board; others provide interactive services to citizens. The Department of Motor Vehicles, for example, allows users to search for available vanity license plate and reserve them if they are available. The Library of Virginia provides a wide array of information online.

Virginia Congressional Delegation

Like all other states, members of Virginia's congressional delegation each have their own homepage. Members of the US House of Representatives can be accessed at http://www.house.gov/. Virginia's Senators can be found at http://www.senate.gov/. These Web sites are generally maintained by someone from the member's staff. Those that do not have an in-house Webmaster are provided with a generic homepage. These generic pages are a standard format with limited resources. Members who maintain their sites in-house offer a customized presentation. Some of these sites are quite sophisticated.

Ten of Virginia's eleven US Representatives have web pages. They are:

Herbert Bateman, 1st District: http://www.house.gov/bateman/

Thomas Bliley, 7th District: http://www.house.gov/bliley/

Rick Boucher, 9th District: http://www.house.gov/boucher/

Tom Davis, 11th District: http://www.house.gov/tomdavis/

Virgil Goode, 5th District: http://www.house.gov/goode/

Bob Goodlatte, 6th District: http://www.house.gov/goodlatte/

Jim Moran, 8th District: http://www.house.gov/moran/

Owen Pickett, 2nd District: http://www.house.gov/pickett/

Norman Sisisky, 4th District: http://www.house.gov/sisisky/

Frank Wolf, 10th District: http://www.house.gov/wolf/

Representative Robert "Bobby" Scott, of the 3rd District, does not appear to have a homepage. He is not listed with the other members on the House Web site, nor is he listed on Project Vote Smart's Web site as having a homepage. Of the ten members of the delegation that do have homepages, the quality of resources on these homepages varies.

Representative Bateman provides a very simple homepage. Aside from its bland presentation, it is little more than a brochure providing basic information with no interactivity. It does offer hyperlinks to Web sites for businesses and institutions in the 1st District. But, for the most part, it tells you to write a postal letter to the Congressman if you actually want something done. This is a good example of an unimpressive homepage.

Representative Wolf's homepage is considerably more impressive. The layout is fresh and the site contains a great deal of information. Still, it does not take full advantage of the technology. It offers no search functions to help citizens find the member's statements on particular subjects. Like most homepages of elected officials, visitors must page through lists of dated titles of press releases and speeches.

Most of these members provide e-mail addresses with which constituents can contact them. This allows a visitor to send a message using their browser's e-mail function. This method, however, does not allow the member's staff to determine easily whether the message is from a constituent, or not. Representative Goodlatte, in contrast, uses a Web mailbox system that requires users to sign up first, indicating their place of residence. This system automatically blocks messages from visitors who do not live in the district. This helps the member's staff avoid sifting through e-mail that they would not answer anyway. It also prevents visitors from sending messages to members outside of their district who may be sponsoring a particular piece of legislation of interest.

Virginia's Senators Robb and Warner also have their own homepages (http://www.senate.gov/~robb/ and http://www.senate.gov/~warner/). Senator Warner's homepage is fairly basic. It contains a biography and press releases, but no search engine. The e-mail link simply opens the browser's mail application. Warner does offer a page that will search the *Congressional Record* for the transcripts of his floor speeches in the Senate. This feature is helpful, but it does not allow for key word or full-text search of these speeches. Actually, the search engine that finds his floor speeches is not on his site, but rather it is on the Library of Congress's Web site.

Senator Robb calls his Web site his "virtual office." This suggests that he and his staff appreciate the power of the Web. Still, his press releases and floor statements are not searchable by key word or full-text, either. Furthermore, Senator Robb's floor speeches are listed directly on one page in his site. Apparently, his staff searches the *Congressional Record* for us and creates links to those speeches. Robb provides visitors with a site map of his Web site. This makes navigation within it much easier. The one area where Senator Robb is taking fuller advantage of the Web than his colleagues in the Virginia delegation is with e-mail. In order to e-mail this Senator, citizens used to fill out a form on of the site's pages that required the user to fill out their name, address, topic of letter, and other vital statistics before they composed their letter. This allowed his staff to fully automate the entry of names and addresses of those who write into their database and to automatically route the e-mail to the staff member responsible for answering letters on that topic.

Recently, however, Senator Robb has eliminated this method of e-mail, leaving only the conventional e-mail available to visitors. The reasons for this switch are revealing. While the forms system would make life very easy for the staff in principle, the technical glitches that always seem to emerge in computer systems undermines the effectiveness. In the end, the maintenance of this system required more time and skill than the staff could provide. Senator Robb, like most members of congress, is unlikely to divert office budget funds to the hiring of a trained Webmaster to manage the site. In Robb's office, the Web site is just one of many responsibilities assigned to his office manager. The key people responsible for maintaining and supporting the Web sites of the members are office managers, legislative correspondents, and mail directors that have little or no formal training in Web development. The Web site, while becoming more recognized as the wave of the future, is still a fairly low priority in Congress.

Local Resources

Many of the cities throughout the Commonwealth of Virginia have their own Web sites. These sites serve to provide constituent services. They also are used for public relations. More and more, people are using the World Wide Web to investigate places before they visit. These local Web sites provide links to the Chamber of Commerce and other organizations that provide an umbrella to various businesses and attraction found in the area.

The official Virginia Web site provides several links to these resources throughout the state (http://www.state.va.us/home/govlocal.html). This page links visitors to a map of Virginia that will take them to many city and county Web sites. It also links to other sites that provide their own links to local Virginia governments.

Unofficial Virginia Web Sites

Unofficial Web sites are not publicly financed. Some are financed by Virginia's political parties (http://www.yahoo.com/Regional/U_S__States/Virginia/Government/Politics/Parties_and_Groups/). Some are available from organizations and businesses around Virginia. Links to these can be found on Yahoo!, as well (http://www.yahoo.com/regional/u_s__states/virginia/).

Other Political Resources

Beyond the offerings from the Commonwealth of Virginia, citizens can access a wide array of political resources on the Web that will be extremely valuable to them. Each of the branches of the federal government has a Web site. There are also a few sites that serve as a clearinghouse of political information. Project Vote Smart, a non-profit, bipartisan organization founded by former Presidents Gerald Ford and Jimmy Carter, provides links to a large number of official and political Web sites (http://www.vote-smart.org). Project Vote Smart also provides original content, including the results of surveys they have sent to political candidates and officials around the nation.

If you want to follow the news in any part of the world, as well as Virginia, the newspapers.com is an invaluable resource (http://www.newspapers.com). From this site, we can access the electronic version of hundreds of newspapers and newsmagazines from around the world. This site links to twenty-seven newspapers in Virginia, alone. These include local newspapers, national newspapers that publish in Virginia (like *USA Today*), and specialty newspapers, like the George Mason University student paper and the *Army Times*.

Conclusion

The World Wide Web is gradually becoming an important part of government and politics. It, and whatever technology will come next, represents the potential to empower all citizens with the information they need to make informed political choices and the communication technology they need to make their opinions known to public officials and other citizens. As more citizens gain the access and skill necessary to use this new technology for their political education and activities we are likely to see changes in how we do politics and what we expect from government. This is an exciting time. This technology is still in its infancy. It has great potential, but it is a potential that may create as many problems as solutions. As its story unfolds, pay close attention to what is happening and how it will affect your lives and the lives of your fellow citizens.

Bibliography

Casey, Chris. 1996. *The Hill on the Net: Congress Enters the Information Age.* New York: AP Professional.

Diamond, Edwin and Robert A. Silverman. 1995. *White House to Your House: Media and Politics in Virtual America.* Cambridge, MA: MIT.

Gilder, George. 1994. *Life After Television: The Coming Transformation of Media and American Life.* New York: Norton.

Grossman, Lawrence K. 1995. *The Electronic Republic: Reshaping Democracy in the Information Age.* New York: Viking.

McLuhan, Marshall. 1994 (1964). *Understanding Media: The Extensions of Man.* Cambridge, MA: MIT.

Postman, Neil. 1985. *Amusing Ourselves to Death: Public Discourse in the Age of Show Business.* New York: Penguin.

Selnow, Gary W. 1998. *Electronic Whistle-Stops: The Impact of the Internet on American Politics.* Westport, CT: Praeger.

Toffler, Alvin and Heidi Toffler. 1994. *Creating a New Civilization: The Politics of the Third Wave.* Atlanta, GA: Turner.

Zaller, John. 1992. *The Nature and Origins of Mass Opinion.* NY: Cambridge.

SECTION THREE:
Public Policy Issues

CHAPTER ELEVEN

Cutting Taxes: Good Public Policy or Political Expediency?

Patrick Lee Plaisance
Daily Press

Of all the strategies that politicians employ, few have the universal appeal of appearing to fight on behalf of people's wallets. Throughout the political history of the United States and of Virginia, politicians have tapped powerful currents of voter sentiment by fighting against new or increased taxes. But taxation as a political issue in Virginia was raised to a new level in 1997 with the campaign promise by Jim Gilmore to eliminate the personal property tax on most private cars and trucks. Gilmore's success in winning a phase-out of the so-called car tax raised the political stakes when it came to taxes. No longer was the quaint promise not to raise taxes a very bold statement by a politician; now the public was shown that serious tax relief could be a reality. But while Gilmore's car-tax pledge proved to be a powerful campaign tool, it also may inflate taxpayer skepticism that government is spending too much money, which may in turn serve to further fuel voter cynicism about government in general. And the economic climate that allows governments to cut taxes may not prove to be enduring enough to support cuts in other taxes such as the state sales tax on food.

America's Historical Dislike of Taxes

Bitter showdowns over the issue of taxes have marked the fabric of American politics since the English tried to force colonists to pay taxes on stamps in 1765. Shortly after the American Revolution, the debate over federal and state taxing powers threatened the unity of the fledgling nation.

Politicians, perhaps more than most, are aware of the adage that there are only two inevitable things in life: death and taxes. As a result, one learns quickly in politics that among the best methods to galvanize voters is to help them keep more of their money. This is especially true in modern American politics, where voter apathy, self-interest and examples of government waste have conspired to leave citizens wondering if the government services they receive are worth the taxes they pay. Whether or not that is the case, politicians have become deft at appealing to this sense of discontent by preaching to peoples' wallets. And unlike other "trigger" issues such as abortion or gun control, which tend to divide voters who already have made up their minds, tax relief has nearly universal appeal.

Taxes have taken center stage and defined recent political campaigns. Most memorably, the issue helped define George Bush in 1988, when the Republican was seeking his first presidential term, and he found himself battling a bid by Massachusetts Gov. Michael Dukakis. "Read my lips: No new taxes!" Bush repeatedly said. The phrase became his mantra, his signature sound-bite beamed to millions on the nightly news. Four years later, however, voters who had watched Bush renege on his promise remembered those words, and he suffered for them in his re-election bid.

Even then, as it has been throughout much of American political history, taxation was a valuable issue only insofar as politicians defined themselves against tax increases. It was far safer to avoid the T-word; most politicians worked hard to be seen as a bulwark against any tax increase, and they embraced any new taxes at their peril.

Virginia's Pattern on Taxes

"Nobody runs and promises to increase taxes," said Hunter B. Andrews, a 32-year veteran of the state senator from Hampton who, as chairman of the Senate Finance Committee for 10 years until his defeat in 1995, was among the most powerful men in Richmond. "You try it, and you won't get very far."

The Bush stance mirrored a common pattern among those who sought the keys to the Governor's Mansion in Virginia. One candidate would raise the stakes by making a no-tax-increase pledge, and all other competitors followed suit. Even when many of those pledges were broken once they won office, the pattern remained a standard one.

Rebuilding Virginia's education system in a post-segregation era was more of a burning issue than taxation when Mills E. Godwin Jr. was first elected governor in 1966—that is, until the Democrat proposed the state's first sales tax. Taxes quickly swept to the forefront when Godwin announced his plan to finance the Virginia community college system. It was a rare case of a politician winning an argument to raise taxes based on the promise of what could be produced from it. Some even suggested Godwin won over a skeptical General Assembly by hinting that new colleges could be built in certain districts depending on the support of certain lawmakers.

"He probably promised a community college here or there," said Andrews. "I got one of them," referring to Thomas Nelson Community College in Hampton.

The bold move didn't doom Godwin as a politician; seven years later, he was asked to switch parties and run as a Republican to counter a populist movement that supported Henry Howell, a maverick Democratic state senator from Norfolk who was crusading to abolish the sales tax on food and non-prescription drugs. Howell was enormously successful in creating a tidal wave of support by making the tax-cut plan the centerpiece of his campaign. Howell's tax-cut campaign drew voters, but his policies could spell disaster for the state budget, Godwin supporters feared. Godwin agreed, seeking his second term—this time as a Republican. Howell's tidal wave soon ebbed when he finally detailed how he was going to compensate for the lost tax revenue—by imposing a host of smaller fee increases including a tax increase on beer. As a result, Godwin won the election.

From then on, politicians routinely made no-tax pledges a part of their campaigns. In 1985, gubernatorial hopeful Gerald Baliles was thrown on the defensive when his opponent, Wyatt Durrette, applied the strategy. Baliles eventually matched Durrette's no-tax pledge before going on to win the race. Not long after his term started, however, Baliles was supporting a plan to tax gasoline to finance a massive highway-construction budget. He was quickly denounced as reneging on his promise, and he defended himself by saying, "I only said it once." Since the state constitution prohibits governors from immediately seeking re-election, there is no way to discern how Baliles' gas-tax record would have affected his political standing.

Another example of the pattern was Marshall Coleman, the Republican candidate for governor in 1989. Though he was the first to stake out a no-tax-increase stand in the race, his Democratic opponent, Doug Wilder, soon followed, neutralizing Coleman's attempt to generate a campaign issue.

Gilmore's Tax Cut "Revolution"

The politics of taxes underwent a revolution on May 8, 1997, when Jim Gilmore launched his bid for governor. A former prosecutor from Henrico County who won statewide election as Attorney General four years earlier, Gilmore had been searching for an issue to seize as a campaign centerpiece. For a law-and-order, socially conservative Republican, the pickings seemed to be slim after the successes of the George Allen administration, which accomplished its landmark goals of abolishing parole, tightening sentencing guidelines for criminals and requiring able-bodied welfare recipients to work.

But there was one issue that resonated powerfully with potential supporters. Intense polling conducted for the Gilmore camp pointed his strategists to one topic: a tax cut. "A lot of traditional issues already had been addressed," said M. Boyd Marcus Jr., Gilmore's chief strategist during the campaign and his chief of staff in office. "We were looking for issues that united the Republican coalition, and a tax cut was one of the few things that united most Republicans."

The only question that remained for Gilmore, then, was which tax to cut.

Should it be the sales tax on food? Should it be the state income tax? Poll results showed all touched a nerve with voters. But in the end, Marcus and Gilmore settled on the one tax that most people had to sit down and write a check to pay: the unpopular personal property tax on vehicles.

"We frankly started looking for a tax cut that made sense," Marcus said. "With those other taxes, the money's taken out drop by drop. The car tax was one that the governor put his finger on right away." Going after the unpopular tax was sure to strike a chord with voters regardless of whether they were Democrats or Republicans, Marcus said.

From that point, Gilmore's task was to sell it to the voters, which he did relentlessly. Reporters covering the 1997 gubernatorial campaign joked about Gilmore's single-minded zeal. He honed his message so well that he could be thrown a question on just about any topic—abortion, the economic health of Newport News Shipbuilding, graduate studies at George Mason University—and Gilmore would find a way to mention his car tax plan as part of his response.

Ironically, the same polls that assured the Gilmore campaign that it had a red-hot issue also revealed that most of the potential voters who said they liked the idea also doubted whether Gilmore could actually deliver. Gilmore had grabbed the voters' attention, but he had not swept away voter cynicism. Indeed, Democrats complained that Gilmore was encouraging that current of cynicism by making promises he may not be able to keep. In this sense, Gilmore's car-tax gambit recast the debate over the relationship between taxes and politics. Could taxes—the revenue on which American democracy depends—be reduced to a simple political argument? Could the modern political campaign do justice to the complexity of government finance, or was it healthy for politicians to foster a suspicion of government spending? Could a politician, despite this era of soundbite-driven campaigns, make a persuasive case that a

Figure 11.1 Gilmore makes good on his campaign promise to end the car tax. Courtesy of the Office of the Governor, State of Virginia.

tax was too burdensome, or were taxes too easily made a scapegoat that voters could feel good about hating?

More than ever, voters were encouraged to feel suspicious that the state government was getting more taxpayer money than it needed. Gilmore intimated that government was too bloated and collecting more tax money than necessary. In his campaign, Gilmore repeatedly made the claim that his car-tax plan would provide a "dividend" for the working families of Virginia who may not otherwise feel the full benefits of a strong state economy. But, that dividend would not be available to families without cars. In addition, those who will benefit will not feel the full effects of Gilmore's plan until after his four-year term ends. Under the planned phase-out, taxpayers will receive state refund checks in the first years for a whopping 12.5 percent of their car-tax bill.

A Democrat, not Gilmore, was the first to view the tax on most privately owned cars and trucks as a source of political capital. In 1995, Democratic state Sen. Charles Colgan of Prince William County had urged the General Assembly to abolish it altogether, but he didn't get very far. Many Democrats urged Gilmore's opponent, former Lt. Gov. Donald S. Beyer Jr., to seize the initiative during his race against Gilmore. But other lawmakers, while they sympathized with the widespread sentiment against the tax, feared doing so would blow a multimillion-dollar hole in the state budget. And public attention wasn't drawn to such proposals, made when the General Assembly gathered in Richmond, in the same way campaign-season advertisements could.

"In Gilmore's case, he stole a page from the Democrats," said Wilder, the former governor who was elected to his four-year term in 1989. "I do think it shocked a lot of people when Gilmore did that."

Although the idea had been floating around Virginia, Gilmore's decision to make it the centerpiece of his campaign threw Beyer, his Democratic opponent, off balance. First Beyer called the proposal reckless and dangerous, saying he had weighed a similar plan but rejected it. Later, Beyer offered a more modest version of tax relief, by phasing out some of the car tax. However, the move did little more than give Gilmore a chance to label him a flip-flopper, putting Beyer on the defensive for much of the campaign season.

"Gilmore stuck with it, and the Democrats had nothing to counter it with," Wilder said. Gilmore's car-tax cut plan, as well as the short-lived alternative plan by Beyer, certainly touched a nerve with voters. But they also prompted a chorus of concern from business leaders in Northern Virginia and Hampton Roads, the state's largest metro areas. In the politicians' eagerness to offer promises they feel voters want to hear, they may be shortchanging Virginia's investment in the future, business leaders said—investment in roads, schools, colleges and job training. Such "investment" inevitably leads to the dreaded "T" word: taxes and the desire by politicians to be responsible for as few of them as possible.

Good Politics and Bad Public Policy

Some observers of the Gilmore/Beyer contest argue that the two politicians were not demonstrating much leadership in refusing to venture beyond so-called feel-good rhetoric. Galvanized by concerns over Gilmore's plan, more than 100 Northern Virginia business executives launched a state campaign in the fall of 1997 to educate voters about the need to spend billions of new state dollars on roads and schools over the next few years.

"Most of the people, particularly those who serve on commissions and bodies, and in leadership roles, all seem to have a general feeling," said the president of a Hampton Roads real estate company during the race for governor. "We're under whelmed with the Republican or Democratic side of the issues, and overwhelmed with the need to look beyond politics and to the needs of the commonwealth. Rather than run for office on tax cuts, which is a very short-term, voter-appeal philosophy, they should be talking about how to spend the money we need to carry Virginia forward. Our area is not terribly well-served by either candidate at this point."

Unlike previous administrations strapped by sagging or slowing state economies, Gilmore was riding a wave of booming job growth and business expansion that was filling the state treasury with nearly $1 billion in surplus tax revenue when Gilmore won election. In other words, the money was available to pay for the first year of his plan, and there was enough projected growth to finance the rest of it. So on Election Day in 1997, the message was clear: by a margin of 56 to 44 percent, Gilmore won the race. His tax-cutting pledge created a wave of popular support that lifted him into the Governor's Mansion.

"During my campaign as governor, I traveled throughout this great commonwealth promising the elimination of this onerous car tax," Gilmore said soon after the General Assembly agreed in early 1998 to start phasing it out. "I am proud to say I have kept my promise, and Virginians will start getting tax relief starting in July."

Once again, a politician harnessed taxes as a galvanizing issue. However, Gilmore did so in a way that may change the nature of the issue itself for years to come. Gilmore's success in winning a phase-out of the so-called car tax raised the political stakes when it came to taxes. No longer was the quaint promise not to raise taxes a very bold statement by a politician; now the public was shown that serious tax relief could be a reality.

"The new mantra will be, 'Which tax will you cut?'" said Larry Sabato, a University of Virginia professor and longtime observer of state politics. "At one point, it was politically popular to say you will not raise taxes, and now you must say which tax you're going to cut. It's not just a flash-in-the-pan issue."

The continued strong growth of the Virginia economy also is likely to keep attention on the possibilities of further tax relief. In 1997, the state economy grew at an impressive 8-percent clip, generating nearly $700 million in new money to throw around in the state budget. The growth was projected to continue at about the same rate in 1998, but the economy grew even faster—a whopping 11 percent. Since every 1 percentage point of economic growth typically generates an additional $85 million in new taxes for the state, such a growth rate pushed the surplus toward the $1 billion mark.

At the same time that the first step in the car-tax phase-out was implemented, another tax break coincidentally took effect: the state 4.5-percent sales tax no longer applied to non-prescription drugs. That tax break was approved in the Wilder administration in 1992, but there was never enough money in the state budget to afford it. Combined, tax relief as a political strategy seemed to be firmly in place—at least as long as a strong state economy could afford it.

"How powerful taxes is as an issue depends on the economics, on the time and place," Marcus said. The taxes on cars and drugs have not been the first ones to take center stage in recent Virginia politics, nor are they likely to be the last. After Gilmore won the election and began pressuring the General Assembly to carry out his car-tax pledge, galvanized Democrats retaliated by suggesting an alternative form of tax relief: removing the state sales tax from grocery items.

The idea, while it drew sudden attention during the 1998 legislative session, was not a new one. The late former Lt. Gov. Henry Howell used the issue, as well as the tax on non-prescription drugs, as a basis for his three unsuccessful campaigns for governor in the late 1960s.

"Is it fair," Howell asked during his first bid for governor in 1969, "to lash Virginians with the sting of a tax on their stomachs and their arthritis?" Breathing new life into the well-worn issue 30 years later, Democrats argued that if Gilmore were truly interested in giving working Virginia families a tax break, he would provide it on something even more universal than vehicles. Removing the tax on food also would benefit poorer families who didn't own cars and therefore would see no relief under Gilmore's plan.

The food-tax proposal proved to be a meager counteroffensive; it was summarily killed in committee in early 1998. However, lawmakers will have to take up the issue again in the 1999 General Assembly session. Sabato and others say it may continue to be the next logical prospect if politicians continue striving to please voters with tax-relief schemes—and if the growing state economy allows them to do so.

However, Gilmore's success may not constitute a tax-cut revolution. Two months after his achievement, polls showed another political truth at play: voter attention spans are about as long as a television commercial break. A May 1998 poll conducted by Virginia Commonwealth University showed that fewer than one in three Virginians—32 percent—were aware that the historic tax cut had even been approved. "The tax cut issue is widely credited with Gilmore's landslide victory and has appeared to be very popular with Virginians," said poll director Scott Keeter, a VCU political scientist. "Yet the fact that only about a third of those interviewed are aware that the cut actually passed suggests that the issue has faded from public consciousness."

A poll taken one month after the Gilmore tax cut was approved showed substantial support for a cut in the food tax—44 percent, compared with 46 percent who said the car-tax cut was the priority. Those numbers suggest that there is enough support for a possible food-tax cut to require Gilmore to fight off attempts to slow or freeze his car-tax phase-out. They also suggest there is enough interest to keep the entire tax-cut issue alive for a while. "A lot of arguments made for it during the General Assembly session are still valid," said Bieber, the director of the state Democratic

Party. "Cutting the food tax benefits everybody. Everybody has to eat. We think it's a much more equitable form of tax relief."

Wilder, the former governor, agreed, going one step further in challenging Gilmore to take the initiative and not stop with his car-tax victory. "I think the ground is still fertile to speak of meaningful tax relief," Wilder said. "As long as you have the food tax out there, it's a good issue. People identify with it. They say, `Look, this is something that can help me.' "

Others have warned that tax cuts may be good politics now but will prove to be bad policy in the future. Gilmore and other politicians may rely on tax cuts to solidify their political support, but many believe they do so at the risk of crippling the state's long-term forecast. Former Gov. Baliles said as much during a tribute to Godwin at the University of Virginia in July 1998. The man responsible for the state's last significant tax increase emphasized the need for investment in services and offered veiled criticism of Gilmore's strategy in his speech to accept an award on Godwin's behalf.

"Mills Godwin did not act in the cause of the next election," Baliles said. "He acted in the cause of the next generation. He helped forge a growing consensus in Virginia, to which I heartily subscribe, that economic growth is a good thing, but that you cannot get there by wishes alone. It takes money. It takes commitment."

Indeed, some Democrats suspect that Gilmore may be willing to sacrifice existing investment in higher education for his car-tax plan. They suspect his new commission to examine how state universities spend their money may be his hedge against any economic downturn that could threaten the phase-out.

"Everybody I've talked to thinks that the commission addressing higher education is going to be his way to justify reducing state funding for state colleges and universities, so that the car tax can be fully phased in," said Craig Beiber, executive director of the Democratic Party of Virginia. "Clearly, we're going to continue to let the public know what it is that's not going to be funded to allow car-tax relief."

Others caution that Virginia simply wouldn't be able to afford it. To accomplish Gilmore's phase-out of the car tax, the state's two-year budget must forgo a whopping $2.26 billion beginning in 2005. "There will be very little play in the budget for many years to come" to accommodate the car-tax relief, said R. Scott Leake, director of the Republican caucus in the General Assembly. The food tax, he said, "might continue to have some political pizzazz, but when people start to understand how much is involved, I think the drive may have less steam to it."

Given the cost of cutting the car tax, Gilmore and others are likely to dig their trenches a little deeper in order to see the phase-out to its completion. Nevertheless, further tax relief could even be envisioned as a desire of the Gilmore administration, given the state has the economic capacity to support it—though the governor continues to warily view the calls for a food-tax cut as a ploy to undermine his car-tax phase-out. "He's certainly against taxes and would look at other ways people can keep more of their money," said Gilmore spokesman Mark Miner. "He's not against it; we just have to do the car tax first."

Conclusion

The motivations of both Democrats and Republicans aside, two things are clear: The phase-out of the tax on cars and trucks begun in 1998 permanently changed the politics of taxes in Virginia, and taxes will continue to be a dominating force in Virginia politics for the foreseeable future as a result. Gilmore's success has proven more than ever that taxes, the mother of all so-called pocketbook issues, can enable a politician to set the agenda for a state if handled shrewdly. Used as the centerpiece of his run for office, the plan to cut the car tax enabled the conservative Gilmore to neutralize potentially divisive social issues and woo a broader spectrum of voters.

Gilmore's opponents may argue that the governor, by placing such a premium on accomplishing his car-tax phase-out, sacrificed sound government for popularity. But Gilmore argued that the best government is limited government. Cutting taxes is both the most effective way to limit the reach of government and to appeal to taxpayers who already feel overburdened.

Moreover, political expedience is not necessarily an evil; Gilmore may demonstrate during his term that the popularity of his car-tax cut is his way of amassing political capital to allow him to accomplish other broader policy objectives that reflect his conservative outlook. His tax-cut strategy could prove to be a means to a greater political end, rather than simply shrewd politics.

That debate is precisely what blurs the line between the politics of taxes and the process of good governance. While the outcome of Gilmore's car-tax phase-out remains to be seen, the debate has focused attention on a crucial dynamic of democracy that is often neglected: the link between state government and the individual taxpayers it depends upon to function. In offering taxpayers the chance of freedom from the annual rite of writing a check to pay an unpopular tax, Gilmore triggered one of the longest sustained debates that had been held on the link between individual and government in years. In their own way, supporters and opponents alike asked Virginians to examine their attitudes toward the state government they supported. Viewed in this sense, the ensuing debate ultimately demonstrated that the issue of taxes is at once personal and political. It also suggested that, as such, the politics of taxes will never be far from the center of public election campaigns.

Bibliography

Allen, Mike. "Tax-Cut Resistance Spreads Beyond N. Va.: Business Leaders Say State's Needs Outweigh Any Election." *The Washington Post,* 24 August 1997, sec. A.

Andrews, Hunter B. Telephone interview 16 July 1998.

Bieber, Craig. Telephone interview 8 July 1998.

Gilmore, James S. 1998. "Gilmore Spearheads Largest Tax Cut in Virginia History," New Release. Richmond: Office of the Governor, 24 April.

Leake, R. Scott. Telephone interview 9 July 1998.

Marcus, M. Boyd. In-person interview 23 June 1998.

Plaisance, Patrick Lee. "Local Leaders Doubt Wisdom of Tax Cut: Candidates' Plans Greeted Skeptically." *Daily Press,* 31 August 1997, sec. C.

Sabato, Larry J. Telephone interview 23 June 1998.

"Most Virginians Unaware of Car Tax Cut, VCU Poll Finds." Richmond: Survey and Evaluation Research Laboratory, Virginia Commonwealth University, 19 May 1998.

Whitley, Tyler. "Godwin Altered Himself, His State: Symposium Looks at Political Career." *Richmond Times-Dispatch*, 19 July 1998, sec. C.

Wilder, L. Douglas. Telephone interview 7 July 1998.

CHAPTER TWELVE

The Criminal Justice System: Providing Public Safety in Virginia

Tom Dempsey
Christopher Newport University

David Coffey
Thomas Nelson Community College

The Virginia criminal justice system is comprised of those components of government established primarily to provide for public safety within a framework of due process protection. The components of the criminal justice system are generally identified as law enforcement, the courts and corrections. These components are not unique to Virginia but operate at all levels of government, federal, state, local and within special jurisdictions.

While the common goal of the system is to provide for public safety, each of the components have specific functions. Those functions may be broadly identified as follows. Law enforcement functions primarily to enforce the law, provide public services not available from other public agencies, maintain public order and protect the rights of the public and the accused. The prosecutor is normally identified within the courts component. The prosecutor's office exists to review information presented for prosecution, usually from law enforcement, and to represent the government at trial. The criminal courts are established to determine truth in dispute, within the procedural framework that is established by law. Corrections agencies exist to carry out the sentence of the courts. There are four widely recognized goals of corrections programs, retribution (punishment), incapacitation, deterrence and rehabilitation. Not every program or sanction will address all of these goals.

Within the guidelines of the U.S. Constitution, the administration of criminal justice is largely a function of state or local government. Certainly, this is true for law enforcement where municipal police departments and county sheriff's offices account for the overwhelming majority of activity. The two primary criminal courts, General District and Circuit, are organized at the state level but actually operate at the local level. The primary actor in the arena of prosecution is the office of Commonwealth's Attorney, which is a county office. The prison system and the Department of Probation and Parole are state agencies. The jails throughout Virginia are either operated by the county sheriffs or as multi-jurisdictional facilities, shared by several counties. Likewise most community-based corrections programs are operated at the county or municipal level.

While legislative bodies are not normally thought of as a component of the criminal justice system, their influence is obvious. These law-making bodies, at all levels of government, formulate the statutes and ordinances which describe criminal conduct. Appellate courts often review the legality of that legislation through the process of appeal. In this chapter we will briefly examine all of these components of the criminal justice system in Virginia. We will close by looking at several criminal justice policy issues.

Law Enforcement

We will pay a great deal of attention to law enforcement because it is the largest of the components and much of the information contained in this section will also apply to the other components. We should keep in mind that the majority of law enforcement activity, throughout the nation and in Virginia, takes place at the local level of government. State legislatures enact the vast majority of the criminal statutes that are enforced by the various law enforcement agencies. To a far lesser extent the federal gov-

Figure 12.1 The largest law enforcement agency in Virginia is the Virginia State Police, with 1,600 officers. Courtesy of Virginia State Police.

ernment defines certain conduct as a criminal violation and empowers enforcement of those violations to law enforcement officers at all levels.

Federal law enforcement agencies operate in Virginia as they do in all states. Because of the large number of federal employees and activities in Virginia, agencies such as the Federal Bureau of Investigation, Drug Enforcement Administration, Bureau of Alcohol, Tobacco and Firearms and Secret Service are relatively active in Virginia. Likewise, the large number of military personnel in Virginia requires significant presence of the various military investigative agencies.

There are nearly 20,000 law enforcement officers in Virginia. Most are employed by the various police departments and sheriff's offices throughout the state. The vast majority of policing agencies in Virginia employ 50 or fewer officers. In fact, there are 19 policing agencies in the Commonwealth that employ only one officer.

The Attorney General of Virginia is the chief legal officer of the Commonwealth. This reference reflects the Attorney General's role with regard to state criminal justice and law enforcement efforts. Although the direct role of the Attorney General in criminal justice is broadly limited to prosecution of very narrowly defined criminal statutes like anti-trust laws, the influence of the office is very significant.

Another state office of importance is the office of the Director of Public Safety. The Director of Public Safety is appointed by the Governor and provides administrative support and oversight for many public safety activities throughout the state.

At the state level, the Virginia State Police (VSP) are the most significant law enforcement agency. In 1998, the VSP employed approximately 1,600 officers statewide, making them the largest law enforcement agency in the state. The VSP follow a model of "full-service" law enforcement, which means they have the statutory authority to serve the general police function throughout the state and they do so in many locales, especially rural areas. The primary function of the state police remains, however, enforcement of traffic laws and investigation of traffic collisions on state highways.

Several other state agencies also perform limited law enforcement functions. These include the Alcoholic Beverage Control Board, Department of Motor Vehicles, Department of Fish and Game and Virginia Marine Resources Commission. One final state agency that merits mention is the Department of Criminal Justice Services (DCJS). DCJS is governed by a board appointed by the Governor and day-to-day operations are supervised by the Executive Director. DCJS establishes guidelines with regard to standards for employment and training of law enforcement officers statewide. DCJS also plays a role in the administration of certain community-based corrections functions not administered by the Virginia Department of Corrections, and establishes training and licensing requirements for private investigators and the private security industry.

At the county level, the most significant role throughout the Commonwealth is played by the county sheriffs. Sheriffs are elected officials within each county and they operate with considerable independence as constitutional officers. Elected sheriffs are typically charged with several functions. Minimally they serve as bailiffs for the courts, maintaining order in the courtrooms and serving legal papers such as subpoenas. In most jurisdictions they are also charged with running county jails, though an increasing number of areas are forming multi-jurisdictional, regional jails. In many areas of the state, especially rural areas, the sheriff is also charged with providing law enforcement for residents of the county. Of approximately 125 sheriffs throughout the state, 90 are involved in law enforcement. Some counties have addressed problems associated with the myriad of tasks required of the sheriff by establishing county police departments to perform the law enforcement function exclusively.

Several important aspects of policing by sheriff's departments should be noted. First, the counties typically have relatively less revenue to support law enforcement than cities and therefore employ fewer deputies than would a city with the same population. This reduced revenue also may translate into lower salaries, less training and less money for equipment. Second, because the chief executive position, sheriff, is elected, the sheriff must be politically astute and must run for re-election every four years. This may take energy that might otherwise be directed to law enforcement activity. Finally, as an elected, constitutional officer, the sheriff is generally recognized to have more freedom than chiefs of police in personnel matters to include hiring, promotion and termination.

Municipal and county police departments in the Commonwealth employ the greatest number of law enforcement officers. The jurisdictions they police include urban, sub-urban and rural communities.

The larger of these agencies perform every conceivable policing function, while smaller departments may perform only patrol, relying on the state police or other agencies to provide specialized services. Police agencies use "sworn" officers, those having police powers as described in the constitution, to perform most of the functions of the

Figure 12.2 DMV office in Virginia. The DMV performs limited law enforcement functions. Courtesy of the Office of the Governor, State of Virginia.

department. These police officers are found in uniformed assignments in patrol and traffic enforcement and investigative assignments like detective or vice and narcotic units. Sworn officers may also perform staff and administrative functions like recruitment, personnel, training, communication, or crime analysis. In many departments, there is a trend toward "civilianization." Civilianization involves employing non-sworn employees to perform many of the functions that do not require the arrest powers of a police officer. Civilianization is generally thought to save money and possibly allow the department to hire employees with more specific job skills.

The chief executive of police departments is normally referred to as the Chief of Police. This is a position that is appointed by the city or county manager. While the position of Chief is a powerful one and one that requires a great deal of political skill it is not an elected position as is the Sheriff.

There are numerous "special jurisdiction" policing agencies throughout the Commonwealth. These agencies perform the policing either within only a narrow range of criminal law or within a narrowly defined geographical area. Among such agencies are airport police, campus police, harbor police or local park rangers.

Policing is largely a function of local government. Typically, the legislature or appellate courts will provide broad guidance but the departments determine how activities are carried out. This is true even in areas of critical public interest like use of force and high-speed pursuits. Guidance may be found in law but application is determined by the departments. The sufficiency of policy in these areas is only scrutinized when practices are challenged in court.

Occasionally issues become so "political" that the General Assembly will directly mandate certain requirements. Policies employed by the police in handling calls of

Figure 12.3 The aftermath of a tornado in Petersburg, Virginia. Part of law enforcement's job is protecting the public during natural disasters. Courtesy of Dennis L. Rubin & Associates.

domestic violence are illustrative. Throughout the 1980s, the public became increasingly convinced that the manner in which the entire criminal justice system had responded to domestic violence, basically a "keep the peace" approach, was not adequate. State legislatures around the country, including Virginia, enacted statutes mandating that the police make a more assertive, proactive effort to intercede in these matters. The specifics of these legislative acts generally required the police to document all calls that fit the definition of domestic violence and gave the police broader authority to arrest in domestic violence matters. These legislative mandates meant that police departments had to change their policies with regard to responding to calls of domestic violence and train officers in new protocols for handling these incidents.

Another important area of change is the adoption by many police departments, especially large urban departments, of a "community based policing" philosophy. Most of what the police do has traditionally been reactive, that is, responding to calls for service after an incident. Under a community based philosophy, departments shift significant resources into areas that are more proactive in an effort to "solve problems rather than handle calls." In order to accomplish the goals of community based policing many departments have de-centralized much of their activities and empowered individual officers with broader problem-solving authority.

Prosecutors

In general, prosecutors perform two critical functions. First, they review police investigations and play a role in deciding which cases will go forward for prosecution. This function is normally referred to as "filing." Once a decision is made to go forward with a criminal case, the prosecutor then becomes the advocate of the people and presents the evidence against the accused at trial.

Criminal prosecutors function at all levels of government. Like law enforcement, the focal point of most criminal prosecution is at the local level. In Virginia, the primary figure is the Commonwealth Attorney for each independent city and county. Commonwealth Attorneys are elected officials. In rural jurisdictions, most prosecutions may be conducted by the Commonwealth Attorney or by a very limited number of assistant Commonwealth Attorneys, many of whom may be part-time prosecutors. In larger, urban areas, the elected Commonwealth Attorney may personally handle very few cases, relying instead on a large staff of assistant and deputy Commonwealth Attorneys.

Commonwealth Attorney's offices prosecute the overwhelming majority of all felony cases in Virginia. With the exception of very rare criminal prosecutions initiated by the state Attorney General's office, it is at this level that serious cases are presented. The Commonwealth Attorney's office also presents evidence at preliminary hearings in felony matters and to the Grand Juries of the various jurisdictions.

Because they are elected state officials, Commonwealth Attorneys must always be aware of the political environment in which they function. Community standards and values may often play a significant role in decisions by the prosecutor with regard to the cases that are aggressively pursued or viewed as less serious than they might be in other jurisdictions. Violations of federal criminal statutes are prosecuted by the Office of the United States Attorney, a division of the US Department of Justice. Federal cases are prosecuted in federal courts rather than state courts.

One issue that merits mention with regard to prosecutors is the concern many citizens have for what is termed the "court house fraternity." While prosecutors may work closely with law enforcement, they are also lawyers who receive the same basic legal training as any other lawyer. The same is true of defense attorneys, private or public, and judges. Some critics of the legal system believe that the common bond among these key actors lends to frequent "gentlemen's agreements" that may undermine the adversary nature of our criminal justice system.

Another issue of significant importance to the public is the frequency with which "negotiated pleas" or "plea bargains" occur. Plea bargaining is a process whereby a defendant in a criminal case agrees with the Commonwealth Attorney to plead guilty in return for a reduced sentence or some other consideration. Many people oppose this process. Some feel that it allows defendants to "get away with murder." Other people fear that it might encourage innocent defendants to plead guilty because they are afraid that they might be found guilty at trial and receive a harsh sentence. Without the use of plea bargaining however, the criminal courts, which are already overcrowded with pending cases, would be overwhelmed.

Courts

There are five levels of criminal courts in the Commonwealth. They are the office of Magistrate, General District Court, Circuit Court, Court of Appeals and the Virginia Supreme Court. The General District and Circuit courts may be thought of primarily as trial courts, that is courts where the main function is to hold criminal trials. The Court of Appeals and Supreme Court are appellate courts. The courts are organized into judicial circuits and districts. There are 31 judicial circuits and 32 judicial districts in the commonwealth.

Magistrates

Many of the duties and functions now performed by magistrates were once performed by justices of the peace. In 1974, as part of a statewide reorganization plan for the court system, Virginia phased out the office of the justice of the peace and established the magistrate system. Magistrates are not judges and do not possess trial jurisdiction; they are however considered judicial officers of the Commonwealth. The principal function of the magistrate is to provide an independent review of complaints and other processes brought to the office by law enforcement and citizens. Magistrates' duties include issuing arrest and search warrants, summons, subpoenas, and civil warrants and bonds. Most magistrates are not lawyers but they do receive special training in order to perform their duties.

Magistrates are appointed judicial officers and can be re-appointed for unlimited consecutive terms. The Chief Circuit Court judges for the various judicial circuits are responsible for the appointment of magistrates in that judicial district. The only qualifications for appointment as a magistrate are US citizenship, residence within the district of appointment and absence of any statutory conflict of interest (such as having a spouse who is a law enforcement officer).

General District Courts

The general district courts do not conduct jury trials. All trial matters in the District Court are heard by a judge alone. The judge determines the guilt or innocence of the accused.

The General District court decides criminal cases involving violations of local city or county ordinances and all misdemeanors under state law. A misdemeanor is any crime for which the punishment can be no more than one year in jail and/or a fine of up to $2,500. All traffic matters are also heard in General District court.

The General District court also conducts preliminary hearings in felony cases. A felony is any charge that is punishable by incarceration for over one year. A preliminary hearing is a review of the evidence against the accused to determine if the matter should be referred to the Grand Jury.

Juvenile and Domestic Relations Courts

In Virginia there are District Courts set up to specifically handle cases involving juveniles and domestic relations matters. These courts are referred to as Juvenile and Domestic Relations District Court (JDR court). The JDR court differs somewhat from other courts in relation to duties and obligations. The welfare of the juvenile and the family is of highest concern to the court. The JDR courts have a duty to protect the confidentiality and privacy of the juveniles with a focus on rehabilitation of the juvenile.

In the Commonwealth, juveniles age 14 and older may, when charged with certain serious felonies, be tried as an adult. In such a situation there is a hearing to determine if the case should be transferred to the Circuit Court for treatment as an adult. Adults charged with committing felonies against children or family members make an initial appearance in JDR court after arrest. A preliminary hearing is conducted in JDR court to determine if there is probable cause to believe that the accused adult committed the felony offense. If the judge determines there is sufficient probable cause, then the case is transferred to the circuit court for further proceedings.

Circuit Courts

The Circuit Court is the only trial court of general jurisdiction in Virginia. This means that the court has authority over a full range of criminal and civil cases. The Circuit Court is the only court that provides jury trials for defendants. The Circuit Court has jurisdiction over all felony matters and misdemeanor charges originating from a grand jury indictment. Circuit Courts also have jurisdiction over juveniles who are charged with felonies where the case has been certified by a JDR judge for trial in Circuit Court. Judges of the Circuit Court are elected for an eight-year term by the majority vote of both houses of the General Assembly.

Court of Appeals

The Court of Appeals is an intermediate appellate court. It was created in 1985 in order to increase the appellate capacity of the court system and expedite the appellate process. A distinction must be made between cases that the courts must review as a matter of right, versus an exercise of discretion. In cases involving appeals as a "matter of right," the Court of Appeals must review the case. In cases where the appeal is a matter of discretion the Court of Appeals considers a "petition for appeal" and may decline to review the matter. The Court of Appeals has jurisdiction to review final orders of the Circuit Court involving convictions in criminal matters, except those criminal matters wherein the death penalty is imposed. Death penalty cases must be reviewed by the Virginia Supreme Court. Ten justices serve on the Court of Appeals, and sit in panels of three when deciding a case.

Virginia Supreme Court

The Supreme Court is an appellate court comprised of seven justices. These justices are nominated by the Governor and confirmed by the Senate. Their appointment is for life. Their primary function with regard to criminal justice is to serve as the court of final appeal. By statute, the Supreme Court must review all death penalty sentences. They select the other cases they choose to review. The Supreme Court normally accepts cases on review when it appears the issues have broad application throughout the state.

The overwhelming majority of cases they review deal with procedural issues concerning due process. Once the Supreme Court rules on a case, a precedent is established which guides similar cases throughout the Commonwealth. Through this process, the Supreme Court has a law making, or policy making, capacity in addition to an interpretation capacity.

Corrections

At a minimum, corrections activities include the operation of local jails, various community-based programs that may include electronic monitoring and house arrest, "boot camp" programs, probation and parole, state prisons and administration of capital sentences. The activity of the corrections component of the criminal justice system in Virginia is supervised primarily by the state Department of Corrections. Some community-based programs, however, are supervised by DCJS.

Sentences imposed by the courts and carried out by the corrections agencies can be divided roughly into several broad categories. Those categories are community-based sanctions, probation, imprisonment (in prison or jail) and capital punishment.

It is important to understand the roles played by jails and by prison. Jails perform two major functions in Virginia. First, they house those offenders who are sentenced by the courts to serve one year or less in secure custody. This is normally upon conviction of a misdemeanor charge. Second, they are used to hold people who have been arrested but who are not yet released on bail. This situation may result from bail being set at an amount the arrested person cannot afford. Or, it may result because the person may not be provided the opportunity to post bail at all due to the nature of the crime she is charged with.

At any given point in time, approximately one half of the people housed in jails are sentenced and the other half have yet to be sentenced. Many of the people who have not been sentenced may only be in jail for a few hours before posting bail or being released on their own recognizance. Both the courts and the jail administrators would like to reduce the number of unsentenced people being held.

Prisons confine people sentenced to incarceration for one year or more, usually for a felony crime. While there are programs in place within the prison system to rehabilitate inmates, the major goals of imprisonment are to incapacitate the offender for a period of time, to discourage the offender from repeating and/or to exact a measure of punishment. As of 1998, Virginia prisons housed approximately 26,000 inmates.

It is within the prison system that executions are also carried out. Virginia is among the leading states in number of executions. Between 1976, when the US Supreme Court re-affirmed the right of the individual states to employ capital punishment under specific conditions, and 1996, Virginia executed 37 inmates. Despite this, a great many inmates who have been sentenced to death remain on "death row" for extended periods of time. The average execution, when it does occur, takes place 7 years after the sentence was imposed.

Probation is by far the most common sentence imposed by the courts. Probation is a sentence under which the offender remains in the community but with conditions and restrictions on his behavior. The focus of a sentence to probation is on rehabilitation through services available within the community. Probationers are monitored and supervised by probation officers and, if they significantly violate the conditions of their probation, may be ordered to incarceration. Probation is not normally used as a sentence for adult offenders who commit violent crimes. The administration of probation is the responsibility of the Department of Probation and Parole.

Parole is a process by which offenders who have been sentenced to imprisonment are released back to the community, with conditions and restrictions, after serving a portion of their sentence. In 1995 the General Assembly passed legislation abolishing parole. Many inmates, however, were sentenced under guidelines which allowed for parole and will continue to be paroled.

Within the broad category of community based corrections programs fall many provisions used throughout the Commonwealth. These include "boot camp" programs, electronic monitoring, community service programs, intensive supervision probation and other innovative programs designed to address the needs of offenders and the public without costly incarceration.

Incarceration of offenders is a very expensive proposition. On average, the cost of housing a single state prison inmate in Virginia has been estimated to be approximately $17,000 per year. Traditional probation costs on average less than $3000 per probationer. These figures do not, however, take into account the cost to the public of additional offenses which may be committed by probationers.

Despite the cost, the Virginia prison system is housing nearly 125% of the number of inmates for which it was designed. Over-crowding in the prisons creates an environment that may not be conducive to "rehabilitation" of inmates, but rather one that promotes violence and one which may expose the state to liability concerns. Overcrowding is generally addressed through the construction of new prisons or by the expanded use of alternatives to incarceration.

The execution of offenders who are sentenced to death by the courts is another very "high profile" issue confronting corrections. While it is true that the sentence is carried out by the corrections component, the death penalty is handed down by a jury and is called for by statute. Proponents and opponents of the death penalty often argue about the appropriateness of the sanction. The majority of the voters of the Commonwealth support the death penalty for some types of murders. The Virginia Supreme Court and United States Supreme Court have both found the Virginia statute constitutional.

Just as overcrowding is a significant issue for prisons and jails, the average case load for probation officers in Virginia is very high. With over 100 cases per probation officer, it may be impossible to effectively supervise probationers. Reducing the caseload will mean employing a greater number of probation officers and therefore additional expense to the taxpayer. Even if the average case-load was reduced to 25 per probation officer, probation would remain, on the surface, a less expensive option than imprisonment.

Development and Implementation of Criminal Justice Policy

There are several aspects of policy making that are significant or unique to the criminal justice system, regardless of specific issues addressed. Perhaps most significant is the role of the political process, particularly the action (or inaction) of legislative bodies such as the General Assembly, county Boards of Supervisors, and city councils. These bodies establish the statutes and ordinances the criminal justice system is charged with enforcing or interpreting. These democratic bodies, along with the appellate courts, provide the framework of law. The criminal justice system must operate within this framework, both in terms of the substantive laws that must be enforced and in terms of the procedural rules that must be followed. Each of the components is directly impacted by legislation. Examples are plentiful and include areas such as drug laws, domestic violence laws, sentencing guidelines that reduce the discretion of judges and abolition of parole.

Likewise, both legislative bodies and appointed executives like the governor, county administrators and city managers influence criminal justice policy making through administrative activity, primarily budgetary allocation. Budgets serve to focus the activity of the components, especially law enforcement and corrections into areas that have political support. Likewise, the availability of state controlled grants may dictate areas in which the components must focus activity. Examples of this process would include funding availability for programs such as community based policing efforts, drug courts or prison construction.

While the actions of legislative bodies and chief executives "set the tone" for criminal justice policy decisions, implementation is nearly always a local function. How the broad mandates of the General Assembly or city council are actually carried out is largely determined by local units of the criminal justice system. It is at the level of the county sheriff, police chief, Commonwealth Attorney, local judge or corrections administrator that the planning process takes place and decisions are made. Issues are local and the programs to address local issues are best developed at the local level. The resources that individual law enforcement agencies, prosecutors or courts devote to drug problems, prostitution, or drunk driving is often contingent on local concern.

At one time local policy making by criminal justice executives was justly criticized for being carried out "in a vacuum" without significant citizen input. The rationale for this was that citizens had input through the political process and did not have the specific understanding of the criminal justice system to make meaningful contributions to "nuts-and-bolts" policy making. Such elitism is rare today as executives from all components seek input from concerned citizens in many areas of policy development.

Any discussion of criminal justice policy making would be incomplete without some mention of the role discretion plays in all criminal justice operational decision making. Employees at all levels and in all components exercise broad discretion in decision making. Decisions involving arrest, filing of charges, pleas, sentencing, eligibility for probation and level of incarceration are all discretionary in almost every case. It is also interesting to note that within law enforcement especially, the greatest amount of discretion over the most critical incidents is normally exercised by the employees with the least amount of experience, uniformed officers.

The fact that many of the key figures in the criminal justice system are elected, most notably sheriffs, Commonwealth's Attorneys and some judges, impacts the policy making process. In order to remain effective in their offices they must seek re-election. Political concerns and public perception may influence policy decisions that would otherwise be based solely on operational factors.

Finally, it is important to recognize that each of the components, through policy, must deal with two distinct features of crime. First is the reality of crime. That is, policy must be established to impact on the actual or potential occurrence of crime. Second, and equally important, the criminal justice system must address public concerns about the perception of crime. Policy decisions must factor in the public perception of how safe, or unsafe, they are in any given community. In general, the public perception of crime is greater than the reality but both impact on the quality of life for citizens.

Bibliography

Allen, Harry E. And Clifford E. Simonsen. 1998. *Corrections in America,* 8th edition, Upper Saddle River, NJ: Prentice Hall.

Del Carmen, Rolando V., Susan E. Ritter and Betsy A. Witt. 1998. *Briefs on Leading Cases in Corrections,* 2nd edition, Cincinnati, OH: Anderson Publishing Co.

Latessa, Edward J. and Harry E. Allen. 1997. *Corrections in the Community,* Cincinnati, OH: Anderson Publishing Co.

Schmalleger, Frank. 1997. *Criminal Justice Today,* 4th ed., Upper Saddle River, NJ: Prentice Hall.

Swanson, Charles R., Leonard Territo and Robert W. Taylor. 1998. *Police Administration: Structure, Processes and Behavior,* 4th edition, Upper Saddle River, NJ: Prentice Hall.

U.S. Department of Justice, Bureau of Justice Statistics, *Capital Punishment Statistics,* http://www.ojp.usdoj.gov/bjs/cp.htm

U.S. Department of Justice, Office of Justice Programs, National Institute of Justice. 1996. *Measuring What Matters.* Washington, D.C.: Department of Justice.

U.S. Department of Justice, Office of Justice Programs, National Institute of Justice. 1996. *Implementation Challenges in Community Policing.* Washington, D.C.: Department of Justice.

U.S. Department of Justice, Office of Justice Programs, National Institute of Justice. 1996. *Implementing Performance-Based Measures in Community Corrections.* Washington, D.C.: Department of Justice.

U.S. Department of Justice. Office of Justice Programs, Bureau of Justice Statistics. 1997. *Capital Punishment,* 1996. Washington, D.C.: Department of Justice.

U.S. Department of Justice, Office of Justice Programs, National Institute of Justice. 1997. *Intermediate Sanctions and Sentencing Guidelines.* Washington, D.C.: Department of Justice.

U.S. Department of Justice, Office of Justice Programs, National Institute of Justice. 1997. *Probation in the United States: Practices and Challenges.* Washington,D.C.: Department of Justice.

U.S. Department of Justice, Office of Justice Programs, National Institute of Justice. 1997. *Prison and Jail Inmates at Midyear 1996.* Washington, D.C.: Department of Justice.

Virginia Department of Corrections, http://www.cns.state.va.us

Virginia Judicial System, http://www.courts.state.va.us

CHAPTER THIRTEEN

Political Ethics and Reform in Virginia: Marching to the Beat of a Different Drummer

Robert N. Roberts
James Madison University

Rebuilding trust in government and public employees and officials constitutes one of the most perplexing problems facing government today. The Vietnam War, the Watergate scandal, campaign finance scandals, negative campaigning, influence peddling by lobbyists and intense media coverage of the personal lives of public officials have seriously weakened public trust in the integrity of public officials. (Frederickson and Frederickson 1995, 163–172). Since the early 1970s, good government groups have lobbied for the enactment of reform legislation directed at controlling the impact of special interest money in politics and preventing public officials from using their public offices for personal financial gain.

The last three decades has seen Congress and state legislatures enact much more stringent campaign finance reform, conflict of interest and lobbying reporting and disclosure laws. Today, federal and state campaign finance reform laws regulate campaign fund raising in almost all federal, state and local elections. Many local, state and federal government employees and officials face disciplinary action for not complying with strict codes of ethics. In addition, federal and state lobbying laws typically require lobbyists to register and to disclose lobbying expenditures and payments received for lobbying.

In sharp contrast to the federal government and the vast majority of states, Virginia has chosen not to adopt the most common campaign finance reform measures, public ethics rules and restrictions on lobbyists. Instead, Virginia has relied upon financial disclosure by political campaigns, public employees and officials, and lob-byists as the primary method of protecting public confidence in state and local gov-ernment officials. To the dismay of some political observers, the majority of Virginia residents seem unconcerned about the apparent weaknesses of Virginia ethics laws.[1]

This chapter provides an overview of Virginia campaign finance, financial conflict-of-interest and lobbying restrictions and their impact upon Virginia state and local politics. The chapter argues that Virginia's traditional political culture has made it difficult for public ethics reform to make much headway in Virginia. Finally, the chapter explores the arguments for maintaining Virginia's relaxed ethics rules and for significantly tightening campaign finance, public ethics and lobbying restrictions.

The Public Integrity Crisis: Fact or Fiction?

A March 1998 study by the Pew Research Center For The People & The Press titled *Deconstructing Distrust: How Americans View Government* confirmed continuing high levels of public distrust in government and elected public officials (Pew 1998). Sixty-four percent of those surveyed agreed with the statement that "Govt is inefficient & wasteful." On the other hand, the public indicated a moderate level of confidence in the ability of state and local governments to operate efficiently. Fifty-nine percent of those surveyed expressed a mostly unfavorable or very unfavorable opinion of the fed-eral government in Washington. Sixty-six percent had a very favorable or mostly fa-vorable impression of their state government and sixty-eight percent expressed a very favorable or mostly favorable impression of their local governments. Twenty-five years earlier, the public had a much higher opinion of the ability of the federal government to get things done and much less confidence in the efficiency and effectiveness of state and local governments.

A closer examination of the Pew survey reveals a relationship between unhappi-ness with the conduct of elected officials and trust in government. Fifty-five percent of those surveyed disagreed with the statement that "most elected officials are trust-worthy." In contrast, sixty-seven percent of those surveyed trusted civil servant em-ployees to do the right thing. Only sixteen percent of respondents trusted politicians to do the right thing. Only thirty-one percent of those surveyed rated the ethical and moral practices of federal government officials as excellent or good. Forty-three per-cent of those surveyed rated the ethical and moral practices of state and local gov-ernment officials as excellent or good.

Little doubt exists that large numbers of Americans question the integrity of elect-ed public officials. Additionally, many Americans doubt the ability of the federal gov-ernment to efficiently manage major government programs. On the other hand, the public appears to have much greater confidence in the ability of state and local offi-cials to do the right thing.

State Political Reform and Rebuilding the Public Trust

At the federal and state level, good government reform groups have focused their en-ergy upon obtaining the enactment of campaign finance reform, public ethics and lobbying reform legislation. By the close of the 1980s, the federal government and the majority of states required political campaigns, their employees and officials and lobbyists to comply with much stricter rules of conduct. Mandatory public financial disclosure by high-level public officials became commonplace at all levels of government. And political campaigns found themselves subject to new requirements that they disclose the amount and sources of campaign contributions.

Campaign Finance Reform and the Money Chase

Even before the Watergate scandal of the early 1970s, reformers saw campaign finance reform as vital to stopping powerful special interests from using campaign contributions to buy access to key decision makers in Washington, state capitols or the local court house. By the end of the 1960s, the rising cost of paying for expensive media campaigns forced candidates to raise larger and larger amounts of campaign contributions. Besides criticizing political campaigns for soliciting campaign contributions from special interests, reformers also argued that the escalating cost of running for public office made it impossible for the vast majority of individuals to run for public office. Consequently, reformers saw campaign finance reform as constituting a way to level the playing field.

The Federal Election Campaign Act (FECA) of 1971 and its subsequent amendments established the blue print for state campaign finance reform. In the aftermath of Watergate, Congress passed the 1974 and 1976 FECA amendments. These amendments "set strict limits on contributions and expenditures, created a system of partial public financing of presidential campaigns, and established an independent agency the Federal Election Commission (FEC) to monitor and enforce tough new disclosure requirements" (Center for Responsive Politics 1998, 1). Although the Supreme Court in the 1976 *Buckley v. Valeo* decision upheld the constitutionality of placing limits on the size of campaign contributions and requiring federal campaigns to disclose the size and name of contributors, the Court found that mandatory limits on campaign expenditures violated the freedom of speech provision of the First Amendment of the Constitution.

Today, the majority of states (1) require full disclosure of campaign contributions, (2) prohibit labor unions and corporations from making campaign contributions, (3) place limits on individual contributions, and (4) limit the size of political contributions by PACs (Blue Book 1993, 62–85). For instance, Florida law prohibits candidates for public office from accepting "a contribution in excess of $500 from any one person per election" (Campaign Finance 1998, 1). A relatively small number of states have instituted some form of public financing of elections. For example, "Florida provides matching public funds for individual contributions of $250 or less to statewide candidates who agree to spending limits (Center for Responsive Politics 1998). A few states, including the state of Virginia, now permit unlimited campaign contributions to state and local political campaigns.

Ethics Codes, Public Service and the Appearance of Impropriety

Besides the passage of new campaign finance reform laws, the two decades following the Watergate scandal saw the federal government and the states adopt new ethics codes for their public employees and officials (Roberts 1994, 485–498). Governments issued the codes to prevent conduct that might raise questions regarding the objectivity or impartiality of their employees and officials in the performance of public business (Roberts 1988, 73–130). The 1970s and 1980s saw twenty-four states adopt new public ethics codes (Huddleston and Sands 1995, 142).

State public ethics codes typically include restrictions on government employees and officials (1) using public positions to obtain personal benefits, (2) using confidential government information for personal gain, (3) receiving certain types of gifts from non-public sources, (4) accepting certain types of honoraria, (5) engaging in outside employment which conflict with the performance of official duties, (6) accepting travel payments from non-governmental sources, (7) representing private clients before public entities and (8) participating in particular matters in which the employee or officials has a financial interest.

In addition, the new ethics codes usually included provisions requiring high-level public officials to file annual public financial disclosure statements. The Ethics in Government Act of 1978 required thousands of high-level federal employees and officials to file public financial disclosure statements (Carroll and Roberts 1988-89, 439–440).

Lobbying Reform and Regulation

Lobbying reform constitutes the third type of political reform pushed by good government groups after 1970. Reformers blamed well paid lobbyists for helping powerful special interests to obtain preferential treatment for clients. To help control the influence of lobbyists, many states enacted laws requiring lobbyists to register and to disclose how much they received for their services and spent on lobbying activities.

At the same time, many states prohibited lobbyists from engaging in specific types of lobbying activities such as (1) making campaign contributions during legislative sessions, (2) lobbying for contingent compensation, (3) participating in fund raising activities of legislative campaigns, (4) giving public officials or employees gifts worth more than a certain value and (5) paying for meals, travel and entertainment worth more than a certain value (Bowman 1996).

The practice of some former state employees and officials becoming lobbyists led many states to enact so-called 'revolving door' rules. Critics of former public officials going into business as lobbyists argued that former public officials could take unfair advantage of their government contacts to obtain preferential treatment for their clients. Consequently, many states now place some type of time restriction on the lobbying activities of former public officials. For instance, the New York State Public Officers Law "prohibits all former State employees from appearing or practicing before their former agencies for two years after they leave their State jobs" (NYS Ethics Commission 1998, 1). The Public Officers Law also imposes a lifetime bar on former state employees appearing before any agency or being paid "for work on matters or transactions in which they were directly concerned and personally participated with working in State government" (NYS Ethics Commission 1998, 1–2).

Public Ethics Management

With the enactment of new state campaign finance laws, ethics codes and lobbying came the problem of how to enforce the new restrictions. During the early twentieth century Progressive era, some states established state election boards to protect election administration from partisan manipulation. Up through the 1970s, however, the majority of states continued to place responsibility for election administration with their popularly elected Secretary of State.

Beginning in the early 1970s, good-government reform groups began to lobby for the establishment of independent commissions to take responsibility for the enforcement of political reform legislation. During the early 1970s, Congress established the Federal Election Commission to oversee enforcement of the new campaign finance legislation. Between 1970 and 1996, the states of Alaska, California, Connecticut, Delaware, Hawaii, Maine, Montana, New Jersey, Missouri, Nebraska, Oklahoma, South Carolina, Texas and Washington established election or ethics commissions. Despite strong pressure from political reform groups, the majority of states did not establish independent election or ethics commissions.

Instead, the majority of states continued to rely upon their Attorney General for the enforcement of criminal ethics laws and campaign finance regulations. Many states divided responsibility for campaign finance disclosure and election administration between election boards and their Secretary of State.

The Old Dominion and the Honor System

The preceding discussion describes how political reform led to major changes in the regulation of political ethics at the state and federal level. The Commonwealth of Virginia, however, has charted a very different course. From the early 1970s through today, the Virginia General Assembly has refused to limit the amount of campaign contributions to state and local candidates. Unlike officials and employees of many states, Virginia state and local government officials may accept free travel and lodging from large corporations and lobbyists. Virginia state and local government officials find themselves subject to much less stringent financial conflict-of-interest restrictions than their counterparts at the federal level. In addition, state law does not prohibit lobbyists from making political contributions to members of the state legislature or providing members of the legislature tickets for sporting events.

Campaign Finance Reform and the Status Quo

As discussed above, Virginia holds the distinction of being one of a handful of states that place no restrictions on the size of campaign contributions to candidates for state or local offices.

For decades, the Virginia legislature has taken the position that candidates and political parties had a right to raise unlimited amounts of political contributions. Instead, the Virginia law requires candidates for state and local office to file detailed reports of political contributions and expenditures (Bowman 1996, 307). Specifically, Virginia candidates "must file contribution and expenditure reports on January 15, July 15, file a number of pre-election reports and a final report 30 days after each election"(Bowman 1996, 307). State law delegates to the Virginia State Board of Elections in Richmond responsibility for collecting the reports and making them available for public inspection (Virginia Board of Elections 1998).

The fact that the Virginia General Assembly has refused to adopt limits on the size of campaign contributions does not mean that reformers have not attempted to persuade legislators to adopt campaign contribution limits. Through the 1980s and much of the 1990s, reformers attempted to persuade the legislature to agree to comprehensive campaign finance reform.

In May of 1992, for example, Virginia Governor L. Douglas Wilder established a commission to look at political ethics in Virginia. Chaired by University of Virginia constitutional scholar A. E. Dick Howard, the commission examined the role of money in Virginia politics.[2] Governor Wilder appointed the commission after he failed to obtain legislative approval of a new tax on the health care industry. He blamed the defeat of his tax proposal on campaign contributions made by health care political action committees to members of the Virginia House of Delegates and Senate.[3]

Instead of welcoming the establishment of the panel, key Democratic legislators criticized Governor Wilder for not notifying key legislators of his plans for creating the blue ribbon ethics panel and for not appointing any legislators to serve on the

Figure 13.1 Governor Douglas Wilder attempted to implement more stringent ethical standards during his administration, but ultimately failed. Courtesy of Associated Press/Wide World Photos.

panel. In early December 1992, the panel released its report proposing sweeping changes in Virginia's campaign finance and lobbying laws which included limiting the size of campaign contributions. During the forthcoming 1993 legislative session, Governor Wilder introduced legislation to put into effect many of the recommendations of the ethics panel, which included limits on campaign contributions.[4] Strong Democratic opposition sealed the fate of Governor Wilder's reform proposals. Surprisingly, many Republican legislators supported Wilder's reform proposals.

The November 1993 election of Republican George Allen as Governor seemed to open the door for campaign finance reform. The Democratic leadership of the state legislature created a new ethics panel made up of legislators to take another look at political reform. The panel recommended that the Virginia General Assembly place limits on the size of campaign contributions in state and local elections.[5] Early optimism regarding the passage of reform legislation proved premature. Contribution limits died after the House of Delegate and Virginia Senate failed to reach agreement on the proposal.

At the beginning of the 1997 legislative session, Governor George Allen resubmitted his ethics reform package to the legislature which included contribution limitations.[6] Neither Republican or Democratic members of the legislature backed the legislation. The upcoming November elections for governor, lieutenant governor, and attorney general made it impossible for either Republicans or Democrats to vote for legislation which might hamper their ability to raise campaign contributions. Both parties found the prospect of limiting the size of campaign contributions simply too frightening.

Employee Standards of Conduct and the Virginia Comprehensive Conflict of Interest Act

Much like the laws that apply to political fund raising in Virginia, ethics rules that apply to Virginia state and local government employees reflect the belief that Virginia residents can trust their public officials and employees to "do the right thing." The integrity of Virginia public officials makes unnecessary requiring state and local government employees to comply with unreasonably restrictive ethics rules and regulations.

Not until the mid-1980s did the Virginia General Assembly undertake a comprehensive revision of ethics rules for Virginia state and local government employees. Today, the State and Local Government Conflict of Interest Act establishes standard of conduct rules for employees and officials working for state and local government agencies (Va. Code 2.1-639.1). The General Assembly Conflict of Interest Act establishes public financial disclosure requirements and ethics rules for members of the Virginia General Assembly (Va. Code 2.1-639.30). And the Virginia Procurement Act includes a number of conflict-of-interest clauses designed to prevent public employees and officials from obtaining preferential treatment in competing for state and local government contracts (Va. Code 11-35)

Virginia's three ethics laws established policies for a number of common types of conflict-of-interest situations faced by state and local government employees and members of the Virginia General Assembly. For instance, the laws prohibit state and local government employees from accepting anything of value from non public sources for performing official duties, helping any person or business obtain a public contract or helping someone obtain a government job (Va. Code 2.1-639.4). Other rules prohibit state and local employees from accepting anything of value intended to influence the employee or official in the performance of official duties.

On the other hand, Virginia law does not prohibit state and local government employees from accepting the private hospitality of private sources as long as the employee or official believes that the items were not given to influence the official or employee in the performance of his official duties. By sanctioning the acceptance of private hospitality by state and local officials, Virginia law differs significantly from ethics rules enforced at the federal level and in many other states.

Gifts and Gratuities and Virginia Public Servants

On June 14, 1998, the *Richmond Times Dispatch* reported that Virginia lawmakers collected $123,700 the previous year in gifts and trips from private sources. The article reported that the majority of gifts came from corporations and special-interest lobbyists who had a history of making large campaign contributions to members of the Virginia General Assembly.[7] The report constituted the first comprehensive examination of private hospitality legally received by the Virginia General Assembly. To the considerable annoyance of critics of the gift acceptance practices of Virginia public officials, the story barely produced a ripple in the tradition bound world of Virginia politics.

The story produced little concern because of the long history of Virginia public officials accepting private hospitality from private sources. For instance, a 1989 *Washington Post* article reported on the tradition of Virginia officials accepting free trips from private sources.[8] In 1992 the *Washington Times* reported on the perks received by high-level state officials from major corporations.[9]

The Virginia Conflict of Interest Act contains two gift acceptance prohibitions. The first prohibits all state and local government employees from accepting any "money, loan, gift, favor, service, or business or professional opportunity" that would influence an official or employee in the performance of their official duties. The provision provides individual employees and their agencies considerable discretion to define permissible and impermissible gifts (Va. Code & 2.1-639.4(5)). In other words, the statute requires that employees and officials refuse to accept gifts that might influence them in their performance of official duties.

The second gift acceptance statute prohibits Virginia state and local government employees from accepting gifts from certain 'interested sources.' Specifically, it directs employees and officials not to accept "a gift from a person who has interests that may be substantially affected by the performance of the officer's or employee's official duties under circumstances where the timing and nature of the gift would cause a reasonable person to question the officer's or employee's impartiality in the matter affecting the donor" (Va. Code & 2.1-639.4). For instance, an employee has to decide on whether to award a contract. One of the contractors offers the employee a free use of a beach house owned by the company. The employee must refuse to accept the use of the beach house.

The two gift acceptance prohibitions establish a flexible approach for regulating the acceptance of gifts by Virginia state and local government employees and officials. Employees and officials must reject any gift which will threaten their ability to perform their duties in a fair and impartial manner.

Disclosure and Protecting the Public Trust

Defenders of the Virginia system for regulating political ethics argue that the disclosure provision of Virginia law provide the public adequate protection against public officials violating the public trust. As discussed earlier, Virginia law requires political campaigns to disclose the amount of campaign contributions and the source of the contributions. Members of the Virginia General Assembly and high-level state officials must disclose all gifts worth more than $50 from lobbyists and corporations. In addition, Virginia law requires lobbyists to disclose the names of public officials who received gifts worth more than $50 from them.[10]

In theory, disclosure gave the media and good government watchdog groups the opportunity to provide the public with information on who gave and received campaign contributions and which public employees received gifts from non-public sources. In fact, the media and good government groups found it extremely difficult to go through thousands of forms and make sense of information provided on the forms.

Although Governor Wilder's 1992 ethics commission recommended that Virginia provide internet access to campaign finance reports, the General Assembly failed to act on the recommendation. With funding provided by a number of state newspapers and broadcast outlets and technical support provided by Virginia Commonwealth's Public Policy Center, the non-partisan Virginia Public Access Project made available over the World Wide Web a vast amount of campaign finance information during the Fall 1997 statewide elections and 1998 Virginia legislative session (Virginia Public Access Project 1998).

Despite the technical success of the project, it did little to build public or legislative support for reforming Virginia's campaign finance laws.

Traditional Political Culture and Political Reform

In the 1960s, political scientist Daniel Elazar developed the theory of political culture as a way to explain the behavior of state political systems. Elazar argued that all states had individualistic, moralistic or traditionalistic political culture (Elazar, 1984). In individualistic states, private motivations or self-interest motivates individual and special interests to become involved in the political system. In moralistic states, substantial numbers of individuals and groups become involved in the political process because they believe that politics "is an effort to establish a good and just society" (Bowman and Kearney 1990, 7). Additionally, in traditionalistic political culture states "politics functions to maintain the existing order, and political participation is confined to elites" (Bowman and Kearney 1990, 7).

Not surprisingly, Elizar found that Virginia had a traditionalistic political culture. In other words, that a small political elite effectively controlled politics in the Old Dominion. From the Civil War through the 1960s the Democratic Party held a near monopoly on political power in Virginia. From the mid-twenties through the 1960s Harry F. Byrd, Sr., assumed effective control of the Virginia Democratic Party (Key 1984, 31). It took the national political turmoil of the 1960s, to begin to weaken the hold of the Byrd political machine over Virginia state politics. Liberal Virginia Democrats openly challenged conservative Democrats for control of the Virginia Democratic Party. Republicans looked to take advantage of this split to persuade conservative Democrats to join their ranks. Through the 1970s, Republican candidates succeeded in winning the governorship of Virginia but the Democratic Party remained in firm control of the General Assembly. The 1980s saw Democrats capture the majority of statewide offices but Republican candidates continued to make progress towards their goal of winning a majority of the Virginia General Assembly.

To the astonishment of Democratic political structure of the state, in 1997 Jim Gilmore won the governorship, John Hager won election as Lieutenant Governor and Mark Early won election as Attorney General. The same year saw the Republican Party obtain parity in the Virginia House of Delegates and in the Virginia Senate. Even more significant, the 1997 election saw the smallest number of Virginia voters cast their vote in 32 years.[11] Throughout the 1970s, 1980s, and 1990s, neither party attempted to make political reform a major part of their political agenda.

Political Reform and Partisan Politics

What explains the reluctance of both political parties to embrace political reform? The answer rests with the fact that both political parties are the products of the traditional political culture of Virginia. In contrast to other Southern states, populist politics has never played well in Virginia. This fact has made it difficult for either Republicans or Democrats to use political reform as a way to attract voters.

As discussed in previous chapters, the 1970s saw the breakup of the conservative Democratic Byrd machine. Out of the turmoil arose populist Henry Howell of Norfolk (Morris and Sabato 1984, 46–47). After the 1970 death of Lieutenant Governor J. Sargent Reynolds, in 1971 Howell beat a Democratic and Republican to win the vacant Lieutenant Governor position as an independent. Howell attempted to put together a coalition of liberals and rural Virginians angry with the political establishment. In 1973, Howell narrowly lost to Republican Miles Godwin in an election where the Democratic Party did not run a candidate for Governor (Morris and Sabato 1984, 46–47). Howell subsequently lost two more runs for Governor. His failure to put together a winning populist coalition sent a message to most Democrats and Republicans that success at the polls depended upon persuading the growing number of suburban voters in Northern Virginia, Richmond and Tidewater that they understood their concerns. Taxes, education and transportation became the issues to sway this key voting block, not placing restrictions on the size of campaign contributions.

Larry Sabato wrote in *Virginia Votes, 1975–1978* that "Virginia is socially and culturally conservative. This conservatism is intertwined with historical traditionalism; Virginia reveres her glorious past and looks to the past as much as to the future.

Change is regarded suspiciously in Virginia, and liberalism represents change" (Morris and Sabato 1984, 49). Sabato's description of Virginia is as accurate today as it was in 1979.

The Future of Political Reform in Virginia

A number of factors make it highly unlikely that political reform will become a major issue in Virginia politics during the foreseeable future.

First, the fact that Virginia has become a competitive two-party state provides both parties little incentive to change the ground rules for the conduct of elections. Both parties understand it will take more and more money to win seats in the General Assembly or to win statewide races. Permitting individuals and corporations to make large contributions greatly reduces the difficulty of meeting fund-raising targets.

Second, like the campaign finance reform issue, neither Republicans or Democrats have any reason to press for the tightening of public ethics rules. The tightening of public ethics rules satisfy the editorial page editors of the *Washington Post, Roanoke Times* and *Virginian-Pilot* but would make the lives of Virginia public officials much more difficult. Tighter financial conflict-of-interest rules might make it more difficult for individuals to serve in government while taking advantage of private business opportunities. This in turn might make it more difficult to recruit individuals to run for political office or accept high-level political appointments.

Third, the elite character of the Virginia electorate will make it extremely difficult for a populist candidate to gain a foothold as long as Virginia's economy remains strong and unemployment remains low. The 1996 presidential election saw 65.36% of the voting age population registered to vote. Only the states of Hawaii and Nevada had lower percentages of their voting age population registered to vote (FEC, 1998: 1–3). A significant minority of voting age Virginians continue to choose not to register to vote. In addition, a significant percentage of those who register to vote do not cast ballots.

Marching to the Beat of a Different Drummer

One can make a persuasive argument that special interest money plays much too great a role in Virginia politics and that Virginia should adopt much tighter public ethics rules and lobbying restrictions. On the other hand, one can also make a persuasive argument that the voters of Virginia have had numerous opportunity to express their dissatisfaction with the status quo and find few problem with the honor system used to maintain public trust in government. A major political corruption scandal could force Virginia to reconsider its approach towards public integrity management. Or, a popular populist political leader might be able to overcome opposition to comprehensive political reform. It remains much more likely that Virginia will continue to march to the beat of a different drummer and continue to rely upon the personal integrity of the state's public employees and officials to put the public interest ahead of their private interest.

Bibliography

Bowman, Ann O'M. and Kearney, Richard C. 1990. *State & Local Government.* Boston, Houghton Mifflin Company.

Bowman, James S., ed. 1996. *Public Integrity Annual.* Lexington, Kentucky: Council of State Governments.

Buckley v. Valeo. 1976. 424 U.S. 1.

Carroll, James D. and Robert Roberts. 1988–89. "If Men Were Angels: Assessing Ethics in the Ethics in Government Act of 1978." *Policy Studies Journal* 17: 435–447.

Center for Responsive Politics. 1998. *A Brief History of Money in Politics: Campaign Finance—and Campaign Finance Reform—in the United States.* URL: http://www.crp.org/pubs/history3.html April 12, 1998.

Center for Responsive Politics. 1998. *The States: Laboratories of Reform.* URL: http://www.crp.org/pubs/history/history4.html April 28, 1998.

Elazar, Daniel J. 1984. *American Federalism: A View from the States,* 3rd. New York: Harper & Row.

Federal Election Commission. 1998. Voter Registration and Turnout-1996, URL: http://www.fec.gov/pages/96to.htm June 1, 1998

Frederickson, George H. and David G. Frederickson. 1995. "Public Perceptions of Ethics in Government." *Annals* 537: 163–172.

Huddleston, Mark W. and Joseph C. Sands. 1995. "Enforcing Administrative Ethics."

Annals 537: 139–172.

Key, V.O. Jr. 1984. "Virginia: Political Museum Piece." In Thomas R. Morris and Larry Sabato, *Virginia Government and Politics: Readings and Comments.* Institute of Government: University of Virginia.

Morris, Thomas H. and Sabato, Larry. 1984. *Virginia Government and Politics: Readings and Commentary.* Charlottesville: University of Virginia and Virginia Chamber of Commerce.

New York State Ethics Commission. 1998. *Revolving Door Restrictions.* URL: http://www.dos.state.ny.us/ethc/rdr.html

Pew Research Center For The People & The Press. 1998. *Deconstructing Distrust: How Americans View Government.* Trust in Government Summary. March 10. URL: http://www.people-press.org/trustrpt.htm

Pew Research Center For The People & The Press. 1998. *Deconstructing Distrust: How Americans View Government. Methodology.* March 10. URL: http://www.people-press.org/trustque.htm

Pew Research Center For The People & The Press. 1998. *Deconstructing Distrust: How Americans View Government: Selected Tables.* March 10. URL: http://www.people-press.org/trusttab.htm

Roberts, Robert. 1988. *White House Ethics: The History of the Politics of Conflict of Interest Regulation.* Westport, CT: Greenwood Press.

Roberts, Robert. 1994. "Regulatory Bias and Conflict of Interest Regulation." In David H. Rosenbloom and Richard D. Schwartz, eds., *Handbook of Regulation and Administrative Law.* New York. Marcel Dekker, Inc: 485–498.

Virginia Conflict of Interest Act, Va. Code, & 2.1-639.1–639.24.

Virginia Public Access Project, URL: http://www.crp.org/vpap/index.html-ssi

Virginia State Board of Elections. URL: www.sbe.state.va.us/

Endnotes

1. "Scandal Waiting to Happen: Money and Politics, Ethics Reform Overdue.," *The Virginian Pilot,* 12 January 1997, sec. A.
2. John F. Harris, "Va Group Will Study Money's Political Role," *Washington Post* 29 May 1992, sec. C.
3. Margaret Edds, "Wilder Angers Legislators in Forming Ethics Panel: Lawmakers Irate They Weren't Told," *The Virginia Pilot,* 1992, sec. A.
4. John F. Harris, "Assembly Rejects Wilder Proposals, Governor Rebuffed on Amendments to Ethics, Environmental Legislation," *Washington Post,* 8 April 1993, sec. C.
5. Donald P. Baker, "Va Commission Proposes Campaign Contributions Limits in Ethics Package," *Washington Post,* 22 January 1994, sec. G.
6. Robert Little, "State Ethics Reform Will Be Hard Sell: Although Allen and the Media Point to Reasons for Change, Law Makers Say Everything's Fine," *The Virginian Pilot,* 12 January 1997.
7. Mollie Gore, "Corporate gifts total $123,700: Lawmakers say practice OK as long as gifts are reported," *Richmond Times Dispatch,* 14 June 1998, sec. A.
8. Donald P. Baker, "Acceptance of Trips Is an Old Va. Tradition," *Washington Post,* 2 December 1989, sec. D.
9. Jim Clardy, "Businesses Pack Pols' Perks with Travel, Tee-Offs, Treasures," *Washington Times,* 17 January 1992 sec. B.
10. Tyler Whitley, "Perks, Power Make Up For Pay: Lawmakers Disclose Gifts of $50 or More," *Gateway Virginia Richmond Times Dispatch,* 9 February 1998, URL: http://www.gateway-va.com/ga98/0209confhtm.
11. Spencer S. Hsu, "Governor's Race Produced Worst Turnout Since '65," *Washington Post,* 7 November 1997, sec. B.

CHAPTER FOURTEEN

The Environment as a Public Policy Issue: Assessing Virginia from a Regional Perspective

Glen Sussman

Old Dominion University

The purpose of this chapter is to provide a political overview of Virginia's environment taking into consideration the relationship between the federal and state governments and the role played by the states regarding environmental quality. We will narrow our focus to several aspects of Virginia and the environment—namely, how Virginia compares with other Southern states regarding selected environmental issues, how the public views environmental protection, environmental (administrative) management, and a brief assessment of the environmental health of the Chesapeake Bay.

In many instances, environmentalism demands trade-offs between the opposing values of preservation and development which results in political conflict. Public opinion polls inform us that despite the cynicism that many citizens have about politics, Americans tend to support governmental efforts to protect the environment rather than business (Bosso 1997, 56). Yet in Virginia, policy-makers have been reluctant to impose state authority over individual actions in order to address environmental problems.[1] Moreover, Virginia is a conservative state where economic interests have had a "decided advantage" in the policy-making process "to promote economic development" (Whelan 1990,177). This has frustrated many efforts to protect the environment.

Intergovernmental Relations, the States, and the Environment

Public policy is subject to several constraints, most notably the fragmentation of power prescribed by the constitutional system of separation of powers and checks and balances and the division of power between the federal government and the fifty states. Although the federal government plays a major role in terms of environmental protection, the jurisdiction for environmental politics is scattered among the executive branch (president and executive agencies), legislative branch (the Congress which is decentralized into numerous committees and subcommittees), and the judicial system. Environmental legislation, once passed by the Congress and signed into law by the president, places demands and responsibilities on the fifty states. For example, the 1970 Clean Air Act required states to develop State Implementation Plans describing how they would achieve federal guidelines by 1982 and thereafter (Rosenbaum 1995, 202–203). The Safe Drinking Water Act passed into law in 1974 mandated that the states would be responsible for enforcing standards that were set by the Congress (Kraft 1996, 91). Rosenbaum (1995, 88) describes the impact of regulatory federalism such that "almost all new federal regulatory programs since 1970 permit, or require, implementation by the states. Thirty-five states, for instance, currently administer water pollution permits under the Clean Water Act of 1972. State implementation of federal laws may vary greatly in scope and detail." Consequently, the devolution of political power from Washington to the states over the last two decades or so has resulted in both policy innovations and recalcitrance among the several states due to the unique social, political, and economic conditions prevalent in each respective state. Nonethe-

Figure 14.1 Dead fish, filth, and debris washed up against the shore, an increasingly common enviromental problem in Virginia.

less, as one political observer has noted, "Virtually all states have taken some steps to go beyond federally imposed requirements, and some have taken the lead in several areas" (John 1994, 80). The point is that while some states have struggled to meet federal environmental guidelines, other states have become models of innovation and efficiency in promoting environmental protection.

State governments play an important role in the environmental policy-making and regulatory process (Ringquist 1993). Yet, as more power and responsibility have passed to the fifty states, variation in the successful effort to achieve an improvement in the quality of their environment is evident. What accounts for differences in a state's commitment and ability to improve environmental quality?

James Lester (1995, 49–53) has described several arguments to help explain the differences in the management of the environment by the states. He informs us that states might vary in their commitment to environmental quality due to the "severity" of the problem within certain states; the amount of "fiscal resources" available to state governments to combat environmental pollution; "partisan" differences which find states with Democrats in control of the government more likely to support environmental initiatives; efforts within states to reform the "organizational capacity" of government in order to achieve environmental goals; and the type of legislature within each state where "professional" legislatures are more inclined to implement environmental legislation in contrast to part-time, amateur state assemblies.

Given the variety of political influences on state management practices, "uneven state performance" regarding environmental protection appears to be the rule rather than the exception (Rabe 1997, 40–41). How does Virginia compare to other states?

Virginia in Comparative Perspective

In order to better understand environmental politics and policy within Virginia, we first turn our attention to the state using a comparative perspective. In our assessment of Virginia, we employ a regional framework which places Virginia within the group of the original eleven states of the South for the purpose of comparison and analysis (Scher 1997). Along with Virginia, the states included in this assessment include Alabama, Arkansas, Florida, Georgia, Louisiana, Mississippi, North Carolina, South Carolina, Tennessee, and Texas. How does Virginia compare with these other ten states within a similar historical and regional context regarding environmental issues?

First, to what extent have the eleven states of the South improved air quality? One way to ascertain air quality within a state is to determine the proportion of the population living in "non-attainment areas" as determined by federal guidelines in the 1990 Clean Air Act. A non-attainment area is a geographic region where air pollution levels exceed the National Ambient Air Quality Standards (Virginia Department of Environmental Quality 1996, 2). The Environmental Protection Agency sets the standards by establishing criteria beyond which the public health is considered threatened due to excessive levels of several types of air pollutants. In six states (Alabama, Arkansas, Florida, Mississippi, North Carolina, South Carolina) an insignificant proportion of the population lives in non-attainment areas (The Council of State Governments 1996). The proportion of the population living in non-attainment areas in the remaining five states is as follows: Louisiana (8.8%), Georgia (9.2%), Virginia (15.1%), Tennessee (16.0%), and Texas (26.5%). Virginia is one among several of the eleven Southern states that needs to do a better job in this policy area. For example, three non-attainment areas have been identified in Virginia including the heavily populated areas of northern Virginia (near Washington, DC), Richmond, and Hampton Roads (consisting of several communities including Norfolk, Virginia Beach and Newport News) in southeastern Virginia. Moreover, the only state in the country to have its Title V Operating Permit Program denied by the Environmental Protection Agency is Virginia (Joint Legislative Audit and Review Commission 1997a, 36–39). A Title V permit is required under the 1990 Clean Air Act Amendments for any major stationary source of air pollution (e.g., industrial plants). Yet, during the Allen administration (1993–1997), Virginia vigorously opposed Environmental Protection Agency guidelines and federal intrusion into the state's affairs.

Second, water quality is a most important aspect of the life of a state and its numerous communities. The Clean Water Act requires that states determine the quality of their waterways. In order to ascertain these conditions, each state must monitor all navigable waters while taking into consideration the Total Daily Maximum Load— namely, "the total amount of pollution a body of water can accept while still remaining healthy" (National Wildlife Federation 1998, 5). Water quality is determined using the following measures: "fully supporting," "partially supporting," "threatened," and "not supporting" designated uses (i.e., fishing and swimming) of waterways. Do the eleven Southern states meet federal guidelines for "fully supporting" the designated uses of its rivers? The eleven states can be ranked from best to worst in terms of water quality which fully supports designated uses: Virginia (87%), Alabama (63%), South Carolina (60%), Louisiana (56%), Tennessee (54%), Florida (46%), Arkansas and Texas (44%), North Carolina (40%), Georgia (36%), and Mississippi (6%) (The Council of State Governments 1996). We can see that water quality varies considerably among the states of the South. Virginia ranks at the top of the eleven Southern states in terms of fully supporting designated uses of its rivers. However, several problems need to be addressed. According to the Chesapeake Bay Foundation (1996a, 6), Virginia is monitoring only sixty percent of its navigable waters and therefore its monitoring program is failing in meeting its compliance with the Clean Water Act. Moreover, based upon data collected from the fifty states, the National Wildlife Federation (1997, 16) has evaluated the states awarding grades of "good," "weak," "poor," or "failing" for each state's water monitoring process. In the South, two states received "weak" grades while "poor" grades were given to four states. Five states, including Virginia, received failing grades. The Virginia state assembly's Joint Legislative Audit and Review Commission (1997a, Ch. IV) has also questioned the monitoring and inspection process used by the Department of Environmental Quality.

Recently, three rivers in Virginia—the Pokomoke, the Mattaponi, and the Potomac—have been included among the twenty most polluted rivers in the United States by environmentalists.[2] Furthermore, the Elizabeth River in southeastern Virginia is a most severely stressed waterway. It is heavily utilized for both commercial and military traffic. As one observer comments, "The main branch of the Elizabeth river between Norfolk and Portsmouth has such high concentrations of mercury and other poisons that it ranks among the great heavy metal bodies of water in North America" (Kirby 1991, 485–486). According to a more recent report by the Chesapeake Bay Foundation (1996b, 21–23), Elizabeth River water poses a dangerous threat to fish. For example, fish suffer from fin and gill damage, cataracts, abnormal growth, and a decline in their immune system.

A third area of importance in investigating the quality of Virginia's environment is to assess the comparative amount of toxic releases by industry into the air, water, and ground. In Table 14.1 toxic releases by manufacturing and industry are presented for the eleven Southern states. How does Virginia rank in comparison to the other Southern states? During the six-year period from 1988–1994, all but one state (Mississippi) succeeded in reducing the discharge of toxic pollutants. It is evident that these states have made a commitment to improving environmental quality with respect to industrial discharges. Nonetheless, some states have improved more than others. Only three Southern states, including Virginia, have done a better job at reducing manufacturing pollutants compared to the average reduction in the other fifty states in the country (U.S. average equals 44.1%). The majority of the states in the South lagged behind the country as a whole. Louisiana has, by far, improved most among the eleven Southern states. However, significantly more toxic pollutants have been discharged over the years in this same state. Tennessee, Arkansas, Florida, and Alabama have improved the least in cutting industrial pollution. As far as Virginia is concerned, the state ranks second behind Louisiana in cutting industrial toxic waste discharges into the environment.

Figure 14.2 So far Virginia has managed to avoid warning signs like these along its shores.
Courtesy of PhotoDisc, Inc.

Table 14.1: Toxic Discharges by Industry, 1988–1994 (in thousands of pounds)

State	1988	1994	Percent Change
Alabama	110,190	88,256	–19.9
Arkansas	40,676	35,042	–13.9
Florida	96,972	82,452	–15.0
Georgia	81,661	45,248	–44.6
Louisiana	435,022	120,017	–72.4
Mississippi	94,357	112,958	+19.7
North Carolina	125,148	79,652	–36.4
South Carolina	61,847	44,786	–27.6
Tennessee	159,647	146,698	–8.0
Texas	310,985	213,061	–31.5
Virginia	115,320	46,243	–59.9

Source: Adapted from U.S.Bureau of the Census, 1997. *Statistical Abstract of the United States: 1997*. Washington, DC: United States Government Printing Office, p. 238. Author's computation.

Fourth, numerous states are being confronted with an increasing number of hazardous waste sites and the inherent threat posed to the environment and public health. Industrial society has provided the means to achieve an improved standard of living; yet at the same time, the quality of life becomes questionable as toxic chemicals and other pollutants have accumulated over the years which have created new challenges for state governments. In 1980, the U.S. Congress passed and President Carter signed into law the Superfund Act which was intended to address the waste site problem. One way to measure the severity of this problem is to examine the number of state sites on the Superfund National Priorities List (NPL). The Superfund cleanup process, based on the "polluter pays" principle, has two primary functions (Hird 1994, 14–22). First, a determination must be made regarding "who pays" for the cleanup. This can include the federal government, state government, or polluter (if identified). Second, waste sites must be identified, classified, and judged in terms of their priority—namely, the severity of the threat posed to the environment and public health. The most severe sites are listed on the NPL. Only after the waste site has been listed on the NPL can the process of cleanup be initiated.

Recent data concerning hazardous waste sites are presented in Table 14.2. Here we can assess: 1) how each state ranks nationally, 2) the change over several years, and 3) how Virginia ranks with respect to its Southern neighbors. First, the states of the Southern region vary in terms of the number of waste sites they have on the NPL. Although five other states in the country, most notably New Jersey, rank above it, Florida has significantly more NPL waste sites than any other Southern state which places it sixth in the country and first in the South. Considerable variation occurs in the Southern states' national ranking from a "high" of 6 for Florida to a "low" of 46 for Mississippi. Second, during the mid-1990s—1994–1996—only Arkansas and Louisiana changed considerably in their overall rankings. In this case, Arkansas moved four steps down in ranking (making progress) while Louisisana moved eight steps up in ranking with more waste sites added to the list. Finally, Virginia ranks about the same both nationally and regionally. Nationally and in the Southern region, it falls within the top third of states in its ranking of NPL sites. This relatively high ranking requires more attention by federal and Virginia state authorities regarding cleanup efforts given the number of NPL waste sites in the state. The result can be harmonious or contentious relations among the federal, state, and local authorities as they go about the process of finding the source of pollution (the polluter), providing adequate funding, and the actual cleanup process.

Table 14.2: Hazardous Waste Sites on the Superfund National Priority List by Rank, 1994–1996

State	Rank in 1994 US	Rank in 1994 South	Rank in 1996 US	Rank in 1996 South
Alabama	31	9	30	8
Arkansas	27	9	31	9
Florida	6	1	6	1
Georgia	26	7	26	7
Louisiana	27	8	19	6
Mississippi	47	10	46	10
North Carolina	18	5	17	5
South Carolina	15	3	15	3
Tennessee	25	6	26	7
Texas	13	2	14	2
Virginia	17	4	16	4

Source: Adapted from U.S. Bureau of the Census. 1997. *Statistical Abstract of the United States: 1997.* Washington, DC: United States Government Printing Office, p. 238; Kathleen O'Leary Morgan, Scott Morgan, Neil Quitro, eds. 1994. *State Rankings 1994:A Statistical View of the 50 United States,* 5th ed., Lawrence, KS: Morgan Quitro Corporation, p. 197, using data from the U.S. Environmental Protection Agency, Hazardous Site Evaluation Division. Author's ranking of the Southern states.

Fifth, wetlands play an important role in the web of life and maintenance of environmental quality. Wetlands act as a buffer between land and waterways and filter pollutants which might otherwise flow into rivers and streams. Several additional salutary benefits of wetlands are "flood control, groundwater recharge, water quality maintenance, erosion control" among others (Council on the Environment 1987, 25). They also provide habitat for a variety of life ensuring the survival of bio-diversity. As Table 14.3 indicates, nationally, the states of the South vary according to the amount of wetlands lost during the two century period, 1780s–1980s. Nine of the 11 Southern states rank in the top third of states losing wetlands. Only South Carolina and Georgia rank near the bottom in wetlands lost. Although Virginia ranks approximately in the middle of the fifty states in the loss of wetlands, it fares better when compared to its Southern neighbors. While Virginia can do a better job in maintaining the integrity of its remaining wetlands as reflected in its national ranking, it can argue that it has been more successful when compared with other Southern states. However, in early 1998, environmentalists who had applauded President Clinton's tightening of wetlands protection, vocalized their concern that thousands of acres of sensitive Virginia wetlands would be threatened by new coastal development as a result of revised Army Corps of Engineer guidelines.[3]

Table 14.3: Total Wetlands Lost, 1780s–1980s

State	Rank		Percent
	US	South	Lost
Alabama	20	4	50
Arkansas	10	1	72
Florida	26	6	46
Georgia	46	9	23
Louisiana	26	6	46
Mississippi	13	2	59
North Carolina	23	5	49
South Carolina	43	8	27
Tennessee	13	2	59
Texas	18	3	52
Virginia	29	7	42

Source: Adapted from T.E. Dahl. 1990. "Wetland Losses in the U.S., 1780s to 1980s." Washington, D.C.: U.S. Department of the Interior, Fish and Wildlife Service. Author's ranking of the Southern States.

Although we have focused on only selected aspects of the environment, a comprehensive study conducted by Hall and Kerr (1991) provides additional comparative data on a range of important environmental indicators with which to make a judgement about Virginia's overall progress and commitment to environmental protection. Hall and Kerr provide two general rankings for the fifty states—one is a Green Policies ranking based upon 77 variables; the second is a Green Index ranking drawing upon 256 variables. The Green Policies ranking is oriented toward innovative state policies while the Green Index addresses a state's overall commitment to environmental quality. Table 14.4 shows Virginia's ranking on both indexes, nationally and regionally. On a national level, Virginia ranked higher in promoting innovative state policies than it did in its overall commitment to environmental protection. In this regard, as Virginia entered the new decade of the 1990s, it ranked near the middle of the fifty states in policy innovation but close to the bottom third of states in its commitment to protecting the environment. However, on a regional basis, only Florida and North Carolina rank higher than Virginia on these two indexes. In comparison to the other Southern states, Virginia ranked third on both "green" indexes demonstrating that it had an overall better environmental record at the regional level than at the national level.

Table 14.4: Environmental Management in the South

State	Green Policies Rank National	Green Policies Rank South	Green Index Rank National	Green Index Rank South
Alabama	49	10	50	11
Arkansas	50	11	48	9
Florida	13	1	18	1
Georgia	29	4	39	5
Louisiana	34	6	49	10
Mississippi	46	9	47	8
North Carolina	18	2	23	2
South Carolina	32	5	36	4
Tennessee	40	8	45	6
Texas	35	7	46	7
Virginia	22	3	32	3

Source: Adapted from Bob Hall and Mary Lee Kerr. 1991. 1991–1992 *Green Index: A State-By-State Guide to the Nation's Environmental Health.* Washington, DC: Island Press, p. 5. Author's ranking of the Southern states.

States have many fiscal responsibilities including the environment, education, health care among others. States vary in terms of the amount of funding expended in different policy areas. The expenditure of tax dollars for the variety of state functions and responsibilities can provide an indicator of the state's orientation toward specific policy issues. Although the federal government spends more on environmental protection than the states, environmental protection budgets in many states have increased along with many new initiatives (John 1994, Ch. 3). At the same time, the federal share for environmental programs provided to the states has decreased as a result of the New Federalism dating back to the 1980s (Fiorino 1995, 88). Given the demands on state finances, what proportion of its state budget does Virginia allocate for environmental protection and natural resources programs? Table 14.5 presents state expenditures for these programs in the eleven Southern states. As the table shows, while some states have increased the amount of funds expended on the environment, other states have actually decreased the amount of funding during the period 1988–1996. In 1988, only two Southern states—Louisiana and Florida—spent more tax dollars on the environment than Virginia. However, by 1996 not only had Virginia's expenditures in this policy area decreased by about 50% but the state ranked last among its Southern neighbors in its funding commitment to the environment. This trend is in stark contrast to Virginia's regional position regarding the green indexes noted above. Virginia spends less than one percent of its state budget on what many Virginians consider to be one of the most important public policy issues.

Table 14.5: Direct Expenditures on Environmental and Natural Resources Programs, 1988–1996 (percent of total state budget)

State	1988	1996	Percent Change
Alabama	1.0	1.4	+.4
Arkansas	1.2	1.9	+.7
Florida	2.5	3.4	+.9
Georgia	1.1	1.8	+.7
Louisiana	2.6	2.3	−.3
Mississippi	1.4	2.0	+.6
North Carolina	1.0	1.9	+.9
South Carolina	1.2	1.4	+.2
Tennessee	1.3	1.2	−.1
Texas	0.6	1.4	+.8
Virginia	1.5	0.8	−.7

Source: Adapted from U.S. Bureau of the Census. Internet address: http://www.census.gov/datamap/www/index.html. Retrieved: March 1998; "Resource Guide to State Environmental Management." 1991. Lexington, KY: Council of State Governments. Author's computation.

Public Opinion and the Environment

For over thirty years, public opinion polls have indicated that citizens in the United States have been concerned about the condition of the environment. While air and water pollution were the primary areas of concern for both policy-makers and citizens, in the early 1960s, Rachel Carson's (1962) book *Silent Spring* called attention to the environmental and public health problems associated with the widespread use of chemical pesticides. Moreover, the first Earth Day in April 1970 demonstrated quite clearly that the environment was a major area of public interest. One intriguing aspect of public opinion polls about the environment is the relative consistency among the public in its support for environmental protection. Anthony Downs (1972) presented an "issue attention" model that indicated that public policy problems emerge, evolve, mature, and decline in a five-stage process. However, Downs found that the dynamics regarding public concern about the environment did not parallel other policy problems. In fact, "environmentalism" did not decline in salience, but rather, remained an important issue for the American public.

Dunlap (1995) conducted a study of public opinion about the environment that provides data to assess the extent to which a trend could be determined about specific environmental issues. During the period beginning in the 1960s through the early 1990s, he examined public attitudes toward the environment regarding air and water pollution, whether environmental laws and regulations went too far or not far enough, spending on the environment, and choosing between opposing environmental and economic goals. Overall, the data indicated that during the last three decades, despite some variation in citizen's attitudes, the public has supported efforts to improve air and water quality, opposed efforts to decrease governmental regulations which protect the environment, believed that spending on the environment is too little rather than too much, and favored environmental protection over economic development. A recent Gallup Poll supports Dunlap's results on this last survey item. When asked to choose between environmental protection and economic growth, over six out of ten Americans chose environmental protection (Gallup, Jr. 1996).

Given the generally pro-environment portrait of the American public, how do Virginians view their state government's role in protecting the environment and what are their views about the environment? Fifteen years ago, a state-wide survey of Virginia citizens sponsored by the Governor's Commission on Virginia's Future (1984:94) found that clean air and water were a high priority for over 80% of Virginians. In 1996, the Virginia Environmental Endowment sponsored a survey of Virginia citizens which was conducted by Democratic pollster Peter Hart and Republican pollster Glen Bolger.[4] Although the environment ranked fourth among key issues behind education, crime, and economy and jobs, more Virginians rather than less believed that not enough was being done to protect the state's air, water, wilderness, and the Chesapeake Bay. Furthermore, more citizens rather than less felt that environmental protection was more important than economic development despite the pro-development orientation of the state generally and popular Governor George Allen in particular. Moreover, despite survey findings which showed that a majority of Virginians believed that penalties for polluters were appropriate, pollution fines actually declined during the administration of Republican governor George Allen (Joint Legislative Audit and Review Commission 1997a, Ch. V). A plurality of Virginians gave the state a grade of "C" in environmental protection and a majority indicated that the nation as a whole was not doing enough to protect the environment.

Environmental Management in Virginia

As the top elected official and chief executive of the state, the governor sets the agenda for state politics. During the last decade or so, a Democrat (L. Douglas Wilder) and a Republican (George Allen) occupied the governor's mansion. Clearly, both governors did not have the environment near the top of their public agenda. In 1989, Wilder became the first African-American to governor in the nation. Despite the enthusiasm his election generated—among citizens expressing concern about the environment, he won 58% of their vote (Sabato 1990, 128)—Wilder had important priorities other than the environment. While gun control and social issues were a fundamental part of his agenda, Wilder was faced with the unpopular task of balancing a state budget which resulted in large cuts in several sensitive areas, including higher education. Moreover, Wilder was contemplating a run for the presidency in 1992 which detracted from his involvement in state politics. Beginning in 1994, the Allen administration made it clear from the outset that Virginia was "open for business" in an effort to bolster economic development in the state. Although he argued that he favored environmental protection and cited positive actions taken by his administration (Governor's Commission on Environmental Stewardship 1996), he quickly antagonized environmental groups in the state which viewed his administration as decidedly "anti-environment."[5] Allen's successor, former Republican Attorney General James Gilmore, has already taken several steps which suggest that he will be a more environmentally-friendly governor than his predecessor.[6]

Although the governor sets the tone for environmental policy in the state, one way to gain a better understanding of the efforts to improve the quality of the environment is through an examination of the role of the state's administrative agencies. State agencies are responsible for implementing and enforcing laws, regulations, and programs to ensure environmental quality. However, state agency performance can be affected by several factors including gubernatorial appointments to head agencies, funding, organizational capacity, staff morale among others. The new position of Secretary of Natural Resources established in the mid-1980s ensured for the first time that the environment would be represented by a member of the governor's cabinet (Council on the Environment 1987, 1). Although the position of Secretary of Natural Resources was established by the Virginia Assembly in 1986, it was not until the early 1990s that legislators decided to consolidate the administration of environmental policy into a single agency. This was a significant change for the regulatory process in Virginia. Despite the early creation of the State Water Control Board in 1946, the State Air Pollution Control Board established in 1966 and the Virginia Waste Management Board which began functioning in 1986, the regulatory process lacked effective leadership and coordination. For instance, one critic of water policy characterized the process in the following way: "The policy-making authority delegated to agencies has generally been under utilized and only marginally successful when exercised. This is in part because each agency in government is established with limited responsibility, with no one state agency having complete responsibility for the management of the state's waters (Walker 1987, 88). In 1992, the Virginia Assembly merged several existing agencies into a new Department of Environmental Quality (DEQ) which began operation in April 1993. The DEQ became Virginia's primary agency for implementing and enforcing the state's Constitutional commitment to protect the environment which was outlined in Article XI to "protect its atmosphere, land, and waters from pollution, impairment, or destruction (Joint Legislative Audit and Review Commission 1997a, 1).

States vary in the level of their regulatory commitment to ensuring the quality of the environment. In Virginia, federal law rather than state action has been the primary motivation for most of the state's regulatory programs (Virginia Department of Environmental Quality 1996, vi). In three primary areas of its regulatory responsibilities—air, water, waste—the state administers programs passed at the federal level (Virginia Department of Environmental Quality 1996, 1–36). While the Air Division is responsible for carrying out the requirements of the Clean Air Act of 1970, the Water Division is responsible for programs established by the Water Pollution Control Act of 1972 (the Clean Water Act) and the Water Quality Act of 1987. At the same time, the Waste Division works within the guidelines set forth by the Resource Conservation and Recovery Act of 1976 and the Comprehensive Environmental Response Compensation and Liability Act (Superfund) of 1980. For example, one of the responsibilities of the Air Division is to determine and monitor "nonattainment areas" for air pollutants in geographic areas (discussed earlier). Moreover, given the increasing realization of the importance of wetlands, the Marine Resources Commission regulates activities in coastal and tidal areas subject to guidelines set forth in the Clean Water Act, Endangered Species Act of 1973, and the National Wild and Scenic Rivers Act of 1968 (Virginia Department of Environmental Quality 1996, 37–39). This is not to say that Virginia state officials have avoided taking action. To the contrary, numerous environmental bills have been passed into law by the General Assembly including the Virginia Air Pollution Control Act, Chesapeake Bay Preservation Act, Virginia Wetlands Act among others. The point is that the federal government has been an active player in encouraging state environmental action.

The DEQ has an important responsibility in protecting the environment. Yet according to the DEQ mission statement, "Under the direction of the Secretary of Natural Resources, DEQ strives to provide efficient, cost-effective services in the Commonwealth of Virginia that promote a proper balance between environmental improvement and economic vitality" (Joint Legislative Audit and Review Commission 1997a, 5). Herein lies the potential for political and partisan conflict—namely, what is the "proper" balance between protecting the environment and economic development?

In 1995, the Virginia General Assembly directed the Joint Legislative Audit and Review Commission (JLARC) to evaluate the performance of the Department of Environmental Quality. Two years later, the JLARC submitted its report to the General Assembly which reviewed whether the DEQ had fulfilled its responsibilities in performing its regulatory function to help improve the quality of Virginia's environment. Overall, despite improvements in some areas, the JLARC report indicated that the DEQ was not meeting its goals.

Figure 14.4 Natural tidal marsh meanders. Courtesy of Dr. Carleton Ray/Photo Researchers, Inc.

According to the JLARC report, the DEQ did a better job in improving the state's air quality but exhibited weaknesses in the area of water quality (Joint Legislative Audit and Review Commission 1997a, Ch. VII). The JLARC expressed concern about the conspicuous decline over the years in the DEQ's assessment of penalties for polluting the state's waters and the decline in water inspections. Also, the JLARC cited the over-all decline in DEQ staff morale resulting from poor leadership and lack of trust. More-over, despite what the JLARC saw as an improvement in air quality, it was still concerned about the decline in the number of air inspections carried out by the DEQ and a fail-ure to establish a long-term plan to ensure the continued improvement in air quali-ty. Consequently, the DEQ faces tough challenges in the future in order to make improvements in the areas of leadership, planning, inspections, and monitoring in order to fulfill its obligation to protect Virginia's environment.

The Chesapeake Bay: Problems and Prospects

The environmental health of the Chesapeake Bay, North America's largest estuary, has been a public policy issue for many years. The health of the Bay is at risk due to various sources of pollution, due in part, to an increasing population which threaten the quality of the water, forests and the oyster population which act as a natural fil-tration process, stocks of a variety of fish, wetlands, Bay grasses among others. Al-though some indicators suggest that there have been improvements in a few areas, the Bay is "terribly subject to environmental stresses" and recovery of this most im-portant ecosystem requires a timely and concerted political effort (Horton and Eich-baum 1991, xxiii).

Over a decade ago, the Virginia Council on the Environment lamented that "our uses of the Bay's resources have become more intense and the resulting pollution and stress on the Bay have drastically affected the beauty and productivity of this incred-ible ecosystem" (Council on the Environment 1987, 35). A major problem threaten-ing the Bay is an excessive buildup of nutrients which are a natural part of the land and water environment and provide the raw materials for organic life. When nitro-gen and phosphorus, in particular, increase too much they have a negative impact on the ecology of the Bay due to an overabundance of algae and a decrease in oxygen (Marshall and de Voursney 1985, 61–62). An important agreement was reached in 1983 to begin the process of reducing the amount of nitrogen and phorphorus in the Bay. In that year, Virginia along with Maryland, Pennsylvania, the District of Columbia, the Environmental Protection Agency, and the Chesapeake Bay Commission established a framework for a cooperative effort to improve the quality of the Bay (Joint Legisla-tive Audit Review Commission 1997a, 3). Subsequent agreements in 1987 and again in 1992 committed the signatories to the agreement to reduce nutrient levels by 40% by the year 2000 and thereafter. A variety of different actions need to be taken by Vir-ginia state officials in order to make progress toward achieving the 40% goal. Unfor-tunately, not only is it unlikely that Virginia will fulfill its Year 2000 commitment, it is also unlikely that it would be able to make progress thereafter (Joint Legislative Audit and Review Commission 1997b). Given the reluctance of Virginia policy-makers to act in an expeditious manner, the health of the Chesapeake Bay remains at risk.

However, there is a larger and perhaps more important issue. If the Chesapeake Bay can recover, then a potential model for other threatened natural environments both national and international will have been established (Horton and Eichbaum 1991, xxiv). This is a most important challenge for Virginia state officials.

Conclusion

This political overview of environmental politics and policy in Virginia has focused on the intergovernmental framework within which Virginia functions, assessing environmental affairs in Virginia compared to its Southern neighbors, and describing how Virginia state officials make and enforce environmental policy. Generally, Virginia appears to do a better job regionally—compared to its Southern neighbors—than it does on a national scale. However, despite successful efforts in some areas, much work remains to be done in the state if it wants to demonstrate its commitment to protection of the environment.

Virginia is, overall, a relatively wealthy state with a long history. It has a generally conservative political orientation, a "mixed" legislature (falling between professional and part-time), a traditionalistic political culture, and a pro-development ethos which suggests that the state would be less likely to promote environmental protection. Yet it also has had a long period of Democratic control of the government which makes it more likely that environmentalism would be important in state policy-making. Perhaps it is best to describe Virginia's orientation toward the environment as one in which the dynamics of state politics are characterized internally by traditional pro-development influences and periodic partisan promotion of pro-environmental initiatives and externally by the carrots and sticks from the federal government.

Bibliography

Bosso, Christopher J. 1997. "Seizing Back the Day: The Challenge to Environmental Activism in the 1990s," pp. 53–74. In Norman J. Vig and Michael E. Kraft, eds. *Environmental Policy in the 1990s: Reform or Reaction?* 3rd ed. Washington, DC: CQ Press.

Carson, Rachel. 1962. *Silent Spring.* Boston: Houghton Mifflin.

Chesapeake Bay Foundation. 1996a. *Virginia's Waters: Still At Risk.* Annapolis, MD: Chesapeake Bay Foundation.

Chesapeake Bay Foundation. 1996b. *Toxic Waters: Failures in the Regulatory System.* Annapolis, MD: Chesapeake Bay Foundation.

Council on the Environment. Commonwealth of Virginia. 1987. *Virginia's Environment: 1984–86 Report.* Richmond, VA: Council on the Environment.

Downs, Anthony. 1972. "Up and Down with Ecology—The 'Issue-Attention Cycle.'" *The Public Interest* 28:38–50.

Dunlap, Riley E. 1995. "Public Opinion and Environmental Policy," pp. 63–114. In James P. Lester, ed. *Environmental Politics and Policy: Theory and Evidence,* 2nd ed. Durham, NC: Duke University Press.

Fiorino, Daniel J. 1995. *Making Environmental Policy.* Berkeley, CA: University of California Press.

Gallup, George Jr. 1996. *The Gallup Poll: Public Opinion 1995.* Wilmington, DE: Scholarly Resources Inc.

Governor's Commission on Environmental Stewardship. 1996. *Report to the Honorable George Allen, Governor of Virginia, December 18, 1996.* Richmond, VA: Office of the Attorney General.

Governor's Commission on Virginia's Future. 1984. *Toward A New Dominion: Choices For Virginians.* Charlottesville, VA: The Institute of Government.

Hall, Bob and Mary Lee Kerr. 1991. *1991–1992 Green Index: A State-By-State Guide to the Nation's Health.* Washington, DC: Island Press.

Hird, John A. 1994. *Superfund: The Political Economy of Environmental Risk.* Baltimore: The Johns Hopkins University Press.

Horton, Tom and William M. Eichbaum. 1991. *Turning the Tide: Saving the Chesapeake Bay.* Washington, DC: Island Press.

John, DeWitt. 1994. *Civic Environmentalism: Alternatives to Regulation in States and Communities.* Washington, DC: CQ Press.

Joint Legislative Audit and Review Commission. 1997a. *Review of the Department of Environmental Quality House Document No. 67.* Richmond, VA: Commonwealth of Virginia.

Joint Legislative Audit and Review Commission. 1997b. *Virginia's Progress Toward Chesapeake Bay Nutrient Reduction Goals.* House Document No. 73. Richmond, VA: Commonwealth of Virginia.

Kirby, Jack Temple. 1991. "Virginia's Environmental History." *The Virginia Magazine of History and Biography* 99:449–488.

Kraft, Michael E. 1996. *Environmental Policy and Politics.* New York: HarperCollins College Publishers.

Lester, James P. 1995. "Federalism and State Environmental Policy," pp. 15–60. In James P. Lester, ed. *Environmental Politics and Policy: Theories and Evidence,* 2nd ed. Durham, NC: Duke Univesity Press.

Marshall, J. Paxton and Robert M. De Voursney, eds. 1985. *The Virginia Assembly on the Future of the Virginia Environment.* Charlottesville, VA: The Institute of Government.

National Wildlife Federation. 1998. "What's a TMDL?" *EnviroAction* 16:5.

National Wildlife Federation. 1997. "Rx for Cleaner Waters." *EnviroAction* 15:16.

Rabe, Barry G. 1997. "Power to the States: The Promise and Pitfalls of Decentralization," pp. 31–52. In Norman J. Vig and Michael E. Kraft, eds. *Environmental Policy in the 1990s: Reform or Reaction?* Washington, DC: CQ Press.

Ringquist, Evan J. 1993. *Environmental Protection at the State Level: Politics and Progress in Controlling Pollution.* Armonk, NY: M.E. Sharpe.

Rosenbaum, Walter A. 1995. *Environmental Politics and Policy,* 3rd ed. Washington, DC: CQ Press.

Sabato, Larry J. 1990. "Virginia's National Election for Governor," pp. 116–138. In Thomas R. Morris and Larry J. Sabato, eds. *Virginia Government and Politics: Readings and Comments,* 3rd revised ed. Charlottesville, VA: University of Virginia and Virginia Chamber of Commerce

Scher, Richard. 1997. *Politics in the South,* 2nd ed. Armonk, NY: M.E. Sharpe.

The Council of State Governments. 1996. *Resource Guide to State Environmental Management,* 4th ed. Lexington, KY: The Council of State Governments.

Virginia Department of Environmental Quality. 1996. *Business and Industry Guide to Environmental Permits in Virginia.* Richmond, VA: Virginia Department of Environmental Quality.

Walker, William R. 1987. "Water Supply in the Year 2000," pp. 85–106. In Joseph L. Fisher and Richard T. Meyer, eds. *Virginia Alternatives for the 1990s: Selected Issues in Public Policy.* Fairfax, VA: George Mason University Press.

Whelan, John T. 1990. "The Interest Group and Lobbying Community in Virginia," pp. 164–180. In Thomas R. Morris and Larry J. Sabato, eds. *Virginia Government and Politics: Reading and Comments,* 3rd revised ed. Charlottesville, VA: University of Virginia and Virginia Chamber of Commerce.

Endnotes

1. Scott Harper, "Farming and Fish Kills," *Virginian-Pilot,* 19 July 1998, sec. A.

2. Scott Harper, "National Environmental Group Puts 3 Virginia Rivers on Endangered List," *Virginian-Pilot,* 7 April 1998, sec. A.

3. Scott Harper, "Wetlands Plan Opens Sensitive Land, Critics Say," *Virginian-Pilot,* 2 February 1998, sec. A.

4. Scott Harper, "Protecting Resources Ranks as Big Concern in Statewide Survey," *Virginian-Pilot,* 1 May 1997, sec. B.

5. Michael Hardy, "Allen Cites Progress Toward Clean Air, Water in Virginia," *Richmond Times-Dispatch,* 31 July 1996, sec. B.

6. "He's No Allen: Gilmore Backs Environmental Policies," *Virginian-Pilot,* 28 February 1998, sec. B.

CHAPTER FIFTEEN

Virginia's Foreign Economic Policy: In Search of Business Opportunities

Tom Lansford and Wayne Lesperance
Old Dominion University

Under the Articles of Confederation, Congress lacked the authority to regulate commerce, making it unable to protect or standardize trade between foreign nations and the various states. In 1784, Congress requested that the states grant it limited power over commerce for a period of fifteen years, but many of the states did not comply. In 1785, a recommendation was made to amend the Articles of Confederation so that Congress would have power over commerce. Although Congress sent the proposed amendment to the state legislatures, along with a letter urging immediate action, few states responded. James Monroe later concluded that the issue was so crucial, and potentially granted so much power to Congress, that the states were afraid to act.

The Constitutional Convention of 1787 was called to revise the ailing Articles of Confederation. However, the Convention soon abandoned the Articles, drafting a new Constitution with a much stronger national government. Nine states had to approve the Constitution before it could go into effect. After a long and often bitter debate, eleven states ratified the Constitution, which instituted a new form of government for the United States. Prominent among the expressed powers of the new federal legislature was its exclusive power, to regulate commerce with foreign nations, found in Article 1, Section 8 of the Constitution. Furthermore, the ability of states to engage in foreign policy was likewise limited in Article 1, Section 10, which reads, "No state shall enter into any treaty, alliance, or confederation. . . ."

Such an evolution of state's rights in the earliest years of the republic would seem to preclude discussion of contemporary foreign and economic policies. Nevertheless, in recent years there has been a new trend among states to pursue commercial interests with foreign governments to exploit new markets in an increasingly interdependent and shrinking world. Such efforts, brought on by reduced federal assistance, the burden placed on state government by un-funded mandates, increased international competition, and the desire for new economic opportunities, has led governors to look abroad, engage in trade missions, and conduct foreign policies on behalf of their states.

The federal government has not resisted these efforts. In fact, there exists a certain degree of complicity by Washington to allow the states latitude when it comes to trade and commercial practices. Across the country, the trend is clear. States are establishing trade missions abroad. Governors are globetrotting to promote trade, tourism and investment. All 50 states have bureaucracies which specifically cultivate foreign economic enterprises and/or tourism. In 1997, for example, nearly 48 million international tourists visited the United States, contributing $94 billion to federal, state, and local coffers.

History

The foreign and economic policy of Virginia has traditionally emphasized the development of external markets for the state's exports. However, one significant non-economic issue emerged following the Civil War. Like other states of the Confederacy, Virginia attempted to develop trade relations with other nations during the conflict and worked unsuccessfully to gain diplomatic recognition of the South by foreign powers. However, the most distinguishing features of Virginia's relations with other nations in the nineteenth-century emerged after the Civil War. The Fourteenth Amendment to the U.S. Constitution discharged all of the debts that the Confederate states had accrued during the war between the states. Nonetheless, conservatives in Virginia were determined to pay off these debts as a point of honor. Before the war the state debt amounted to $37 million, by 1871 it had grown to $47 million, most of which was owed to Europeans and Northerners. Although the state government ultimately repudiated part of the debt, the economic burden of the repayment effort significantly hampered the development of public infrastructure until the 1930's. After the world wars, Virginia began an effort to expand its export trade beyond the traditional agricultural products and coal that had marked the bulk of the state's external trade.

The Old Dominion's position on the eastern seaboard has led the state to engage in external trade with Europe throughout its history. The state is the fourth largest on the Atlantic coast and it possesses the world's largest deep-water harbor in Hampton Roads. Virginia is the twelfth most populous state with some 6.6 million residents. More than 70 percent of its population live in metropolitan areas with the largest population centered in the greater Tidewater area. Since 1980, the state population has increased by some 15 percent as the economy has outperformed that of much of the rest of the nation, and the large concentration of military facilities in Virginia has provided a recession-resistant economic base.

Virginia's most important exports have traditionally been agricultural. Between 1940 and 1950, the number of people employed in agriculture was surpassed by those employed in non-agricultural jobs, such as manufacturing and retail businesses. Since the 1940s, the total number of Virginia farms has declined by approximately one-half. By the late 1960s, chemical manufacturing, food and tobacco products, and textile production had become the fastest growing industries in the state. Technology and communications have recently become the state's growth industry with some 2,450 high-tech firms now located in the state. Official state estimates predict that by 2002, 63 percent of Virginia's gross state product will be tied to these companies. Manufacturing has also gained an increased importance in the state. Industrial machinery now accounts for 10 percent of the state's exports, and is Virginia's second leading export commodity. In addition, transport equipment accounts for 8 percent of the state's export while chemicals make up 7 percent.

In spite of this trend, agriculture and mineral products remain among the most significant Virginia exports. Half of Virginia's farm income is concentrated in poultry and livestock. Crops such as corn, peanuts, and potatoes make-up the next largest source of income. However, these products are mainly grown for domestic consumption. With the exception of tobacco, agricultural products only accounted for 7 percent of the state's exports in 1996. Tobacco is Virginia's main export crop. It regularly accounts for at least a third of Virginia's total exports. In 1996, tobacco exports provided the state with some $3.6 billion. Similarly, while Virginia produces a variety of mineral products, including sand, gravel, limestone, and zinc, coal is the state's main mineral export to foreign markets. In 1996, coal exports amounted to $673.6 million. Taken together, tobacco and coal have traditionally been Virginia's top export commodities. They account for approximately 40 percent of the state's exports.

Virginia and the World Economy

The state economy has increasingly been tied to exports. Virginia ranks as the nation's sixteenth largest exporter in 1996. In the Southeast region, Virginia ranked third, behind Florida and North Carolina as an exporter. The state is also the region's top exporter to Western Europe. A 1996 survey ranked the Richmond-Petersburg area as the nation's eighteenth largest exporter among 265 other metropolitan areas. Exports now account for approximately 10 percent of Virginia's gross state product. In addition, since 1993, exports have grown by some 27 percent, and economists predict that they will continue to grow at a rate of some 5 percent per year.

Virginia's foreign economic policy has concentrated on two broad goals: the promotion of exports; and the attraction of foreign direct investments (FDI). In 1996, exports provided the state economy with some $10.9 billion. In addition, industrial machinery and other manufactured products have gained an increased amount of importance in the state's exports. For all of the state's history, Western Europe has been Virginia's main international trading partner. The state economy has greatly diversified over the years, and Virginia now exports products to more than 190 nations. Nonetheless, Europe remains the key to the state's foreign trade. Europe is both Virginia's largest export market and the leading source of direct investment in the state. In 1996, Europe accounted for nearly 34 percent of Virginia's exports, or $3.6 billion. In an effort to expand existing trade relations with the nations of Western Europe and open markets in Eastern Europe, Governor George Allen opened the Virginia

Department of Economic Development's (VDED) Trade and Investment office in Frankfurt, Germany in 1995.

Of particular concern to state politicians is the effort to expand direct exports. For instance, Belgium is the leading destination for Virginia exports to Europe, but most of the products shipped to that nation are not consumed there. Instead they are stored or immediately shipped to other markets. Tobacco accounted for some $1.13 billion of the state's exports to Belgium in 1996, and almost all of that was transshipped elsewhere. In contrast, the next leading export to Belgium was chemical products at $67 million. Since tobacco exports have continued to increase over the past several years, they rose 15 percent from 1995 to 1996, attempts to develop direct markets are of utmost importance to the future of the state economy.

Europe is also Virginia's leading source of FDI. Of the $16.6 billion that international companies invested in the state in 1995, $10.2 billion or some 61 percent came from Europe. Most significantly, 77 percent of the FDI for manufacturing industries came from Europe. In addition, 76 percent of employment related to FDI comes from Europe. European nations have 485 firms located in Virginia and European FDI supports some 90,000 jobs. Of the individual nations, Great Britain has the most FDI in Virginia, followed by Germany and France. The state government has embarked on a number of programs to attract new FDI to Virginia.

While Europe as a region is the key to Virginia's foreign economic policy, East Asia ranks as the second leading destination for the state's exports and accounts for 24 percent of total exports. Outside of Europe, Japan is the single leading recipient of the state's products, and in 1996 it purchased some $1.38 billion goods from Virginia. However, the continuing economic problems in the region have resulted in a yearly decline in the overall volume of exports over the past five years. Nonetheless, the state continues to promote trade and investment in the region, and has invited

Figure 15.1 A major component of Virginia's economic prosperity is export activity through the ports in Hampton Roads. Courtesy of Alex S. MacLean/Peter Arnold, Inc.

representatives from Japan and Korea to serve with VDED as liaisons with their respective nations. In total, East Asia provides Virginia with some $3 billion in FDI and 83 firms from the region are responsible for 11,200 jobs in the state. Although this makes East Asia the second largest source of FDI in the state, it only accounts for 13 percent of the total figure.

In 1993, after the signing of the North American Free Trade Agreement (NAFTA) between Canada, Mexico and the United States, Virginia initiated an effort to expand commerce with the nation's NAFTA partners. In 1994, Governor Allen's first trade mission was to the NAFTA countries. He also directed VDED to make expanded trade with the NAFTA states a priority. Taken together, exports to Canada and Mexico account for 16 percent of Virginia's total exports. In spite of the state government's efforts, Virginia has found itself unable to compete with Florida and Texas which have much more developed trade relations with Mexico, and has seen overall exports to Canada decline over the past several years.

The state's trade policy has also centered around efforts to promote the Port of Hampton Roads as the primary conduit for goods on the East Coast. Hampton Roads is the world's largest deep-water port. The port is actually three different port facilities that are all operated by the Virginia Port Authority (VPA). These ports include the Norfolk International Terminal, the Portsmouth Marine Terminal, and the Newport News Marine Terminal. The VPA operates a total of 20 cargo terminals. Regionally, some 244,000 jobs are related to the port in one form or another. Hampton Roads ranks as the sixth largest port in the United States and the twenty-eighth largest in the world. In 1996, it handled some 58 percent of the exports from the Atlantic region, and 9 percent of the region's imports. This amounted to some $10.4 billion in products or some 9.1 million tons of cargo. Since 1982, trade through the Port of Hampton Roads has increased by 300-percent, and the port now services some 75 different cargo companies. Each year more than 4,000 ships dock in the port and provide service to more than 100 countries. Most significantly, 80 percent of the export cargo shipped through the port comes from outside of the Old Dominion. In overall terms, the port has become the most important gateway for goods and products shipped form the Midwest region of the United States. In line with the state's general orientation toward trade with Western Europe, the majority of goods and products shipped through the port are either being sent to or coming from Europe.

Efforts at Promoting Trade

Throughout the 1990's, Virginia has steadily improved its efforts to bring together Virginia producers and international buyers, resulting in a 27 percent increase in the volume of Virginia exports since 1993. Today, exports constitute approximately 10 percent of the Commonwealth's Gross State Product with some $14 billion in products and services being exported to destinations around the world.

At the forefront of Virginia's efforts to promote trade is the Virginia Economic Development Partnership (VEDP) which was created in 1995. Since its inception, VEDP has successfully courted over 300 companies, which have announced decisions to expand or build new facilities within the state. Early commitment figures estimate the growth will bring an additional $6 billion and more than 30,000 jobs to Virginia. VEDP's success has not been limited to US industries alone, however. In 1996, 33 new foreign direct investment announcements amounted to $1.24 billion, adding 3,290 new jobs to the Virginia work force. They originated from ten different countries. These additions bring the state's total number of foreign firms to 628 with cumulative investments of $8.7 billion and 61,550 employees.

With an eye to the future, VEDP has taken additional steps to promote international trade. The International Market Planning (IMP) program has been used to provide firms with targeted marketing information and strategies to compete successfully in the global marketplace. The IMP program is based on cooperative arrangements between VEDP and graduate programs from different universities around the state. Specifically, the IMP has three emphases identified in its mission statement:

- Increasing the export of Virginia products and services and the number of Virginia exporters;
- Increasing the awareness abroad of quality Virginia products and services; and
- Attracting foreign direct investment by promoting Virginia strategic business advantages.

VEDP is also involved with a number of other related agencies such as the International InfoCenter, the Virginia Small Business Financing Authority, and the International Marketing Managers. The ultimate focus is on keeping Virginia businesses competitive in the international marketplace and helping those businesses take advantage of the global economy.

The Future of the Old Dominion's Foreign Policy

In the near term, Virginia's economic future looks bright. During the first 100 days of the Gilmore administration, employment increased by 14,000 jobs. Industries from around the world have committed to relocating in the Commonwealth or have expanded existing sites. Within that same 100 days, Governor Gilmore led a trade and marketing mission to Europe to court British and German business leaders. It is clear that the Gilmore administration will aggressively seek out foreign investment in the Commonwealth.

Another interesting future trend will be the increased importance of technology industries in the region. Governor Gilmore appointed the Commonwealth's first Secretary of Technology who, among others, will work with VEDP officials to attract international technology and telecommunications firms to the region. Governor Gilmore, who has been at the forefront of government officials who oppose the taxation or regulation of the internet, has also aggressively pursued high technology firms like Siemens, Oracle and Gateway 2000 to what is now being referred to as the "Silicon Dominion." VEDP, in conjunction with several universities, is creating research and development centers to ensure future private industry investment.

One dark cloud appears to be hovering on the horizon, however. As the tobacco industry languishes under national disapproval, the future of the industry remains unknown. While the Commonwealth is working towards greater diversification of industries, tobacco remains prominent among its export commodities. If tobacco regulation increases in the United States, it is plausible that the Port of Hampton Roads may find itself shipping more tobacco products to overseas markets in an effort to alleviate the revenue loss.

In sum, the future of the state appears to be consistent with its recent past. The strong national economy is a reflection of strong state economies, which will likely continue to remain robust. While there has been a change in Republican gubernatorial administrations in Richmond, the trends appear to remain consistently in favor of promoting business friendly environments, aggressively undertaking international marketing and trade missions, and renewing support for the modernization and expansion of existing industries.

Bibliography

Allen, George, and Robert T. Skunda. 1995. *Opportunity Virginia: A Strategic Plan for Jobs and Prosperity*. Richmond: Commonwealth of Virginia.

Dabney, Virginius. 1983. *Virginia: The New Dominion, a History From 1607 to the Present*. Charlottesville: University Press of Virginia.

European-American Chamber of Commerce (EACC). 1996. *The United States & Europe: Jobs, Trade & Investment*, 3rd ed. Washington, D.C.: EACC.

Hampton Roads Chamber of Commerce. 1998. *Hampton Roads Business Contact*. 12.

Salmon, Emily J. 1983. *A Hornbook of Virginia History*, 3rd ed. Richmond: Virginia State Library.

Virginia Economic Development Partnership (VEDP). 1996. *VA Business Incentives*. Richmond: VEDP.

Virginia Port Authority (VPA). [various dates]. *Virginia Maritimer*.

Ward, Gerard W. 1993. *Industrial Modernization in Virginia*. Richmond: Virginia Department of Planning and Budget.

APPENDIX

The Constitution of Virginia

Effective July 1, 1971
with
Amendments—January 1, 1997

Issued by the Clerk's Office
The House of Delegates

Bruce F. Jamerson
Clerk of the House of Delegates
and
Keeper of the Rolls of the Commonwealth

Commonwealth of Virginia
Richmond
January 1997

The Constitution of Virginia

Foreword

The Virginia Constitution of 1971 was approved by vote of the people on November 3, 1970, and became effective on July 1, 1971. The 1971 Constitution is the fifth complete revision of Virginia's fundamental law since 1776—other complete revisions having been effective in 1830, 1851, 1870, and 1902.[1]

The revision which led to the adoption of the Constitution of 1971 began with the creation of the Commission on Constitutional Revision, authorized by joint resolution at the General Assembly's 1968 Session and appointed by Governor Mills E. Godwin, Jr. The Commission, chaired by former Governor Albertis S. Harrison, Jr., reported to the Governor and the General Assembly in January 1969. The revisions took the form of amendments—one of two ways to change the Virginia Constitution (the other way being by the calling of a constitutional convention).[2]

The General Assembly, at a special session called in 1969, approved amendments which, with two exceptions,[3] were approved for a second time at the Assembly's regular session in 1970 and then laid before the people at the general election in November 1970. There were four proposals on the November ballot—a general question containing the main body of the revised Constitution and three separate questions (one repealing the constitutional prohibition on lotteries, and two dealing with borrowing by the Commonwealth). All four questions passed.[4]

Since the Constitution's effective date in 1971, there have been additional amendments. [See Additional Notes.)

In addition to the body of Virginia constitutional law (including judicial decisions) already in being, several documents will be helpful to a fuller understanding of the Constitution of 1971. They include

(1) 'The Report of the Commission on Constitutional Revision (January 1, 1969). Many of the Commission's recommendations were adopted by the General Assembly; to that extent, the commentary in the Commission's report will be relevant.

(2) The debates in the 1969 Special Session and 1970 Regular Session of the General Assembly. It was at these sessions, especially that of 1969, that the revisions were debated in detail. The debates have been published in two volumes: *Proceedings and Debates of the House of Delegates [Senate of Virginia] pertaining to Amendment of the Constitution,* ed. Charles K. Woltz (Richmond, n.d.).

(3) The revised Constitution is commented on section by section in A. E. Dick Howard's *Commentaries on the Constitution of Virginia* (2 vols.; Charlottesville, 1975). These commentaries trace the historical origins and evolution of the Constitution's provisions, as well as discussing the present-day interpretation. The Commentaries are available from the University Press of Virginia, Charlottesville.

Footnotes

1. This does not count the Constitution of 1864, which was drafted under wartime conditions and whose legal status was never certain. This count also does not include the revision of 1928, in which fewer than half of the sections of the Constitution of 1902 were changed at all.

2. See Article XII, infra.

3. One amendment dealt with State aid to handicapped children in private schools, the other with the boundaries of the capital city; both failed of passage at the 1970 Session.

4. Proposal No. 1, generally revising the Constitution, passed by a vote of 576,776 to 226,219. Proposal No. 2, repealing Section 60 of the existing Constitution, passed by a vote of 491,124 to 290,168. Proposal No. 3, which appears as Article X, Section 9(b) of this Constitution, infra, was approved by a vote of 504,315 to 261,220. Proposal No. 4, which appears as Article X, Section 9(c) of this Constitution, infra, was approved by a vote of 484,274 to 265,784. (These figures do not include a small number of ballots whose validity depended on the outcome of pending federal court litigation involving residence requirements.)

Additional Notes

5. In November 1972, the people approved an amendment to Article II, Section 1, specifying the voting age as eighteen (thus conforming Virginia's Constitution to the Twenty-sixth Amendment to the Federal Constitution). The voters also approved an amendment to Article VII, Section 1, to preserve city and town status for those municipalities that had city or town status before July 1, 1971, even though they may fail to meet the population minimum otherwise required by Section 1.

6. In November 1974, the people approved an amendment to Article VIII, Section 11, authorizing the General Assembly to provide for grants to students in certain institutions of higher education (Section I I had already permitted loans to such students) and, further, authorizing the Assembly to provide contracts between the Commonwealth or its political subdivisions and those educational institutions for the provision of educational or related services.

7. In November 1976, the people approved amendments to Article II, Sections 1, 2, 4 and 5, changing certain residence qualifications to vote, permitting absentee registration by persons temporarily residing outside the country, and requiring the residency for an office seeker to be at least one year prior to his election; an amendment to Article VI, Section 12, to permit judicial appointments of elected local officials to fill vacancies for less than sixty days; and an amendment to Article X, Section 6, to permit tax exemptions for certain property: subject to flooding, owned by disabled persons, used for solar energy, and tangible farm property and products. [The 1976 amendment to Article II, Section 4 was superseded by the 1994 amendment.]

8. In November 1978, the people approved an amendment to Article X, Section 6, to permit certain tax exemptions for property which due to age or use has been renovated, rehabilitated or replaced.

9. In November 1980, the people approved amendments to Article IV, Section 6, and Article V, Section 6, to provide that the General Assembly reconvene after each session to consider legislation returned by the Governor without his signature; an amendment to Article IV, Section 11, relating to the signing of enrolled bills; an amendment to Article IV, Section 13, relating to the date on which laws shall take effect; an amendment to Article VII, Section 10, decreasing the maximum indebtedness of a city or town; and amendments to Article X, Section 6, permitting certain tax exemptions for personal property of the aged or disabled, and permitting certain tax exemptions for property whose purpose is to replace oil or natural gas generating equipment. [The 1980 amendment to Article V, Section 6 was superseded by the 1994 amendment.]

10. In November 1982, the people approved an amendment to Article II, Section 2, relating to information required from persons applying to register.

11. In November 1984, the people approved an amendment to Article VII, Section 6, relating to multiple offices; and an amendment to Article X, Section 7, relating to collection and disposition of State revenues.

12. In November 1986, the people approved an amendment to Article II, Section 4, relating to powers and duties of the General Assembly with respect to registration and voting; an amendment to Article II, Section 8, relating to elections and election officials; and amendments to Article VI, Section 1, pertaining to judicial power and jurisdiction. [The 1986 amendment to Article II, Section 4 was superseded by the 1994 amendment.]

13. In November 1990, the people approved an amendment to Article VIII, Section 8, relating to the Literary Fund; and an amendment to Article X, Section 1, relating to taxable property.

14. In November 1992, the people approved an amendment to Article X, Section 8, creating the Revenue Stabilization Fund.

15. In November 1994, the people approved amendments to Article II, Sections 2, 3 and 4, deleting the constitutional requirement for voters to register in person and allowing the General Assembly to revise laws for canceling a person's registration for not voting; an amendment to Article IV, Section 14, allowing the General Assembly to revise the time period for filing lawsuits involving past injuries to children; and an amendment to Article V, Section 6, revising the options available to the Governor for acting on bills presented to him and the procedures available to the General Assembly when acting on bills returned by the Governor.

16. In November 1996, the people approved an amendment to Article I by creating Section 8-A, relating to the rights of victims of crime; amendments to Article II, Sections I and 2, relating to voter franchise and registration; an amendment to Article VI, Section 1, authorizing the General Assembly to expand the Commonwealth's right to appeal; and an amendment to Article X, Section 11, relating to a governmental employees retirement system.

Editor's Note

The Foreword, Footnotes, and Additional Notes 5 and 6 were written by Dr. A. E. Dick Howard, who was the Executive Director of the Commission on Constitutional Revision, and is now Professor of Law at the University of Virginia.

The Constitution of Virginia

Table of Contents

ARTICLE III
Division of Powers

ARTICLE IV
Legislature

ARTICLE V
Executive

ARTICLE VI
Judiciary

ARTICLE VII
Local Government

ARTICLE VIII
Education

ARTICLE IX
Corporations

ARTICLE X
Taxation and Finance

ARTICLE XI
Conservation

ARTICLE XII
Future Changes

SCHEDULE

The Constitution of Virginia

ARTICLE I
Bill of Rights

A DECLARATION OF RIGHTS made by the good people of Virginia in the exercise of their sovereign powers, which rights do pertain to them and their posterity, as the basis and foundation of government.

Section 1. Equality and rights of men.

That all men are by nature equally free and independent and have certain inherent rights, of which, when they enter into a state of society, they cannot, by any compact, deprive or divest their posterity; namely, the enjoyment of life and liberty, with the means of acquiring and possessing property, and pursuing and obtaining happiness and safety.

Section 2. People the source of power.

That all power is vested in, and consequently derived from, the people, that magistrates are their trustees and servants, and at all times amenable to them.

Section 3. Government instituted for common benefit.

That government is, or ought to be, instituted for the common benefit, protection, and security of the people, nation, or community; of all the various modes and forms of government, that is best which is capable of producing the greatest degree of happiness and safety, and is most effectually secured against the danger of maladministration; and, whenever any government shall be found inadequate or contrary to these purposes, a majority of the community hath an indubitable, inalienable, and indefeasible right to reform, alter, or abolish it, in such manner as shall be judged most conducive to the public weal.

Section 4. No exclusive emoluments or privileges; offices not to be hereditary.

That no man, or set of men, is entitled to exclusive or separate emoluments or privileges from the community, but in consideration of public services; which not being descendible, neither ought the offices of magistrate, legislator, or judge to be hereditary.

Section 5. Separation of legislative, executive, and judicial departments; periodical elections.

That the legislative, executive, and judicial departments of the Commonwealth should be separate and distinct; and that the members thereof may be restrained from oppression, by feeling and participating the burthens of the people, they should, at fixed periods, be reduced to a private station, return into that body from which they were originally taken, and the vacancies be supplied by regular elections, in which all or any part of the former members shall be again eligible, or ineligible, as the laws may direct.

Section 6. Free elections; consent of governed.

That all elections ought to be free; and that all men, having sufficient evidence of permanent common interest with, and attachment to, the community, have the right of suffrage, and cannot be taxed, or deprived of, or damaged in, their property for public uses, without their own consent, or that of their representatives duly elected, or bound by any law to which they have not, in like manner, assented for the public good.

Section 7. Laws should not be suspended.

That all power of suspending laws, or the execution of laws, by any authority, without consent of the representatives of the people, is injurious to their rights, and ought not to be exercised.

Section 8. Criminal prosecutions.

That in criminal prosecutions a man hath a right to demand the cause and nature of his accusation, to be confronted with the accusers and witnesses, and to call for evidence in his favor, and he shall enjoy the right to a speedy and public trial, by an impartial jury of his vicinage, without whose unanimous consent he cannot be found guilty. He shall not be deprived of life or liberty, except by the law of the land or the judgment of his peers, nor be compelled in any criminal proceeding to give evidence against himself, nor be put twice in jeopardy for the same offense.

Laws may be enacted providing for the trial of offenses not felonious by a court not of record without a jury, preserving the right of the accused to an appeal to and a trial by jury in some court of record having original criminal jurisdiction. Laws may also provide for juries consisting of less than twelve, but not less than five, for the trial of offenses not felonious, and may classify such cases, and prescribe the number of jurors for each class.

In criminal cases, the accused may plead guilty. If the accused plead not guilty, he may, with his consent and the concurrence of the Commonwealth's Attorney and of the court entered of record, be tried by a smaller number of jurors, or waive a jury. In case of such waiver or plea of guilty, the court shall try the case.

The provisions of this section shall be self-executing.

Section 8-A. Rights of victims of crime.

That in criminal prosecutions, the victim shall be accorded fairness, dignity and respect by the officers, employees and agents of the Commonwealth and its political subdivisions and officers of the courts and, as the General Assembly may define and provide by law, may be accorded rights to reasonable and appropriate notice, information, restitution, protection, and access to a meaningful role in the criminal justice process. These rights may include, but not be limited to, the following:

1. The right to protection from further harm or reprisal through the imposition of appropriate bail and conditions of release;
2. The right to be treated with respect, dignity and fairness at all stages of the criminal justice system;
3. The right to address the circuit court at the time sentence is imposed;
4. The right to receive timely notification of judicial proceedings;
5. The right to restitution;
6. The right to be advised of release from custody or escape of the offender, whether before or after disposition; and
7. The right to confer with the prosecution.

This section does not confer upon any person a right to appeal or modify any decision in a criminal proceeding, does not abridge any other right guaranteed by the Constitution of the United States or this Constitution, and does not create any cause of action for compensation or damages against the Commonwealth or any of its political subdivisions, any officer, employee or agent of the Commonwealth or any of its political subdivisions, or any officer of the court.

The amendment ratified November 5, 1996 and effective January 1, 1997—Added a new section (8-A).

Section 9. Prohibition of excessive bail and fines, cruel and unusual punishment, suspension of habeas corpus, bills of attainder, and ex post facto laws.

That excessive bail ought not to be required, nor excessive fines imposed, nor cruel and unusual punishments inflicted; that the privilege of the writ of habeas corpus shall not be suspended unless when, in cases of invasion or rebellion, the public safety may require; and that the General Assembly shall not pass any bill of attainder, or any ex post facto law.

Section 10. General warrants of search or seizure prohibited.

That general warrants, whereby an officer or messenger may be commanded to search suspected places without evidence of a fact committed, or to seize any person or persons not named, or whose offense is not particularly described and supported by evidence, are grievous and oppressive, and ought not to be granted.

Section 11. Due process of law; obligation of contracts; taking of private property; prohibited discrimination; jury trial in civil cases.

That no person shall be deprived of his life, liberty, or property without due process of law; that the General Assembly shall not pass any law impairing the obligation of contracts, nor any law whereby private property shall be taken or damaged for public uses, without just compensation, the term "public uses" to be defined by the General Assembly; and that the right to be free from any governmental discrimination upon the basis of religious conviction, race, color, sex, or national origin shall not be abridged, except that the mere separation of the sexes shall not be considered discrimination.

That in controversies respecting property, and in suits between man and man, trial by jury is preferable to any other, and ought to be held sacred. The General Assembly may limit the number of jurors for civil cases in courts of record to not less than five.

Section 12. Freedom of speech and of the press; right peaceably to assemble, and to petition.

That the freedoms of speech and of the press are among the great bulwarks of liberty, and can never be restrained except by despotic governments; that any citizen may freely speak, write, and publish his sentiments on all subjects, being responsible for the abuse of that right; that the General Assembly shall not pass any law abridging the freedom of speech or of the press, nor the right of the people peaceably to assemble, and to petition the government for the redress of grievances.

Section 13. Militia; standing armies; military subordinate to civil power.

That a well regulated militia, composed of the body of the people, trained to arms, is the proper, natural, and safe defense of a free state, therefore, the right of the people to keep and bear arms shall not be infringed; that standing armies, in time of peace, should be avoided as dangerous to liberty; and that in all cases the military should be under strict subordination to, and governed by, the civil power.

Section 14. Government should be uniform.

That the people have a right to uniform government; and, therefore, that no government separate from, or independent of, the government of Virginia, ought to be erected or established within the limits thereof.

Section 15. Qualities necessary to preservation of free government.

That no free government, nor the blessings of liberty, can be preserved to any people, but by a firm adherence to justice, moderation, temperance, frugality, and virtue; by frequent recurrence to fundamental principles; and by the recognition by all citizens that they have duties as well as rights, and that such rights cannot be enjoyed save in a society where law is respected and due process is observed.

That free government rests, as does all progress, upon the broadest possible diffusion of knowledge, and that the Commonwealth should avail itself of those talents which nature has sown so liberally among its people by assuring the opportunity for their fullest development by an effective system of education throughout the Commonwealth.

Section 16. Free exercise of religion; no establishment of religion.

That religion or the duty which we owe to our Creator, and the manner of discharging it, can be directed only by reason and conviction, not by force or violence; and, therefore, all men are equally entitled to the free exercise of religion, according to the dictates of conscience; and that it is the mutual duty of all to practice Christian forbearance, love, and charity towards each other. No man shall be compelled to frequent or support any religious worship, place, or ministry whatsoever, nor shall be enforced, restrained, molested, or burthened in his body or goods, nor shall otherwise suffer on account of his religious opinions or belief; but all men shall be free to profess and by argument to maintain their opinions in matters of religion, and the same shall in nowise diminish, enlarge, or affect their civil capacities. And the General Assembly shall not prescribe any religious test whatever, or confer any peculiar privileges or advantages on any sect or denomination, or pass any law requiring or authorizing any religious society, or the people of any district within this Commonwealth, to levy on themselves or others, any tax for the erection or repair of any house of public worship, or for the support of any church or ministry; but it shall be left free to every person to select his religious instructor, and to make for his support such private contract as he shall please.

Section 17. Construction of the Bill of Rights.

The rights enumerated in this Bill of Rights shall not be construed to limit other rights of the people not therein expressed.

ARTICLE II
Franchise and Officers

Section 1. Qualifications of voters.

In elections by the people, the qualifications of voters shall be as follows: Each voter shall be a citizen of the United States, shall be eighteen years of age, shall fulfill the residence requirements set forth in this section, and shall be registered to vote pursuant to this article. No person who has been convicted of a felony shall be qualified to vote unless his civil rights have been restored by the Governor or other appropriate authority. As prescribed by law, no person adjudicated to be mentally incompetent shall be qualified to vote until his competency has been reestablished.

The residence requirements shall be that each voter shall be a resident of the Commonwealth and of the precinct where he votes. Residence, for all purposes of qualification to vote, requires both domicile and a place of abode. The General Assembly may provide for persons who are qualified to vote except for having moved their residence from one precinct to another within the Commonwealth to continue to vote in a former precinct subject to conditions and time limits defined by law. The General Assembly may also provide, in elections for President and Vice-President of the United States, alternatives to registration for new residents of the Commonwealth.

Any person who will be qualified with respect to age to vote at the next general election shall be permitted to register in advance and also to vote in any intervening primary or special election.

The amendment ratified November 7, 1972 and effective January 1, 1973—In paragraph one, the voting age, formerly "twenty-one", was reduced to "eighteen".

The amendment ratified November 2, 1976 and effective January 1, 1977—In paragraph two, substituted "be" for "have been" and removed the durational residency requirement of "six months" in the Commonwealth and "thirty days" in the precinct in the first sentence. The second sentence removed the language "fewer than thirty days prior to an election" and after the word "may" added the language "in the following November general election and (in any) intervening". In the last sentence of the paragraph the less than six months residency requirement for presidential elections was removed to conform with the first sentence.

The amendment ratified November 5, 1996 and effective January 1, 1997—In paragraph two, deleted the second sentence: "A person who is qualified to vote except for having moved his residence from one precinct to another may in the following November general election and in any intervening election vote in the precinct from which he has moved.", added a next-to-the-last sentence: "The General Assembly may provide for persons who are qualified to vote . . .", and added "also" preceding "provide" in the last sentence.

Section 2. Registration of voters.

The General Assembly shall provide by law for the registration of all persons otherwise qualified to vote who have met the residence requirements contained in this article, and shall ensure that the opportunity to register is made available. Registrations accomplished prior to the effective date of this section shall be effective hereunder. The registration records shall not be closed to new or transferred registrations more than thirty days before the election in which they are to be used.

Applications to register shall require the applicant to provide the following information on a standard form: full name; date of birth; residence address; social security number, if any; whether the applicant is presently a United States citizen; and such additional information as may be required by law. All applications to register shall be completed by or at the direction of the applicant and signed by the applicant, unless physically disabled. No fee shall be charged to the applicant incident to an application to register.

Nothing in this article shall preclude the General Assembly from requiring as a prerequisite to registration to vote the ability of the applicant to read and complete in his own handwriting the application to register.

The amendment ratified November 2, 1976 and effective January 1, 1977—In paragraph two, substituted "date of residence in the precinct" for "length of residence in the Commonwealth and in the precinct" and removed "time" of any previous registrations to vote.

The amendment ratified November 2, 1982 and effective January 1, 1983—In paragraph two, after "maiden" added "and any other prior legal" and deleted "of a woman, if married" and after "birth;" deleted "marital status; occupation;".

The amendment ratified November 8, 1994 and effective January 1, 1995—In paragraph two, after "to provide" deleted "under oath", after "has been restored." deleted "Except as otherwise provided in this Constitution,", and after "shall be completed" deleted "in person before the register and".

The amendment ratified November 5, 1996 and effective January 1, 1997—In paragraph two, after "full name", deleted ", including the maiden and any other prior legal name; age", after "date", deleted "and place", added "residence address;" after "of birth;", and substituted "and such additional information as may be required by law" for "address and place of abode and date of residence in the precinct; place of any previous registrations to vote; and whether the applicant has ever been adjudicated to be mentally incompetent or convicted of a felony, and if so, under what circumstances the applicant's right to vote has been restored".

Section 3. Method of voting.

In elections by the people, the following safeguards shall be maintained: Voting shall be by ballot or by machines for receiving, recording, and counting votes cast. No ballot or list of candidates upon any voting machine shall bear any distinguishing mark or symbol, other than words identifying political party affiliation; and their form, including the offices to be filled and the listing of candidates or nominees, shall be as uniform as is practicable throughout the Commonwealth or smaller governmental unit in which the election is held.

In elections other than primary elections, provision shall be made whereby votes may be cast for persons other than the listed candidates or nominees. Secrecy in casting votes shall be maintained, except as provision may be made for assistance to handicapped voters, but the ballot box or voting machine shall be kept in public view and shall not be opened, nor the ballots canvassed nor the votes counted, in secret. Votes may be cast in person or by absentee ballot as provided by law.

The amendment ratified November 8, 1994 and effective January 1, 1995—In paragraph two, after "Votes may be cast" deleted "only in person, except as otherwise provided in this article" and added "in person or by absentee ballot as provided by law".

Section 4. Powers and duties of General Assembly.

The General Assembly shall establish a uniform system for permanent registration of voters pursuant to this Constitution, including provisions for appeal by any person denied registration, correction of illegal or fraudulent registrations, penalties for illegal, fraudulent, or false registrations, proper transfer of all registered voters, and cancellation of registrations in other jurisdictions of persons who apply to register to vote in the Commonwealth. The General Assembly shall provide for maintenance of accurate and current registration records and may provide for the cancellation of registrations for such purpose.

The General Assembly shall provide for the nomination of candidates, shall regulate the time, place, manner, conduct, and administration of primary, general, and special elections, and shall have power to make any other law regulating elections not inconsistent with this Constitution.

The amendment ratified November 8, 1994 and effective January 1, 1995—In paragraph one, after "fraudulent registrations," added "penalties for illegal, fraudulent, or false registrations," and replaced "shall provide for cancellation" with "may provide for the cancellation". Deleted provision for canceling a voter's registration for not having voted for four years, allowing the General Assembly to revise laws for canceling a person's registration for not voting. Deleted a paragraph relating to registration and voting by absentee application and ballot for those in the armed forces or temporarily employed out of the country, and for other qualified voters. [The amendment to this section ratified November 2, 1976 and effective January 1, 1977 and the amendment to this section ratified November 4, 1986 and effective July 1, 1987 were superseded by the 1994 amendment.]

Section 5. Qualifications to hold elective office.

The only qualification to hold any office of the Commonwealth or of its governmental units, elective by the people, shall be that a person must have been a resident of the Commonwealth for one year next preceding his election and be qualified to vote for that office, except as otherwise provided in this Constitution, and except that:

(a) the General Assembly may impose more restrictive geographical residence requirements for election of its members, and may permit other governing bodies in the Commonwealth to impose more restrictive geographical residence requirements for election to such governing bodies, but no such requirements shall impair equal representation of the persons entitled to vote;

(b) the General Assembly may provide that residence in a local governmental unit is not required for election to designated elective offices in local governments, other than membership in the local governing body; and

(c) nothing in this Constitution shall limit the power of the General Assembly to prevent conflict of interests, dual officeholding, or other incompatible activities by elective or appointive officials of the Commonwealth or of any political subdivision.

The amendment ratified November 2, 1976 and effective January 1, 1977—In paragraph one, after "one year" added the language "next preceding his election".

Section 6. Apportionment.

Members of the House of Representatives of the United States and members of the Senate and of the House of Delegates of the General Assembly shall be elected from electoral districts established by the General Assembly. Every electoral district shall be composed of contiguous and compact territory and shall be so constituted as to give, as nearly as is practicable, representation in proportion to the population of the district. The General Assembly shall reapportion the Commonwealth into electoral districts in accordance with this section in the year 1971 and every ten years thereafter.

Any such reapportionment law shall take effect immediately and not be subject to the limitations contained in Article IV, Section 13, of this Constitution.

Section 7. Oath or affirmation.

All officers elected or appointed under or pursuant to this Constitution shall, before they enter on the performance of their public duties, severally take and subscribe the following oath or affirmation:

"I do solemnly swear (or affirm) that I will support the Constitution of the United States, and the Constitution of the Commonwealth of Virginia, and that I will faithfully and impartially discharge all the duties incumbent upon me as ...., according to the best of my ability (so help me God)."

Section 8. Electoral boards; registrars and officers of election.

There shall be in each county and city an electoral board composed of three members, selected as provided by law. In the appointment of the electoral boards, representation, as far as practicable, shall be given to each of the two political parties which, at the general election next preceding their appointment, cast the highest and the next highest number of votes. The present members of such boards shall continue in office until the expiration of their respective terms; thereafter their successors shall be appointed for the term of three years. Any vacancy occurring in any board shall be filled by the same authority for the unexpired term.

Each electoral board shall appoint the officers of election and general registrar for its county or city. In appointing such officers of election, representation, as far as practicable, shall be given to each of the two political parties which, at the general election next preceding their appointment, cast the highest and next highest number of votes.

No person, nor the deputy of any person, who is employed by or holds any office or post of profit or emolument, or who holds any elective office of profit or trust, under the governments of the United States, the Commonwealth, or any county, city, or town, shall be appointed a member of the electoral board or general registrar. No person, nor the deputy or the employee of any person, who holds any elective office of profit or trust under the government of the United States, the Commonwealth, or any county, city, or town of the Commonwealth shall be appointed an assistant registrar or officer of election.

The amendment ratified November 4, 1986 and effective January 1, 1987—In paragraph two, after "officers" deleted the words "and registrars" and added "and general registrar" after "of election". In paragraph three, after "the electoral board or" added the word "general" before "registrar" and deleted a reference to officer of election, and added the last sentence: "No person, nor the deputy or the employee of any person . . .".

Section 9. Privileges of voters during election.

No voter, during the time of holding any election at which he is entitled to vote, shall be compelled to perform military service, except in time of war or public danger, nor to attend any court as suitor, juror, or witness; nor shall any such voter be subject to arrest under any civil process during his attendance at election or in going to or returning therefrom.

Article III
Division of Powers

Section 1. Departments to be distinct.

The legislative, executive, and judicial departments shall be separate and distinct, so that none exercise the powers properly belonging to the others, nor any person exercise the power of more than one of them at the same time; provided, however, administrative agencies may be created by the General Assembly with such authority and duties as the General Assembly may prescribe. Provisions may be made for judicial review of any finding, order, or judgment of such administrative agencies.

ARTICLE IV
Legislature

Section 1. Legislative power.

The legislative power of the Commonwealth shall be vested in a General Assembly, which shall consist of a Senate and House of Delegates.

Section 2. Senate.

The Senate shall consist of not more than forty and not less than thirty-three members, who shall be elected quadrennially by the voters of the several senatorial districts on the Tuesday succeeding the first Monday in November.

Section 3. House of Delegates.

The House of Delegates shall consist of not more than one hundred and not less than ninety members, who shall be elected biennially by the voters of the several house districts on the Tuesday succeeding the first Monday in November.

Section 4. Qualifications of senators and delegates.

Any person may be elected to the Senate who, at the time of the election, is twenty-one years of age, is a resident of the senatorial district which he is seeking to represent, and is qualified to vote for members of the General Assembly. Any person may be elected to the House of Delegates who, at the time of the election, is twenty-one years of age, is a resident of the house district which he is seeking to represent, and is qualified to vote for members of the General Assembly. A senator or delegate who moves his residence from the district for which he is elected shall thereby vacate his office.

No person holding a salaried office under the government of the Commonwealth, and no judge of any court, attorney for the Commonwealth, sheriff, treasurer, assessor of taxes, commissioner of the revenue, collector of taxes, or clerk of any court shall be a member of either house of the General Assembly during his continuance in office; and his qualification as a member shall vacate any such office held by him. No person holding any office or post of profit or emolument under the United States government, or who is in the employment of such government, shall be eligible to either house.

Section 5. Compensation; election to civil office of profit.

The members of the General Assembly shall receive such salary and allowances as may be prescribed by law, but no increase in salary shall take effect for a given member until after the end of the term for which he was elected. No member during the term for which he shall have been elected shall be elected by the General Assembly to any civil office of profit in the Commonwealth.

Section 6. Legislative sessions.

The General Assembly shall meet once each year on the second Wednesday in January. Except as herein provided for reconvened sessions, no regular session of the General Assembly convened in an even-numbered year shall continue longer than sixty days; no regular session of the General Assembly convened in an odd-numbered year shall continue longer than thirty days; but with the concurrence of two-thirds of the members elected to each house, any regular session may be extended for a period not exceeding thirty days. Neither house shall, without the consent of the other, adjourn to another place, nor for more than three days.

The Governor may convene a special session of the General Assembly when, in his opinion, the interest of the Commonwealth may require and shall convene a special session upon the application of two-thirds of the members elected to each house.

The General Assembly shall reconvene on the sixth Wednesday after adjournment of each regular or special session for the purpose of considering bills which may have been returned by the Governor with recommendations for their amendment and bills and items of appropriation bills which may have been returned by the Governor with his objections. No other business shall be considered at a reconvened session. Such reconvened session shall not continue longer than three days unless the session be extended, for a period not exceeding seven additional days, upon the vote of the majority of the members elected to each house.

The amendment ratified November 4, 1980 and effective January 1, 1981—After the first sentence in the first paragraph added "Except as herein provided for reconvened sessions,", and added a third paragraph "The General Assembly shall reconvene on the sixth Wednesday . . .".

Section 7. Organization of General Assembly.

The House of Delegates shall choose its own Speaker; and, in the absence of the Lieutenant Governor, or when he shall exercise the office of Governor, the Senate shall choose from its own body a president pro tempore. Each house shall select its officers and settle its rules of procedure. The houses may jointly provide for legislative continuity between sessions occurring during the term for which members of the House of Delegates are elected. Each house may direct writs of election for supplying vacancies which may occur during a session of the General Assembly. If vacancies exist while the General Assembly is not in session, such writs may be issued by the Governor under such regulations as may be prescribed by law. Each house shall judge of the election, qualification, and returns of its members, may punish them for disorderly behavior, and, with the concurrence of two-thirds of its elected membership, may expel a member.

Section 8. Quorum.

A majority of the members elected to each house shall constitute a quorum to do business, but a smaller number may adjourn from day to day and shall have power to compel the attendance of members in such manner and under such penalty as each house may prescribe. A smaller number, not less than two-fifths of the elected membership of each house, may meet and may, notwithstanding any other provision of this Constitution, enact legislation if the Governor by proclamation declares that a quorum of the General Assembly cannot be convened because of enemy attack upon the soil of Virginia. Such legislation shall remain effective only until thirty days after a quorum of the General Assembly can be convened.

Section 9. Immunity of legislators.

Members of the General Assembly shall, in all cases except treason, felony, or breach of the peace, be privileged from arrest during the sessions of their respective houses; and for any speech or debate in either house shall not be questioned in any other place. They shall not be subject to arrest under any civil process during the sessions of the

General Assembly, or during the fifteen days before the beginning or after the ending of any session.

Section 10. Journal of proceedings.

Each house shall keep a journal of its proceedings, which shall be published from time to time. The vote of each member voting in each house on any question shall, at the desire of one-fifth of those present, be recorded in the journal. On the final vote on any bill, and on the vote in any election or impeachment conducted in the General Assembly or on the expulsion of a member, the name of each member voting in each house and how he voted shall be recorded in the journal.

Section 11. Enactment of laws.

No law shall be enacted except by bill. A bill may originate in either house, may be approved or rejected by the other, or may be amended by either, with the concurrence of the other.

No bill shall become a law unless, prior to its passage:

(a) it has been referred to a committee of each house, considered by such committee in session, and reported;

(b) it has been printed by the house in which it originated prior to its passage therein;

(c) it has been read by its title, or its title has been printed in a daily calendar, on three different calendar days in each house; and

(d) upon its final passage a vote has been taken thereon in each house, the name of each member voting for and against recorded in the journal, and a majority of those voting in each house, which majority shall include at least two-fifths of the members elected to that house, recorded in the affirmative.

Only in the manner required in subparagraph (d) of this section shall an amendment to a bill by one house be concurred in by the other, or a conference report be adopted by either house, or either house discharge a committee from the consideration of a bill and consider the same as if reported. The printing and reading, or either, required in subparagraphs (b) and (c) of this section, may be dispensed with in a bill to codify the laws of the Commonwealth, and in the case of an emergency by a vote of four-fifths of the members voting in each house, the name of each member voting and how he voted to be recorded in the journal.

No bill which creates or establishes a new office, or which creates, continues, or revives a debt or charge, or which makes, continues, or revives any appropriation of public or trust money or property, or which releases, discharges, or commutes any claim or demand of the Commonwealth, or which imposes, continues, or revives a tax, shall be passed except by the affirmative vote of a majority of all the members elected to each house, the name of each member voting and how he voted to be recorded in the journal.

Every law imposing, continuing, or reviving a tax shall specifically state such tax. However, any law by which taxes are imposed may define or specify the subject and provisions of such tax by reference to any provision of the laws of the United States as those laws may be or become effective at any time or from time to time, and may prescribe exceptions or modifications to any such provision.

The presiding officer of each house or upon his inability or failure to act a person designated by a majority of the members elected to each house shall, not later than three days after each bill is enrolled, sign each bill that has been passed by both houses and duly enrolled. The fact of signing shall be recorded in the journal.

The amendment ratified November 4, 1980 and effective January 1, 1981—In the last paragraph substituted "or upon his inability or failure to act a person designated by a majority of the members elected to each house shall, not later than three days after each bill is enrolled, sign each" for "shall, not later than twenty days after adjournment, sign every".

Section 12. Form of laws.

No law shall embrace more than one object, which shall be expressed in its title. Nor shall any law be revived or amended with reference to its title, but the act revived or the section amended shall be reenacted and published at length.

Section 13. Effective date of laws.

All laws enacted at a regular session, including laws which are enacted by reason of actions taken during the reconvened session following a regular session, but excluding a general appropriation law, shall take effect on the first day of July following the adjournment of the session of the General Assembly at which it has been enacted; and all laws enacted at a special session, including laws which are enacted by reason of actions taken during the reconvened session following a special session but excluding a general appropriation law, shall take effect on the first day of the fourth month following the month of adjournment of the special session; unless in the case of an emergency (which emergency shall be expressed in the body of the bill) the General Assembly shall specify an earlier date by a vote of four-fifths of the members voting in each house, the name of each member voting and how he voted to be recorded in the journal, or unless a subsequent date is specified in the body of the bill or by general law.

The amendment ratified November 4, 1980 and effective January 1, 1981—Rewrote the section so that all laws enacted at regular sessions and reconvened sessions which follow will take effect on July 1 rather than on the first day of the fourth month following the month of adjournment, and all laws enacted at special sessions and reconvened sessions which follow will take effect on the fourth month following the month of adjournment, excluding the general appropriation laws.

Section 14. Powers of General Assembly; limitations.

The authority of the General Assembly shall extend to all subjects of legislation not herein forbidden or restricted; and a specific grant of authority in this Constitution upon a subject shall not work a restriction of its authority upon the same or any other subject. The omission in this Constitution of specific grants of authority heretofore conferred shall not be construed to deprive the General Assembly of such authority, or to indicate a change of policy in reference thereto, unless such purpose plainly appear.

The General Assembly shall confer on the courts power to grant divorces, change the names of persons, and direct the sales of estates belonging to infants and other persons under legal disabilities, and shall not, by special legislation, grant relief in these or other cases of which the courts or other tribunals may have jurisdiction.

The General Assembly may regulate the exercise by courts of the right to punish for contempt.

The General Assembly's power to define the accrual date for a civil action based on an intentional tort committed by a natural person against a person who, at the time of the intentional tort, was a minor shall include the power to provide for the retroactive application of a change in the accrual date. No natural person shall have a constitutionally protected property right to bar a cause of action based on intentional torts as described herein on the ground that a change in the accrual date for the action has been applied retroactively or that a statute of limitations or statute of repose has expired.

The General Assembly shall not enact any local, special, or private law in the following cases:

(1) For the punishment of crime.

(2) Providing a change of venue in civil or criminal cases.

(3) Regulating the practice in, or the jurisdiction of, or changing the rules of evidence in any judicial proceedings or inquiry before the courts or other tribunals, or providing or changing the methods of collecting debts or enforcing judgments or prescribing the effect of judicial sales of real estate.

(4) Changing or locating county seats.

(5) For the assessment and collection of taxes, except as to animals which the General Assembly may deem dangerous to the farming interests.

(6) Extending the time for the assessment or collection of taxes.

(7) Exempting property from taxation.

(8) Remitting, releasing, postponing, or diminishing any obligation or liability of any person, corporation, or association to the Commonwealth or to any political subdivision thereof.

(9) Refunding money lawfully paid into the treasury of the Commonwealth or the treasury of any political subdivision thereof.

(10) Granting from the treasury of the Commonwealth, or granting or authorizing to be granted from the treasury of any political subdivision thereof, any extra compensation to any public officer, servant, agent, or contractor.

(11) For registering voters, conducting elections, or designating the places of voting.

(12) Regulating labor, trade, mining, or manufacturing, or the rate of interest on money.

(13) Granting any pension.

(14) Creating, increasing, or decreasing, or authorizing to be created, increased, or decreased, the salaries, fees, percentages, or allowances of public officers during the term for which they are elected or appointed.

(15) Declaring streams navigable, or authorizing the construction of booms or dams therein, or the removal of obstructions therefrom.

(16) Affecting or regulating fencing or the boundaries of land, or the running at large of stock.

(17) Creating private corporations, or amending, renewing, or extending the charters thereof.

(18) Granting to any private corporation, association, or individual any special or exclusive right, privilege, or immunity.

(19) Naming or changing the name of any private corporation or association.

(20) Remitting the forfeiture of the charter of any private corporation, except upon the condition that such corporation shall thereafter hold its charter subject to the provisions of this Constitution and the laws passed in pursuance thereof.

The General Assembly shall not grant a charter of incorporation to any church or religious denomination, but may secure the title to church property to an extent to be limited by law.

The amendment ratified November 8, 1994 and effective January 1, 1995—Added a new paragraph after paragraph three.

Section 15. General laws.

In all cases enumerated in the preceding section, and in every other case which, in its judgment, may be provided for by general laws, the General Assembly shall enact general laws. Any general law shall be subject to amendment or repeal, but the amendment or partial repeal thereof shall not operate directly or indirectly to enact, and shall not have the effect of enactment of, a special, private, or local law.

No general or special law shall surrender or suspend the right and power of the Commonwealth, or any political subdivision thereof, to tax corporations and corporate property, except as authorized by Article X. No private corporation, association, or individual shall be specially exempted from the operation of any general law, nor shall a general law's operation be suspended for the benefit of any private corporation, association, or individual.

Section 16. Appropriations to religious or charitable bodies.

The General Assembly shall not make any appropriation of public funds, personal property, or real estate to any church or sectarian society, or any association or institution of any kind whatever which is entirely or partly, directly or indirectly, controlled by any church or sectarian society. Nor shall the General Assembly make any like appropriation to any charitable institution which is not owned or controlled by the Commonwealth; the General Assembly may, however, make appropriations to nonsectarian institutions for the reform of youthful criminals and may also authorize counties, cities, or towns to make such appropriations to any charitable institution or association.

Section 17. Impeachment.

The Governor, Lieutenant Governor, Attorney General, judges, members of the State Corporation Commission, and all officers appointed by the Governor or elected by the General Assembly, offending against the Commonwealth by malfeasance in office, corruption, neglect of duty, or other high crime or misdemeanor may be impeached by the House of Delegates and prosecuted before the Senate, which shall have the sole power to try impeachments. When sitting for that purpose, the senators shall be on oath or affirmation, and no person shall be convicted without the concurrence of two-thirds of the senators present. Judgment in case of impeachment shall not extend further than removal from office and disqualification to hold and enjoy any office of honor, trust, or profit under the Commonwealth; but the person convicted shall nevertheless be subject to indictment, trial, judgment, and punishment according to law. The Senate may sit during the recess of the General Assembly for the trial of impeachments.

Section 18. Auditor of Public Accounts.

An Auditor of Public Accounts shall be elected by the joint vote of the two houses of the General Assembly for the term of four years. His powers and duties shall be prescribed by law.

ARTICLE V
Executive

Section 1. Executive power; Governor's term of office.

The chief executive power of the Commonwealth shall be vested in a Governor. He shall hold office for a term commencing upon his inauguration on the Saturday after the second Wednesday in January, next succeeding his election, and ending in the fourth year thereafter immediately upon the inauguration of his successor. He shall be ineligible to the same office for the term next succeeding that for which he was elected, and to any other office during his term of service.

Section 2. Election of Governor.

The Governor shall be elected by the qualified voters of the Commonwealth at the time and place of choosing members of the General Assembly. Returns of the election shall be transmitted, under seal, by the proper officers, to the State Board of Elections, or such other officer or agency as may be designated by law, which shall cause the returns to be opened and the votes to be counted in the manner prescribed by law. The person having the highest number of votes shall be declared elected; but if two or more shall have the highest and an equal number of votes, one of them shall be chosen Governor by a majority of the total membership of the General Assembly. Contested elections for Governor shall be decided by a like vote. The mode of proceeding in such cases shall be prescribed by law.

Section 3. Qualifications of Governor.

No person except a citizen of the United States shall be eligible to the office of Governor; nor shall any person be eligible to that office unless he shall have attained the age of thirty years and have been a resident of the Commonwealth and a registered voter in the Commonwealth for five years next preceding his election.

Section 4. Place of residence and compensation of Governor.

The Governor shall reside at the seat of government. He shall receive for his services a compensation to be prescribed by law, which shall neither be increased nor diminished during the period for which he shall have been elected. While in office he shall receive no other emolument from this or any other government.

Section 5. Legislative responsibilities of Governor.

The Governor shall communicate to the General Assembly, at every regular session, the condition of the Commonwealth, recommend to its consideration such measures as he may deem expedient, and convene the General Assembly on application of two-thirds of the members elected to each house thereof, or when, in his opinion, the interest of the Commonwealth may require.

Section 6. Presentation of bills; powers of Governor; vetoes and amendments.

(a) Every bill which passes the Senate and House of Delegates, before it becomes law, shall be presented to the Governor.

(b) During a regular or special session, the Governor shall have seven days in which to act on the bill after it is presented to him and to exercise one of the three options set out below. If the Governor does not act on the bill, it shall become law without his signature.

(i) The Governor may sign the bill if he approves it, and the bill shall become law.

(ii) The Governor may veto the bill if he objects to it by returning the bill with his objections to the house in which the bill originated. The house shall enter the objections in its journal and reconsider the bill. The house may override the veto by a two-thirds vote of the members present, which two-thirds shall include a majority of the members elected to that house. If the house of origin overrides the Governor's veto, it shall send the bill and Governor's objections to the other house where the bill shall be reconsidered. The second house may override the Governor's veto by a two-thirds vote of the members present, which two-thirds shall include a majority of the members elected to that house. If both houses override the Governor's veto, the bill shall become law without his signature. If either house fails to override the Governor's veto, the veto shall stand and the bill shall not become law.

(iii) The Governor may recommend one or more specific and severable amendments to a bill by returning it with his recommendation to the house in which it originated. The house shall enter the Governor's recommendation in its journal and reconsider the bill. If both houses agree to the Governor's entire recommendation, the bill, as amended, shall become law. Each house may agree to the Governor's amendments by a majority vote of the members present. If both houses agree to the bill in the form originally sent to the Governor by a two-thirds vote of all members present in each house, which two-thirds shall include a majority of the members elected to that house, the original bill shall become law. If the Governor sends down specific and severable amendments then each house may determine, in accordance with its own procedures, whether to act on the Governor's amendments en bloc or individually, or any combination thereof. If the house of origin agrees to one or more of the Governor's amendments, it shall send the bill and the entire recommendation to the other house. The second house may also agree to one or more of the Governor's amendments. If either house fails to agree to the Governor's entire recommendation or fails to agree to at least one of the Governor's amendments agreed to by the other house, the bill, as originally presented to the Governor, shall be returned to the Governor. If both houses agree to one or more amendments but not to the entire recommendation of the Governor, the bill shall be reenrolled with the Governor's amendments agreed to by both houses and shall be returned to the Governor. If the Governor fails to send down specific and severable amendments as determined by the majority vote of the members present in either house, then the bill shall be before that house, in the form originally sent to the Governor and may be acted upon in accordance with Article IV, Section 11 of this Constitution and returned to the Governor. The Governor shall either sign or veto a bill returned as provided in this subsection or, if there are fewer than seven days remaining in the session, as provided in subsection (c).

(c) When there are fewer than seven days remaining in the regular or special session from the date a bill is presented to the Governor and the General Assembly adjourns to a reconvened session, the Governor shall have thirty days from the date of adjournment of the regular or special session in which to act on the bills presented to him and to exercise one of the three options set out below. If the Governor does not act on any bill, it shall become law without his signature.

(i) The Governor may sign the bill if he approves it, and the bill shall become law.

(ii) The Governor may veto the bill if he objects to it by returning the bill with his objections to the house in which the bill originated. The same procedures for overriding his veto are applicable as stated in subsection (b) for bills vetoed during the session.

(iii) The Governor may recommend one or more specific and severable amendments to a bill by returning it with his recommendation to the house in which it originated. The same procedures for considering his recommendation are applicable as stated in subsection (b) (iii) for bills returned with his recommendation. The

Governor shall either sign or veto a bill returned to him from a reconvened session. If the Governor vetoes the bill, the veto shall stand and the bill shall not become law. If the Governor does not act on the bill within thirty days after the adjournment of the reconvened session, the bill shall become law without his signature.

(d) The Governor shall have the power to veto any particular item or items of an appropriation bill, but the veto shall not affect the item or items to which he does not object. The item or items objected to shall not take effect except in the manner provided in this section for a bill vetoed by the Governor.

(e) In all cases set forth above, the names of the members voting for and against the bill, the amendment or amendments to the bill, or the item or items of an appropriation bill shall be entered on the journal of each house.

The amendment ratified November 8, 1994 and effective January 1, 1995—Rewrote the section to provide that the Governor may offer only one set of amendments to any bill, to require the Governor to take action to veto a bill, to allow the General Assembly to sever the Governor's amendments, acting on them individually or en bloc, and to allow the General Assembly to propose its own amendments if it determines the Governor's amendments are not severable. [The amendment to this section ratified November 4, 1980 and effective January 1, 1981 was superseded by the 1994 amendment.]

Section 7. Executive and administrative powers.

The Governor shall take care that the laws be faithfully executed.

The Governor shall be commander-in-chief of the armed forces of the Commonwealth and shall have power to embody such forces to repel invasion, suppress insurrection, and enforce the execution of the laws.

The Governor shall conduct, either in person or in such manner as shall be prescribed by law, all intercourse with other and foreign states.

The Governor shall have power to fill vacancies in all offices of the Commonwealth for the filling of which the Constitution and laws make no other provision. If such office be one filled by the election of the people, the appointee shall hold office until the next general election, and thereafter until his successor qualifies, according to law. The General Assembly shall, if it is in session, fill vacancies in all offices which are filled by election by that body.

Gubernatorial appointments to fill vacancies in offices which are filled by election by the General Assembly or by appointment by the Governor which is subject to confirmation by the Senate or the General Assembly, made during the recess of the General Assembly, shall expire at the end of thirty days after the commencement of the next session of the General Assembly.

Section 8. Information from administrative officers.

The Governor may require information in writing, under oath, from any officer of any executive or administrative department, office, or agency, or any public institution upon any subject relating to their respective departments, offices, agencies, or public institutions; and he may inspect at any time their official books, accounts, and vouch-

Appendix 237

ers, and ascertain the conditions of the public funds in their charge, and in that connection may employ accountants. He may require the opinion in writing of the Attorney General upon any question of law affecting the official duties of the Governor.

Section 9. Administrative organization.

The functions, powers, and duties of the administrative departments and divisions and of the agencies of the Commonwealth within the legislative and executive branches may be prescribed by law.

Section 10. Appointment and removal of administrative officers.

Except as may be otherwise provided in this Constitution, the Governor shall appoint each officer serving as the head of an administrative department or division of the executive branch of the government, subject to such confirmation as the General Assembly may prescribe. Each officer appointed by the Governor pursuant to this section shall have such professional qualifications as may be prescribed by law and shall serve at the pleasure of the Governor.

Section 11. Effect of refusal of General Assembly to confirm an appointment by the Governor.

No person appointed to any office by the Governor, whose appointment is subject to confirmation by the General Assembly, under the provisions of this Constitution or any statute, shall enter upon, or continue in, office after the General Assembly shall have refused to confirm his appointment, nor shall such person be eligible for reappointment during the recess of the General Assembly to fill the vacancy caused by such refusal to confirm.

Section 12. Executive clemency.

The Governor shall have power to remit fines and penalties under such rules and regulations as may be prescribed by law; to grant reprieves and pardons after conviction except when the prosecution has been carried on by the House of Delegates; to remove political disabilities consequent upon conviction for offenses committed prior or subsequent to the adoption of this Constitution; and to commute capital punishment.

He shall communicate to the General Assembly, at each regular session, particulars of every case of fine or penalty remitted, of reprieve or pardon granted, and of punishment commuted, with his reasons for remitting, granting, or commuting the same.

Section 13. Lieutenant Governor; election and qualifications.

A Lieutenant Governor shall be elected at the same time and for the same term as the Governor, and his qualifications and the manner and ascertainment of his election, in all respects, shall be the same, except that there shall be no limit on the terms of the Lieutenant Governor.

Section 14. Duties and compensation of Lieutenant Governor.

The Lieutenant Governor shall be President of the Senate but shall have no vote except in case of an equal division. He shall receive for his services a compensation to be prescribed by law, which shall not be increased nor diminished during the period for which he shall have been elected.

Section 15. Attorney General.

An Attorney General shall be elected by the qualified voters of the Commonwealth at the same time and for the same term as the Governor; and the fact of his election shall be ascertained in the same manner. No person shall be eligible for election or appointment to the office of Attorney General unless he is a citizen of the United States, has attained the age of thirty years, and has the qualifications required for a judge of a court of record. He shall perform such duties and receive such compensation as may be prescribed by law, which compensation shall neither be increased nor diminished during the period for which he shall have been elected. There shall be no limit on the terms of the Attorney General.

Section 16. Succession to the office of Governor.

When the Governor-elect is disqualified, resigns, or dies following his election but prior to taking office, the Lieutenant Governor-elect shall succeed to the office of Governor for the full term. When the Governor-elect fails to assume office for any other reason, the Lieutenant Governor-elect shall serve as Acting Governor.

Whenever the Governor transmits to the President pro tempore of the Senate and the Speaker of the House of Delegates his written declaration that he is unable to discharge the powers and duties of his office and until he transmits to them a written declaration to the contrary, such powers and duties shall be discharged by the Lieutenant Governor as Acting Governor.

Whenever the Attorney General, the President pro tempore of the Senate, and the Speaker of the House of Delegates, or a majority of the total membership of the General Assembly, transmit to the Clerk of the Senate and the Clerk of the House of Delegates their written declaration that the Governor is unable to discharge the powers and duties of his office, the Lieutenant Governor shall immediately assume the powers and duties of the office as Acting Governor.

Thereafter, when the Governor transmits to the Clerk of the Senate and the Clerk of the House of Delegates his written declaration that no inability exists, he shall resume the powers and duties of his office unless the Attorney General, the President pro tempore of the Senate, and the Speaker of the House of Delegates, or a majority of the total membership of the General Assembly, transmit within four days to the Clerk of the Senate and the Clerk of the House of Delegates their written declaration that the Governor is unable to discharge the powers and duties of his office. Thereupon the General Assembly shall decide the issue, convening within forty-eight hours for that purpose if not already in session. If within twenty-one days after receipt of the latter declaration or, if the General Assembly is not in session, within twenty-one days after the General Assembly is required to convene, the General Assembly determines by three-fourths vote of the elected membership of each house of the General Assembly that the Governor is unable to discharge the powers and duties of his office, the Lieutenant Governor shall become Governor; otherwise, the Governor shall resume the powers and duties of his office.

In the case of the removal of the Governor from office or in the case of his disqualification, death, or resignation, the Lieutenant Governor shall become Governor.

If a vacancy exists in the office of Lieutenant Governor when the Lieutenant Governor is to succeed to the office of Governor or to serve as Acting Governor, the Attorney General, if he is eligible to serve as Governor, shall succeed to the office of Governor for the unexpired term or serve as Acting Governor. If the Attorney General is ineligible to serve as Governor, the Speaker of the House of Delegates, if he is eligible to serve as Governor, shall succeed to the office of Governor for the unexpired term or serve as Acting Governor. If a vacancy exists in the office of the Speaker of the House of Delegates or if the Speaker of the House of Delegates is ineligible to serve as Governor, the House of Delegates shall convene and fill the vacancy.

Section 17. Commissions and grants.

Commissions and grants shall run in the name of the Commonwealth of Virginia, and be attested by the Governor, with the seal of the Commonwealth annexed.

ARTICLE VI
Judiciary

Section 1. Judicial power; jurisdiction.

The judicial power of the Commonwealth shall be vested in a Supreme Court and in such other courts of original or appellate jurisdiction subordinate to the Supreme Court as the General Assembly may from time to time establish. Trial courts of general jurisdiction, appellate courts, and such other courts as shall be so designated by the General Assembly shall be known as courts of record.

The Supreme Court shall, by virtue of this Constitution, have original jurisdiction in cases of habeas corpus, mandamus, and prohibition, in matters of judicial censure, retirement, and removal under Section 10 of this article, and to answer questions of state law certified by a court of the United States or the highest appellate court of any other state. All other jurisdiction of the Supreme Court shall be appellate. Subject to such reasonable rules as may be prescribed as to the course of appeals and other procedural matters, the Supreme Court shall, by virtue of this Constitution, have appellate jurisdiction in cases involving the constitutionality of a law under this Constitution or the Constitution of the United States and in cases involving the life or liberty of any person.

The General Assembly may allow the Commonwealth the right to appeal in all cases, including those involving the life or liberty of a person, provided such appeal would not otherwise violate this Constitution or the Constitution of the United States.

Subject to the foregoing limitations, the General Assembly shall have the power to determine the original and appellate jurisdiction of the courts of the Commonwealth.

The amendment ratified November 4, 1986 and effective December 1, 1986—In paragraph two, after "mandamus, and prohibition" deleted "and" and added to the sentence ", and to answer questions of state law certified by a court of the United States . . .".

The amendment ratified November 4, 1986 and effective December 1, 1986—In paragraph three, after "relating to the State revenue." added the last sentence "The General Assembly may also allow the Commonwealth . . .".

The amendment ratified November 5, 1996 and effective January 1, 1997—Deleted the third paragraph: "No appeal shall be allowed to the Commonwealth . . ." and added a next-to-the-last paragraph: "The General Assembly may allow the Commonwealth . . .".

Section 2. Supreme Court.

The Supreme Court shall consist of seven justices. The General Assembly may, if three-fifths of the elected membership of each house so vote at two successive regular sessions, increase or decrease the number of justices of the Court, provided that the Court shall consist of no fewer than seven and no more than eleven justices. The Court may sit and render final judgment en banc or in divisions as may be prescribed by law. No decision shall become the judgment of the Court, however, except on the concurrence of at least three justices, and no law shall be declared unconstitutional under either this Constitution or the Constitution of the United States except on the concurrence of at least a majority of all justices of the Supreme Court.

Section 3. Selection of Chief Justice.

The Chief Justice shall be selected from among the justices in a manner provided by law.

Section 4. Administration of the judicial system.

The Chief Justice of the Supreme Court shall be the administrative head of the judicial system. He may temporarily assign any judge of a court of record to any other court of record except the Supreme Court and may assign a retired judge of a court of record, with his consent, to any court of record except the Supreme Court. The General Assembly may adopt such additional measures as it deems desirable for the improvement of the administration of justice by the courts and for the expedition of judicial business.

Section 5. Rules of practice and procedure.

The Supreme Court shall have the authority to make rules governing the course of appeals and the practice and procedures to be used in the courts of the Commonwealth, but such rules shall not be in conflict with the general law as the same shall, from time to time, be established by the General Assembly.

Section 6. Opinions and judgments of the Supreme Court.

When a judgment or decree is reversed, modified, or affirmed by the Supreme Court, or when original cases are resolved on their merits, the reasons for the Court's action shall be stated in writing and preserved with the record of the case. The Court may, but need not, remand a case for a new trial. In any civil case, it may enter final judgment, except that the award in a suit or action for unliquidated damages shall not be increased or diminished.

Section 7. Selection and qualification of judges.

The justices of the Supreme Court shall be chosen by the vote of a majority of the members elected to each house of the General Assembly for terms of twelve years. The judges of all other courts of record shall be chosen by the vote of a majority of the members elected to each house of the General Assembly for terms of eight years. During any vacancy which may exist while the General Assembly is not in session, the Governor may appoint a successor to serve until thirty days after the commencement of the next session of the General Assembly. Upon election by the General Assembly, a new justice or judge shall begin service of a full term.

All justices of the Supreme Court and all judges of other courts of record shall be residents of the Commonwealth and shall, at least five years prior to their appointment or election, have been admitted to the bar of the Commonwealth. Each judge of a trial court of record shall during his term of office reside within the jurisdiction of one of the courts to which he was appointed or elected; provided, however, that where the boundary of such jurisdiction is changed by annexation or otherwise, no judge thereof shall thereby become disqualified from office or ineligible for reelection if, except for such annexation or change, he would otherwise be qualified.

Section 8. Additional judicial personnel.

The General Assembly may provide for additional judicial personnel, such as judges of courts not of record and magistrates or justices of the peace, and may prescribe their jurisdiction and provide the manner in which they shall be selected and the terms for which they shall serve.

The General Assembly may confer upon the clerks of the several courts having probate jurisdiction, jurisdiction of the probate of wills and of the appointment and qualification of guardians, personal representatives, curators, appraisers, and committees of persons adjudged insane or convicted of felony, and in the matter of the substitution of trustees.

Section 9. Commission; compensation; retirement.

All justices of the Supreme Court and all judges of other courts of record shall be commissioned by the Governor. They shall receive such salaries and allowances as shall be prescribed by the General Assembly, which shall be apportioned between the Commonwealth and its cities and counties in the manner provided by law. Unless expressly prohibited or limited by the General Assembly, cities and counties shall be permitted to supplement from local funds the salaries of any judges serving within their geographical boundaries. The salary of any justice or judge shall not be diminished during his term of office.

The General Assembly may enact such laws as it deems necessary for the retirement of justices and judges, with such conditions, compensation, and duties as it may prescribe. The General Assembly may also provide for the mandatory retirement of justices and judges after they reach a prescribed age, beyond which they shall not serve, regardless of the term to which elected or appointed.

Section 10. Disabled and unfit judges.

The General Assembly shall create a Judicial Inquiry and Review Commission consisting of members of the judiciary, the bar, and the public and vested with the power to investigate charges which would be the basis for retirement, censure, or removal of a judge. The Commission shall be authorized to conduct hearings and to subpoena witnesses and documents. Proceedings before the Commission shall be confidential.

If the Commission finds the charges to be well-founded, it may file a formal complaint before the Supreme Court.

Upon the filing of a complaint, the Supreme Court shall conduct a hearing in open court and, upon a finding of disability which is or is likely to be permanent and which seriously interferes with the performance by the judge of his duties, shall retire the judge from office. A judge retired under this authority shall be considered for the purpose of retirement benefits to have retired voluntarily.

If the Supreme Court after the hearing on the complaint finds that the judge has engaged in misconduct while in office, or that he has persistently failed to perform the duties of his office, or that he has engaged in conduct prejudicial to the proper administration of justice, it shall censure him or shall remove him from office. A judge removed under this authority shall not be entitled to retirement benefits, but only to the return of contributions made by him, together with any income accrued thereon. This section shall apply to justices of the Supreme Court, to judges of other courts of record, and to members of the State Corporation Commission. The General Assembly also may provide by general law for the retirement, censure, or removal of judges of any court not of record, or other personnel exercising judicial functions.

Section 11. Incompatible activities.

No justice or judge of a court of record shall, during his continuance in office, engage in the practice of law within or without the Commonwealth, or seek or accept any nonjudicial elective office, or hold any other office of public trust, or engage in any other incompatible activity.

Section 12. Limitation; judicial appointment.

No judge shall be granted the power to make any appointment of any local governmental official elected by the voters except to fill a vacancy in office pending the next ensuing general election or, if the vacancy occurs within one hundred twenty days prior to such election, pending the second ensuing general election, unless such election falls within sixty days of the end of the term of the office to be filled.

The amendment ratified November 2, 1976 and effective January 1, 1977—At the end of the section, after the word "election" added the language ", unless such election falls within sixty days of the end of the term of the office to be filled".

ARTICLE VII
Local Government

Section 1. Definitions.

As used in this article (1) "county" means any existing county or any such unit hereafter created, (2) "city" means an independent incorporated community which became a city as provided by law before noon on the first day of July, nineteen hundred seventy-one, or which has within defined boundaries a population of 5,000 or more and which has become a city as provided by law, (3) "town" means any existing town or an incorporated community within one or more counties which became a town before noon, July one, nineteen hundred seventy-one, as provided by law or which has within defined boundaries a population of 1,000 or more and which has become a town as provided by law, (4) "regional government" means a unit of general government organized as provided by law within defined boundaries, as determined by the General Assembly, (5) "general law" means a law which on its effective date applies alike to all counties, cities, towns, or regional governments or to a reasonable classification thereof, and (6) "special act" means a law applicable to a county, city, town, or regional government and for enactment shall require an affirmative vote of two-thirds of the members elected to each house of the General Assembly.

The General Assembly may increase by general law the population minima provided in this article for cities and towns. Any county which on the effective date of this Constitution had adopted an optional form of government pursuant to a valid statute that does not meet the general law requirements of this article may continue its form of government without regard to such general law requirements until it adopts a form of government provided in conformity with this article. In this article, whenever the General Assembly is authorized or required to act by general law, no special act for that purpose shall be valid unless this article so provides.

The amendment ratified November 7, 1972—Added language to the definition of city in (2) to include those communities which became cities before July 1, 1971. Added language to the definition of town in (3) to include those communities which became towns before July 1, 1971.

Section 2. Organization and government.

The General Assembly shall provide by general law for the organization, government, powers, change of boundaries, consolidation, and dissolution of counties, cities, towns, and regional governments. The General Assembly may also provide by general law optional plans of government for counties, cities, or towns to be effective if approved by a majority vote of the qualified voters voting on any such plan in any such county, city, or town.

The General Assembly may also provide by special act for the organization, government, and powers of any county, city, town, or regional government, including such powers of legislation, taxation, and assessment as the General Assembly may determine, but no such special act shall be adopted which provides for the extension or contraction of boundaries of any county, city, or town.

Every law providing for the organization of a regional government shall, in addition to any other requirements imposed by the General Assembly, require the approval of the organization of the regional government by a majority vote of the qualified voters voting thereon in each county and city which is to participate in the regional government and of the voters voting thereon in a part of a county or city where only the part is to participate.

Section 3. Powers.

The General Assembly may provide by general law or special act that any county, city, town, or other unit of government may exercise any of its powers or perform any of its functions and may participate in the financing thereof jointly or in cooperation with the Commonwealth or any other unit of government within or without the Commonwealth. The General Assembly may provide by general law or special act for transfer to or sharing with a regional government of any services, functions, and related facilities of any county, city, town, or other unit of government within the boundaries of such regional government.

Section 4. County and city officers.

There shall be elected by the qualified voters of each county and city a treasurer, a sheriff, an attorney for the Commonwealth, a clerk, who shall be clerk of the court in the office of which deeds are recorded, and a commissioner of revenue. The duties and compensation of such officers shall be prescribed by general law or special act.

Regular elections for such officers shall be held on Tuesday after the first Monday in November. Such officers shall take office on the first day of the following January unless otherwise provided by law and shall hold their respective offices for the term of four years, except that the clerk shall hold office for eight years.

The General Assembly may provide for county or city officers or methods of their selection, including permission for two or more units of government to share the officers required by this section, without regard to the provisions of this section, either (1) by general law to become effective in any county or city when submitted to the qualified voters thereof in an election held for such purpose and approved by a majority of those voting thereon in each such county or city, or (2) by special act upon the request, made after such an election, of each county or city affected. No such law shall reduce the term of any person holding an office at the time the election is held. A county or city not required to have or to elect such officers prior to the effective date of this Constitution shall not be so required by this section.

The General Assembly may provide by general law or special act for additional officers and for the terms of their office.

Section 5. County, city, and town governing bodies.

The governing body of each county, city, or town shall be elected by the qualified voters of such county, city, or town in the manner provided by law.

If the members are elected by district, the district shall be composed of contiguous and compact territory and shall be so constituted as to give, as nearly as is practicable, representation in proportion to the population of the district. When members are so elected by district, the governing body of any county, city, or town may, in a manner provided by law, increase or diminish the number, and change the boundaries, of districts, and shall in 1971 and every ten years thereafter, and also whenever the boundaries of such districts are changed, reapportion the representation in the governing body among the districts in a manner provided by law. Whenever the governing body of any such unit shall fail to perform the duties so prescribed in the manner herein directed, a suit shall lie on behalf of any citizen thereof to compel performance by the governing body.

Unless otherwise provided by law, the governing body of each city or town shall be elected on the second Tuesday in June and take office on the first day of the following September. Unless otherwise provided by law, the governing body of each county shall be elected on the Tuesday after the first Monday in November and take office on the first day of the following January.

Section 6. Multiple offices.

Unless two or more units exercise functions jointly as authorized in Sections 3 and 4, no person shall at the same time hold more than one office mentioned in this article. No member of a governing body shall be eligible, during the term of office for which he was elected or appointed, to hold any office filled by the governing body by election or appointment, except that a member of a governing body may be named a member of such other boards, commissions, and bodies as may be permitted by general law and except that a member of a governing body may be elected or appointed to fill a vacancy in the office of mayor or board chairman if permitted by general law or special act.

The amendment ratified November 6, 1984 and effective January 1, 1985—After "as may be permitted by general law" added "and except that a member of a governing body may be elected or appointed to fill a vacancy in the office of mayor or board chairman if permitted by general law or special act".

Section 7. Procedures.

No ordinance or resolution appropriating money exceeding the sum of five hundred dollars, imposing taxes, or authorizing the borrowing of money shall be passed except by a recorded affirmative vote of a majority of all members elected to the governing body. In case of the veto of such an ordinance or resolution, where the power of veto exists, it shall require for passage thereafter a recorded affirmative vote of two-thirds of all members elected to the governing body.

On final vote on any ordinance or resolution, the name of each member voting and how he voted shall be recorded.

Section 8. Consent to use public property.

No street railway, gas, water, steam or electric heating, electric light or power, cold storage, compressed air, viaduct, conduit, telephone, or bridge company, nor any corporation, association, person, or partnership engaged in these or like enterprises shall be permitted to use the streets, alleys, or public grounds of a city or town without the previous consent of the corporate authorities of such city or town.

Section 9. Sale of property and granting of franchises by cities and towns.

No rights of a city or town in and to its waterfront, wharf property, public landings, wharves, docks, streets, avenues, parks, bridges, or other public places, or its gas, water, or electric works shall be sold except by an ordinance or resolution passed by a recorded affirmative vote of three-fourths of all members elected to the governing body.

No franchise, lease, or right of any kind to use any such public property or any other public property or easement of any description in a manner not permitted to the general public shall be granted for a longer period than forty years, except for air rights together with easements for columns of support, which may be granted for a period not exceeding sixty years. Before granting any such franchise or privilege for a term in excess of five years, except for a trunk railway, the city or town shall, after due advertisement, publicly receive bids therefor. Such grant, and any contract in pursuance thereof, may provide that upon the termination of the grant, the plant as well as the property, if any, of the grantee in the streets, avenues, and other public places shall thereupon, without compensation to the grantee, or upon the payment of a fair valuation therefor, become the property of the said city or town; but the grantee shall be entitled to no payment by reason of the value of the franchise. Any such plant or property acquired by a city or town may be sold or leased or, unless prohibited by general law, maintained, controlled, and operated by such city or town. Every such grant shall specify the mode of determining any valuation therein provided for and shall make adequate provisions by way of forfeiture of the grant, or otherwise, to secure efficiency of public service at reasonable rates and the maintenance of the property in good order throughout the term of the grant.

Section 10. Debt.

(a) No city or town shall issue any bonds or other interest-bearing obligations which, including existing indebtedness, shall at any time exceed ten per centum of the assessed valuation of the real estate in the city or town subject to taxation, as shown by the last preceding assessment for taxes. In determining the limitation for a city or town there shall not be included the following classes of indebtedness:

(1) Certificates of indebtedness, revenue bonds, or other obligations issued in anticipation of the collection of the revenues of such city or town for the then current year; provided that such certificates, bonds, or other obligations mature within one year from the date of their issue, be not past due, and do not exceed the revenue for such year.

(2) Bonds pledging the full faith and credit of such city or town authorized by an ordinance enacted in accordance with Section 7, and approved by the affirmative vote of the qualified voters of the city or town voting upon the question of their issuance, for a supply of water or other specific undertaking from which the city or town may derive a revenue; but from and after a period to be determined by the governing body not exceeding five years from the date of such election, whenever and for so long as such undertaking fails to produce sufficient revenue to pay for cost of operation and administration (including interest on bonds issued therefor), the cost of insurance against loss by injury to persons or property, and an annual amount to be placed into a sinking fund sufficient to pay the bonds at or before maturity, all outstanding bonds issued on account of such undertaking shall be included in determining such limitation.

(3) Bonds of a city or town the principal and interest on which are payable exclusively from the revenues and receipts of a water system or other specific undertaking or undertakings from which the city or town may derive a revenue or secured, solely or together with such revenues, by contributions of other units of government.

(4) Contract obligations of a city or town to provide payments over a period of more than one year to any publicly owned or controlled regional project, if the project has been authorized by an interstate compact or if the General Assembly by general law or special act has authorized an exclusion for such project purposes.

(b) No debt shall be contracted by or on behalf of any county or district thereof or by or on behalf of any regional government or district thereof except by authority conferred by the General Assembly by general law. The General Assembly shall not authorize any such debt, except the classes described in paragraphs (1) and (3) of subsection (a), refunding bonds, and bonds issued, with the consent of the school board and the governing body of the county, by or on behalf of a county or district thereof for capital projects for school purposes and sold to the Literary Fund, the Virginia Supplemental Retirement System, or other State agency prescribed by law, unless in the general law authorizing the same, provision be made for submission to the qualified voters of the county or district thereof or the region or district thereof, as the case may be, for approval or rejection by a majority vote of the qualified voters voting in an election on the question of contracting such debt. Such approval shall be a prerequisite to contracting such debt.

Any county may, upon approval by the affirmative vote of the qualified voters of the county voting in an election on the question, elect to be treated as a city for the purposes of issuing its bonds under this section. If a county so elects, it shall thereafter be subject to all of the benefits and limitations of this section applicable to cities, but in determining the limitation for a county there shall be included, unless otherwise excluded under this section, indebtedness of any town or district in that county empowered to levy taxes on real estate.

The amendment ratified November 4, 1980 and effective January 1, 1981—In subsection (a) substituted "ten per centum" for "eighteen per centum".

ARTICLE VIII
Education

Section 1. Public schools of high quality to be maintained.

The General Assembly shall provide for a system of free public elementary and secondary schools for all children of school age throughout the Commonwealth, and shall seek to ensure that an educational program of high quality is established and continually maintained.

Section 2. Standards of quality; State and local support of public schools.

Standards of quality for the several school divisions shall be determined and prescribed from time to time by the Board of Education, subject to revision only by the General Assembly.

The General Assembly shall determine the manner in which funds are to be provided for the cost of maintaining an educational program meeting the prescribed standards of quality, and shall provide for the apportionment of the cost of such program between the Commonwealth and the local units of government comprising such school divisions. Each unit of local government shall provide its portion of such cost by local taxes or from other available funds.

Section 3. Compulsory education; free textbooks.

The General Assembly shall provide for the compulsory elementary and secondary education of every eligible child of appropriate age, such eligibility and age to be determined by law. It shall ensure that textbooks are provided at no cost to each child attending public school whose parent or guardian is financially unable to furnish them.

Section 4. Board of Education.

The general supervision of the public school system shall be vested in a Board of Education of nine members, to be appointed by the Governor, subject to confirmation by the General Assembly. Each appointment shall be for four years, except that those to fill vacancies shall be for the unexpired terms. Terms shall be staggered, so that no more than three regular appointments shall be made in the same year.

Section 5. Powers and duties of the Board of Education.

The powers and duties of the Board of Education shall be as follows:

(a) Subject to such criteria and conditions as the General Assembly may prescribe, the Board shall divide the Commonwealth into school divisions of such geographical area and school-age population as will promote the realization of the prescribed standards of quality, and shall periodically review the adequacy of existing school divisions for this purpose.

(b) It shall make annual reports to the Governor and the General Assembly concerning the condition and needs of public education in the Commonwealth, and shall in such report identify any school divisions which have failed to establish and maintain schools meeting the prescribed standards of quality.

(c) It shall certify to the school board of each division a list of qualified persons for the office of division superintendent of schools, one of whom shall be selected to fill the post by the division school board. In the event a division school board fails to select a division superintendent within the time prescribed by law, the Board of Education shall appoint him.

(d) It shall have authority to approve textbooks and instructional aids and materials for use in courses in the public schools of the Commonwealth.

(e) Subject to the ultimate authority of the General Assembly, the Board shall have primary responsibility and authority for effectuating the educational policy set forth in this article, and it shall have such other powers and duties as may be prescribed by law.

Section 6. Superintendent of Public Instruction.

A Superintendent of Public Instruction, who shall be an experienced educator, shall be appointed by the Governor, subject to confirmation by the General Assembly, for a term coincident with that of the Governor making the appointment, but the General Assembly may alter by statute this method of selection and term of office. The powers and duties of the Superintendent shall be prescribed by law.

Section 7. School boards.

The supervision of schools in each school division shall be vested in a school board, to be composed of members selected in the manner, for the term, possessing the qualifications, and to the number provided by law.

‎‎

Section 8. The Literary Fund.

The General Assembly shall set apart as a permanent and perpetual school fund the present Literary Fund; the proceeds of all public lands donated by Congress for free public school purposes, of all escheated property, of all waste and unappropriated lands, of all property accruing to the Commonwealth by forfeiture except as hereinafter provided, of all fines collected for offenses committed against the Commonwealth, and of the annual interest on the Literary Fund; and such other sums as the General Assembly may appropriate. But so long as the principal of the Fund totals as much as eighty million dollars, the General Assembly may set aside all or any part of additional moneys received into its principal for public school purposes, including the teachers retirement fund.

The General Assembly may provide by general law an exemption from this section for the proceeds from the sale of all property seized and forfeited to the Commonwealth for a violation of the criminal laws of this Commonwealth proscribing the manufacture, sale or distribution of a controlled substance or marijuana. Such proceeds shall be paid into the state treasury and shall be distributed by law for the purpose of promoting law enforcement.

The Literary Fund shall be held and administered by the Board of Education in such manner as may be provided by law. The General Assembly may authorize the Board to borrow other funds against assets of the Literary Fund as collateral, such borrowing not to involve the full faith and credit of the Commonwealth.

The principal of the Fund shall include assets of the Fund in other funds or authorities which are repayable to the Fund.

The amendment ratified November 6, 1990 and effective January 1, 1991—In paragraph one, after "forfeiture" added "except as hereinafter provided". Added a new paragraph after paragraph one.

Section 9. Other educational institutions.

The General Assembly may provide for the establishment, maintenance, and operation of any educational institutions which are desirable for the intellectual, cultural, and occupational development of the people of this Commonwealth. The governance of such institutions, and the status and powers of their boards of visitors or other governing bodies, shall be as provided by law.

Section 10. State appropriations prohibited to schools or institutions of learning not owned or exclusively controlled by the State or some subdivision thereof; exceptions to rule.

No appropriation of public funds shall be made to any school or institution of learning not owned or exclusively controlled by the State or some political subdivision thereof; provided, first, that the General Assembly may, and the governing bodies of the several counties, cities and towns may, subject to such limitations as may be imposed by the General Assembly, appropriate funds for educational purposes which may be expended in furtherance of elementary, secondary, collegiate or graduate education of Virginia students in public and nonsectarian private schools and institutions of learning, in addition to those owned or exclusively controlled by the State or any such county, city or town; second, that the General Assembly may appropriate funds to an agency, or to a school or institution of learning owned or controlled by an agency, created and established by two or more States under a joint agreement to which this State is a party for the purpose of providing educational facilities for the citizens of the several States joining in such agreement; third, that counties, cities, towns, and districts may make appropriations to nonsectarian schools of manual, industrial, or technical training, and also to any school or institution of learning owned or exclusively controlled by such county, city, town, or school district.

Section 11. Aid to nonpublic higher education.

The General Assembly may provide for loans to, and grants to or on behalf of, students attending nonprofit institutions of higher education in the Commonwealth whose primary purpose is to provide collegiate or graduate education and not to provide religious training or theological education. The General Assembly may also provide for a State agency or authority to assist in borrowing money for construction of educational facilities at such institutions, provided that the Commonwealth shall not be liable for any debt created by such borrowing. The General Assembly may also provide for the Commonwealth or any political subdivision thereof to contract with such institutions for the provision of educational or other related services.

The amendment ratified November 5, 1974 and effective January 1, 1975—Provided for "grants to or on behalf of" in addition to loans to students, in the first sentence. Added the last sentence to permit "the Commonwealth or any political subdivision thereof to contract with" nonprofit institutions of higher education.

ARTICLE IX
Corporations

Section 1. State Corporation Commission.

There shall be a permanent commission which shall be known as the State Corporation Commission and which shall consist of three members. The General Assembly may, by majority vote of the members elected to each house, increase the size of the Commission to no more than five members. Members of the Commission shall be elected by the General Assembly and shall serve for regular terms of six years. At least one member of the Commission shall have the qualifications prescribed for judges of courts of record, and any Commissioner may be impeached or removed in the manner provided for the impeachment or removal of judges of courts of record. The General Assembly may enact such laws as it deems necessary for the retirement of the

Commissioners, with such conditions, compensation, and duties as it may prescribe. The General Assembly may also provide for the mandatory retirement of Commissioners after they reach a prescribed age, beyond which they shall not serve, regardless of the term to which elected or appointed. Whenever a vacancy in the Commission shall occur or exist when the General Assembly is in session, the General Assembly shall elect a successor for such unexpired term. If the General Assembly is not in session, the Governor shall forthwith appoint pro tempore a qualified person to fill the vacancy for a term ending thirty days after the commencement of the next regular session of the General Assembly and the General Assembly shall elect a successor for such unexpired term.

The Commission shall annually elect one of its members chairman. Its subordinates and employees, and the manner of their appointment and removal, shall be as provided by law, except that its heads of divisions and assistant heads of divisions shall be appointed and subject to removal by the Commission.

Section 2. Powers and duties of the Commission.

Subject to the provisions of this Constitution and to such requirements as may be prescribed by law, the Commission shall be the department of government through which shall be issued all charters, and amendments or extensions thereof, of domestic corporations and all licenses of foreign corporations to do business in this Commonwealth.

Except as may be otherwise prescribed by this Constitution or by law, the Commission shall be charged with the duty of administering the laws made in pursuance of this Constitution for the regulation and control of corporations doing business in this Commonwealth. Subject to such criteria and other requirements as may be prescribed by law, the Commission shall have the power and be charged with the duty of regulating the rates, charges, and services and, except as may be otherwise authorized by this Constitution or by general law, the facilities of railroad, telephone, gas, and electric companies.

The Commission shall in proceedings before it ensure that the interests of the consumers of the Commonwealth are represented, unless the General Assembly otherwise provides for representation of such interests.

The Commission shall have such other powers and duties not inconsistent with this Constitution as may be prescribed by law.

Section 3. Procedures of the Commission.

Before promulgating any general order, rule, or regulation, the Commission shall give reasonable notice of its contents.

In all matters within the jurisdiction of the Commission, it shall have the powers of a court of record to administer oaths, to compel the attendance of witnesses and the production of documents, to punish for contempt, and to enforce compliance with its lawful orders or requirements by adjudging and enforcing by its own appropriate process such fines or other penalties as may be prescribed or authorized by law. Before the Commission shall enter any finding, order, or judgment against a party it shall afford such party reasonable notice of the time and place at which he shall be afforded an opportunity to introduce evidence and be heard.

The Commission may prescribe its own rules of practice and procedure not inconsistent with those made by the General Assembly. The General Assembly shall have the power to adopt such rules, to amend, modify, or set aside the Commission's rules, or to substitute rules of its own.

Section 4. Appeals from actions of the Commission.

The Commonwealth, any party in interest, or any party aggrieved by any final finding, order, or judgment of the Commission shall have, of right, an appeal to the Supreme Court. The method of taking and prosecuting an appeal from any action of the Commission shall be prescribed by law or by the rules of the Supreme Court. All appeals from the Commission shall be to the Supreme Court only.

No other court of the Commonwealth shall have jurisdiction to review, reverse, correct, or annul any action of the Commission or to enjoin or restrain it in the performance of its official duties, provided, however, that the writs of mandamus and prohibition shall lie from the Supreme Court to the Commission.

Section 5. Foreign corporations.

No foreign corporation shall be authorized to carry on in this Commonwealth the business of, or to exercise any of the powers or functions of, a public service enterprise, or be permitted to do anything which domestic corporations are prohibited from doing, or be relieved from compliance with any of the requirements made of similar domestic corporations by the Constitution and laws of this Commonwealth. However, nothing in this section shall restrict the power of the General Assembly to enact such laws specially applying to foreign corporations as the General Assembly may deem appropriate.

Section 6. Corporations subject to general laws.

The creation of corporations, and the extension and amendment of charters whether heretofore or hereafter granted, shall be provided for by general law, and no charter shall be granted, amended, or extended by special act, nor shall authority in such matters be conferred upon any tribunal or officer, except to ascertain whether the applicants have, by complying with the requirements of the law, entitled themselves to the charter, amendment, or extension applied for and to issue or refuse the same accordingly. Such general laws may be amended, repealed, or modified by the General Assembly. Every corporation chartered in this Commonwealth shall be deemed to hold its charter and all amendments thereof under the provisions of, and subject to all the requirements, terms, and conditions of, this Constitution and any laws passed in pursuance thereof. The police power of the Commonwealth to regulate the affairs of corporations, the same as individuals, shall never be abridged.

Section 7. Exclusions from term "corporation" or "company."

The term "corporation" or "company" as used in this article shall exclude all municipal corporations, other political subdivisions, and public institutions owned or controlled by the Commonwealth.

ARTICLE X
Taxation and Finance

Section 1. Taxable property; uniformity; classification and segregation.

All property, except as hereinafter provided, shall be taxed. All taxes shall be levied and collected under general laws and shall be uniform upon the same class of subjects within the territorial limits of the authority levying the tax, except that the General Assembly may provide for differences in the rate of taxation to be imposed upon real estate by a city or town within all or parts of areas added to its territorial limits, or by a new unit of general government, within its area, created by or encompassing two or more, or parts of two or more, existing units of general government. Such differences in the rate of taxation shall bear a reasonable relationship to differences between non-revenue-producing governmental services giving land urban character which are furnished in one or several areas in contrast to the services furnished in other areas of such unit of government.

The General Assembly may by general law and within such restrictions and upon such conditions as may be prescribed authorize the governing body of any county, city, town or regional government to provide for differences in the rate of taxation imposed upon tangible personal property owned by persons not less than sixty-five years of age or persons permanently and totally disabled as established by general law who are deemed by the General Assembly to be bearing an extraordinary tax burden on said tangible personal property in relation to their income and financial worth.

The General Assembly may define and classify taxable subjects. Except as to classes of property herein expressly segregated for either State or local taxation, the General Assembly may segregate the several classes of property so as to specify and determine upon what subjects State taxes, and upon what subjects local taxes, may be levied.

The amendment ratified November 6, 1990 and effective January 1, 1991——Added a new paragraph after paragraph one.

Section 2. Assessments.

All assessments of real estate and tangible personal property shall be at their fair market value, to be ascertained as prescribed by law. The General Assembly may define and classify real estate devoted to agricultural, horticultural, forest, or open space uses, and may by general law authorize any county, city, town, or regional government to allow deferral of, or relief from, portions of taxes otherwise payable on such real estate if it were not so classified, provided the General Assembly shall first determine that classification of such real estate for such purpose is in the public interest for the preservation or conservation of real estate for such uses. In the event the General Assembly defines and classifies real estate for such purposes, it shall prescribe the limits, conditions, and extent of such deferral or relief. No such deferral or relief shall be granted within the territorial limits of any county, city, town, or regional government except by ordinance adopted by the governing body thereof.

So long as the Commonwealth shall levy upon any public service corporation a State franchise, license, or other similar tax based upon or measured by its gross receipts or gross earnings, or any part thereof, its real estate and tangible personal property shall be assessed by a central State agency, as prescribed by law.

Section 3. Taxes or assessments upon abutting property owners.

The General Assembly by general law may authorize any county, city, town, or regional government to impose taxes or assessments upon abutting property owners for such local public improvements as may be designated by the General Assembly; however, such taxes or assessments shall not be in excess of the peculiar benefits resulting from the improvements to such abutting property owners.

Section 4. Property segregated for local taxation; exceptions.

Real estate, coal and other mineral lands, and tangible personal property, except the rolling stock of public service corporations, are hereby segregated for, and made subject to, local taxation only, and shall be assessed for local taxation in such manner and at such times as the General Assembly may prescribe by general law.

Section 5. Franchise taxes; taxation of corporate stock.

The General Assembly, in imposing a franchise tax upon corporations, may in its discretion make the same in lieu of taxes upon other property, in whole or in part, of such corporations. Whenever a franchise tax shall be imposed upon a corporation doing business in this Commonwealth, or whenever all the capital, however invested, of a corporation chartered under the laws of this Commonwealth shall be taxed, the shares of stock issued by any such corporation shall not be further taxed.

Section 6. Exempt property.

(a) Except as otherwise provided in this Constitution, the following property and no other shall be exempt from taxation, State and local, including inheritance taxes:

(1) Property owned directly or indirectly by the Commonwealth or any political subdivision thereof, and obligations of the Commonwealth or any political subdivision thereof exempt by law.

(2) Real estate and personal property owned and exclusively occupied or used by churches or religious bodies for religious worship or for the residences of their ministers.

(3) Private or public burying grounds or cemeteries, provided the same are not operated for profit.

(4) Property owned by public libraries or by institutions of learning not conducted for profit, so long as such property is primarily used for literary, scientific, or educational purposes or purposes incidental thereto. This provision may also apply to leasehold interests in such property as may be provided by general law.

(5) Intangible personal property, or any class or classes thereof, as may be exempted in whole or in part by general law.

(6) Property used by its owner for religious, charitable, patriotic, historical, benevolent, cultural, or public park and playground purposes, as may be provided by classification or designation by a three-fourths vote of the members elected to each house of the General Assembly and subject to such restrictions and conditions as may be prescribed.

(7) Land subject to a perpetual easement permitting inundation by water as may be exempted in whole or in part by general law.

(b) The General Assembly may by general law authorize the governing body of any county, city, town, or regional government to provide for the exemption from local property taxation, or a portion thereof, within such restrictions and upon such conditions as may be prescribed, of real estate and personal property designed for continuous habitation owned by, and occupied as the sole dwelling of, persons not less than sixty-five years of age or persons permanently and totally disabled as established by general law who are deemed by the General Assembly to be bearing an extraordinary tax burden on said property in relation to their income and financial worth.

(c) Except as to property of the Commonwealth, the General Assembly by general law may restrict or condition, in whole or in part, but not extend, any or all of the above exemptions.

(d) The General Assembly may define as a separate subject of taxation any property, including real or personal property, equipment, facilities, or devices, used primarily for the purpose of abating or preventing pollution of the atmosphere or waters of the Commonwealth or for the purpose of transferring or storing solar energy, and by general law may allow the governing body of any county, city, town, or regional government to exempt or partially exempt such property from taxation, or by general law may directly exempt or partially exempt such property from taxation.

(e) The General Assembly may define as a separate subject of taxation household goods, personal effects and tangible farm property and products, and by general law may allow the governing body of any county, city, town, or regional government to exempt or partially exempt such property from taxation, or by general law may directly exempt or partially exempt such property from taxation.

(f) Exemptions of property from taxation as established or authorized hereby shall be strictly construed; provided, however, that all property exempt from taxation on the effective date of this section shall continue to be exempt until otherwise provided by the General Assembly as herein set forth.

(g) The General Assembly may by general law authorize any county, city, town, or regional government to impose a service charge upon the owners of a class or classes of exempt property for services provided by such governments.

(h) The General Assembly may by general law authorize the governing body of any county, city, town, or regional government to provide for a partial exemption from local real property taxation, within such restrictions and upon such conditions as may be prescribed, of real estate whose improvements, by virtue of age and use, have undergone substantial renovation, rehabilitation or replacement.

(i) The General Assembly may by general law allow the governing body of any county, city, or town to exempt or partially exempt from taxation any generating equipment installed after December thirty-one, nineteen hundred seventy-four, for the purpose of converting from oil or natural gas to coal or to wood, wood bark, wood residue, or to any other alternate energy source for manufacturing, and any co-generation equipment installed since such date for use in manufacturing.

The amendment ratified November 2, 1976 and effective January 1, 1977—After (a)(6) added subdivision "(7) Land subject to a perpetual easement . . .". In subsection (b) after "sixty-five years of age" added the language "or persons permanently and totally disabled as established by general law". In subsection (d) after "Commonwealth" added the language "or for the purpose of transferring or storing solar energy". In subsection (e) after "personal effects" added the language "and tangible farm property and products".

The amendment ratified November 7, 1978 and effective January 1, 1979—Added a new subsection (h).

The amendment ratified November 4, 1980 and effective January 1, 1981—In subsection (b) substituted "exemption from local property taxation" for "exemption from local real property taxation". After "of real estate" added "and personal property designed for continuous habitation". Substituted "property" for "real estate" near the end of subsection (b).

The amendment ratified November 4, 1980 and effective January 1, 1981—Added a new subsection (i).

Section 7. Collection and disposition of State revenues.

All taxes, licenses, and other revenues of the Commonwealth shall be collected by its proper officers and paid into the State treasury. No money shall be paid out of the State treasury except in pursuance of appropriations made by law; and no such appropriation shall be made which is payable more than two years and six months after the end of the session of the General Assembly at which the law is enacted authorizing the same.

Other than as may be provided for in the debt provisions of this Constitution, the Governor, subject to such criteria as may be established by the General Assembly, shall ensure that no expenses of the Commonwealth be incurred which exceed total revenues on hand and anticipated during a period not to exceed the two years and six months period established by this section of the Constitution.

The amendment ratified November 6, 1984 and effective July 1, 1986—Added the second paragraph.

Section 8. Limit of tax or revenue.

No other or greater amount of tax or revenues shall, at any time, be levied than may be required for the necessary expenses of the government, or to pay the indebtedness of the Commonwealth.

The General Assembly shall establish the Revenue Stabilization Fund. The Fund shall consist of an amount not to exceed ten percent of the Commonwealth's average annual tax revenues derived from taxes on income and retail sales as certified by the Auditor of Public Accounts for the three fiscal years immediately preceding. The Auditor of Public Accounts shall compute the ten percent limitation of such fund annually and report to the General Assembly not later than the first day of December. "Certified tax revenues" means the Commonwealth's annual tax revenues derived from taxes on income and retail sales as certified by the Auditor of Public Accounts.

The General Assembly shall make deposits to the Fund to equal at least fifty percent of the product of the certified tax revenues collected in the most recently ended fiscal year times the difference between the annual percentage increase in the certified tax revenues collected for the most recently ended fiscal year and the average annual percentage increase in the certified tax revenues collected in the six fiscal years immediately preceding the most recently ended fiscal year. However, growth in certified tax revenues, which is the result of either increases in tax rates on income or retail sales or the repeal of exemptions therefrom, may be excluded, in whole or in part, from the computation immediately preceding for a period of time not to exceed six calendar years from the calendar year in which such tax rate increase or exemption repeal was effective. Additional appropriations may be made at any time so long as the ten percent limitation established herein is not exceeded. All interest earned on the Fund shall be part thereof; however, if the Fund's balance exceeds the limitation, the amount in excess of the limitation shall be paid into the general fund after appropriation by the General Assembly.

The General Assembly may appropriate an amount for transfer from the Fund to compensate for no more than one-half of the difference between the total general fund revenues appropriated and a revised general fund revenue forecast presented to the General Assembly prior to or during a subsequent regular or special legislative session. However, no transfer shall be made unless the general fund revenues appropriated exceed such revised general fund revenue forecast by more than two percent of certified tax revenues collected in the most recently ended fiscal year. Furthermore, no appropriation or transfer from such fund in any fiscal year shall exceed more than one-half of the balance of the Revenue Stabilization Fund. The General Assembly may enact such laws as may be necessary and appropriate to implement the Fund.

The amendment ratified November 3, 1992 and effective January 1, 1993—Added the second, third, and fourth paragraphs.

Section 9. State debt.

No debt shall be contracted by or in behalf of the Commonwealth except as provided herein.

(a) Debts to meet emergencies and redeem previous debt obligations.

The General Assembly may (1) contract debts to suppress insurrection, repel invasion, or defend the Commonwealth in time of war; (2) contract debts, or may authorize the Governor to contract debts, to meet casual deficits in the revenue or in anticipation of the collection of revenues of the Commonwealth for the then current fiscal year within the amount of authorized appropriations, provided that the total of such indebtedness shall not exceed thirty per centum of an amount equal to 1.15 times the average annual tax revenues of the Commonwealth derived from taxes on income and retail sales, as certified by the Auditor of Public Accounts, for the preceding fiscal year and that each such debt shall mature within twelve months from the date such debt is incurred; and (3) contract debts to redeem a previous debt obligation of the Commonwealth.

The full faith and credit of the Commonwealth shall be pledged to any debt created under this subsection. The amount of such debt shall not be included in the limitations on debt hereinafter established, except that the amount of debt incurred pursuant to clause (3) above shall be included in determining the limitation on the aggregate amount of general obligation debt for capital projects permitted elsewhere in this article unless the debt so incurred pursuant to clause (3) above is secured by a pledge of net revenues from capital projects of institutions or agencies administered solely by the executive department of the Commonwealth or of institutions of higher learning of the Commonwealth, which net revenues the Governor shall certify are anticipated to be sufficient to pay the principal of and interest on such debt and to provide such reserves as the law authorizing the same may require, in which event the amount thereof shall be included in determining the limitation on the aggregate amount of debt contained in the provision of this article which authorizes general obligation debt for certain revenue-producing capital projects.

(b) General obligation debt for capital projects and sinking fund.

The General Assembly may, upon the affirmative vote of a majority of the members elected to each house, authorize the creation of debt to which the full faith and credit of the Commonwealth is pledged, for capital projects to be distinctly specified in the law authorizing the same; provided that any such law shall specify capital projects constituting a single purpose and shall not take effect until it shall have been submitted to the people at an election and a majority of those voting on the question shall have approved such debt. No such debt shall be authorized by the General Assembly if the amount thereof when added to amounts approved by the people or authorized by the General Assembly and not yet submitted to the people for approval, under this subsection during the three fiscal years immediately preceding the authorization by the General Assembly of such debt and the fiscal year in which such debt is authorized shall exceed twenty-five per centum of an amount equal to 1.15 times the average annual tax revenues of the Commonwealth derived from taxes on income and retail sales, as certified by the Auditor of Public Accounts, for the three fiscal years immediately preceding the authorization of such debt by the General Assembly.

No debt shall be incurred under this subsection if the amount thereof when added to the aggregate amount of all outstanding debt to which the full faith and credit of the Commonwealth is pledged other than that excluded from this limitation by the provisions of this article authorizing the contracting of debts to redeem a previous debt obligation of the Commonwealth and for certain revenue-producing capital projects, less any amounts set aside in sinking funds for the repayment of such outstanding debt, shall exceed an amount equal to 1.15 times the average annual tax revenues of the Commonwealth derived from taxes on income and retail sales, as certified by the Auditor of Public Accounts, for the three fiscal years immediately preceding the incurring of such debt.

All debt incurred under this subsection shall mature within a period not to exceed the estimated useful life of the projects as stated in the authorizing law, which statement shall be conclusive, or a period of thirty years, whichever is shorter; and all debt incurred to redeem a previous debt obligation of the Commonwealth, except that which is secured by net revenues anticipated to be sufficient to pay the same and provide reserves therefor, shall mature within a period not to exceed thirty years. Such debt shall be amortized, by payment into a sinking fund or otherwise, in annual installments of principal to begin not later than one-tenth of the term of the bonds, and any such sinking fund shall not be appropriated for any other purpose; if such debt be for public road purposes, such payment shall be first made from revenues segregated by law for the construction and maintenance of State highways. No such installment shall exceed the smallest previous installment by more than one hundred per centum. If sufficient funds are not appropriated in the budget for any fiscal year for the timely payment of the interest upon and installments of principal of such debt, there shall be set apart by direction of the Governor, from the first general fund revenues received during such fiscal year and thereafter, a sum sufficient to pay such interest and installments of principal.

(c) Debt for certain revenue-producing capital projects.

The General Assembly may authorize the creation of debt secured by a pledge of net revenues derived from rates, fees, or other charges and the full faith and credit of the Commonwealth, and such debt shall not be included in determining the limitation on general obligation debt for capital projects as permitted elsewhere in this article, provided that

(1) the creation of such debt is authorized by the affirmative vote of two-thirds of the members elected to each house of the General Assembly; and

(2) such debt is created for specific revenue-producing capital projects (including the enlargement or improvement thereof), which shall be distinctly specified in the law authorizing the same, of institutions and agencies administered solely by the executive department of the Commonwealth or of institutions of higher learning of the Commonwealth.

Before any such debt shall be authorized by the General Assembly, and again before it shall be incurred, the Governor shall certify in writing, filed with the Auditor of Public Accounts, his opinion, based upon responsible engineering and economic estimates, that the anticipated net revenues to be pledged to the payment of principal of and interest on such debt will be sufficient to meet such payments as the same become due and to provide such reserves as the law authorizing such debt may require, and that the projects otherwise comply with the requirements of this subsection, which certifications shall be conclusive.

No debt shall be incurred under this subsection if the amount thereof when added to the aggregate amount of all outstanding debt authorized by this subsection and the amount of all outstanding debt incurred to redeem a previous debt obligation of the Commonwealth which is to be included in the limitation of this subsection by virtue of the provisions of this article authorizing the contracting of debts to redeem a previous debt obligation of the Commonwealth, less any amounts set aside in sinking funds for the payment of such debt, shall exceed an amount equal to 1.15 times the average annual tax revenues of the Commonwealth derived from taxes on income and retail sales, as certified by the Auditor of Public Accounts, for the three fiscal years immediately preceding the incurring of such debt.

This subsection shall not be construed to pledge the full faith and credit of the Commonwealth to the payment of any obligation of the Commonwealth, or any institution, agency, or authority thereof, or to any refinancing or reissuance of such obligation which was incurred prior to the effective date of this subsection.

(d) Obligations to which section not applicable.

The restrictions of this section shall not apply to any obligation incurred by the Commonwealth or any institution, agency, or authority thereof if the full faith and credit of the Commonwealth is not pledged or committed to the payment of such obligation.

Section 10. Lending of credit, stock subscriptions, and works of internal improvement.

Neither the credit of the Commonwealth nor of any county, city, town, or regional government shall be directly or indirectly, under any device or pretense whatsoever, granted to or in aid of any person, association, or corporation; nor shall the Commonwealth or any such unit of government subscribe to or become interested in the stock or obligations of any company, association, or corporation for the purpose of aiding in the construction or maintenance of its work; nor shall the Commonwealth become a party to or become interested in any work of internal improvement, except public roads and public parks, or engage in carrying on any such work; nor shall the Commonwealth assume any indebtedness of any county, city, town, or regional government, nor lend its credit to the same. This section shall not be construed to prohibit the General Assembly from establishing an authority with power to insure and guarantee loans to finance industrial development and industrial expansion and from making appropriations to such authority.

Section 11. Governmental employees retirement system.

The General Assembly shall maintain a retirement system for state employees and employees of participating political subdivisions and school divisions. The funds of the retirement system shall be deemed separate and independent trust funds, shall be segregated from all other funds of the Commonwealth, and shall be invested and administered solely in the interests of the members and beneficiaries thereof. Neither the General Assembly nor any public officer, employee, or agency shall use or authorize the use of such trust funds for any purpose other than as provided in law for benefits, refunds, and administrative expenses, including but not limited to legislative oversight of the retirement system. Such trust funds shall be invested as authorized by law. Retirement system benefits shall be funded using methods which are consistent with generally accepted actuarial principles. The retirement system shall be subject to restrictions, terms, and conditions as may be prescribed by the General Assembly.

The amendment ratified November 5, 1996 and effective January 1, 1997—In the heading of the section, substituted "employees" for "employee" and deleted "fund" after "retirement system". In the text, substituted "retirement system for state employees and employees of participating political subdivisions and school divisions" for "state employees retirement system to be administered in the best interest of the beneficiaries thereof and subject to such restrictions or conditions as may be prescribed by the General Assembly" and added the remainder of the paragraph.

ARTICLE XI
Conservation

Section 1. Natural resources and historical sites of the Commonwealth.

To the end that the people have clean air, pure water, and the use and enjoyment for recreation of adequate public lands, waters, and other natural resources, it shall be the policy of the Commonwealth to conserve, develop, and utilize its natural resources, its public lands, and its historical sites and buildings. Further, it shall be the Commonwealth's policy to protect its atmosphere, lands, and waters from pollution, impairment, or destruction, for the benefit, enjoyment, and general welfare of the people of the Commonwealth.

Section 2. Conservation and development of natural resources and historical sites.

In the furtherance of such policy, the General Assembly may undertake the conservation, development, or utilization of lands or natural resources of the Commonwealth, the acquisition and protection of historical sites and buildings, and the protection of its atmosphere, lands, and waters from pollution, impairment, or destruction, by agencies of the Commonwealth or by the creation of public authorities, or by leases or other contracts with agencies of the United States, with other states, with units of government in the Commonwealth, or with private persons or corporations. Notwithstanding the time limitations of the provisions of Article X, Section 7, of this Constitution, the Commonwealth may participate for any period of years in the cost of projects which shall be the subject of a joint undertaking between the Commonwealth and any agency of the United States or of other states.

Section 3. Natural oyster beds.

The natural oyster beds, rocks, and shoals in the waters of the Commonwealth shall not be leased, rented, or sold but shall be held in trust for the benefit of the people of the Commonwealth, subject to such regulations and restriction as the General Assembly may prescribe, but the General Assembly may, from time to time, define and determine such natural beds, rocks, or shoals by surveys or otherwise.

ARTICLE XII
Future Changes

Section 1. Amendments.

Any amendment or amendments to this Constitution may be proposed in the Senate or House of Delegates, and if the same shall be agreed to by a majority of the members elected to each of the two houses, such proposed amendment or amendments shall be entered on their journals, the name of each member and how he voted to be recorded, and referred to the General Assembly at its first regular session held after the next general election of members of the House of Delegates. If at such regular session or any subsequent special session of that General Assembly the proposed amendment or amendments shall be agreed to by a majority of all the members elected to each house, then it shall be the duty of the General Assembly to submit such proposed amendment or amendments to the voters qualified to vote in elections by the people, in such manner as it shall prescribe and not sooner than ninety days after final passage by the General Assembly. If a majority of those voting vote in favor of any amendment, it shall become part of the Constitution on the date prescribed by the General Assembly in submitting the amendment to the voters.

Section 2. Constitutional convention.

The General Assembly may, by a vote of two-thirds of the members elected to each house, call a convention to propose a general revision of, or specific amendments to, this Constitution, as the General Assembly in its call may stipulate.

The General Assembly shall provide by law for the election of delegates to such a convention, and shall also provide for the submission, in such manner as it shall prescribe and not sooner than ninety days after final adjournment of the convention, of the proposals of the convention to the voters qualified to vote in elections by the people. If a majority of those voting vote in favor of any proposal, it shall become effective on the date prescribed by the General Assembly in providing for the submission of the convention proposals to the voters.

Schedule

Section 1. *Effective date of revised Constitution.*

This revised Constitution shall, except as is otherwise provided herein, go into effect at noon on the first day of July, nineteen hundred and seventy-one.

Section 2. *Officers and elections.*

Unless otherwise provided herein or by law, nothing in this revised Constitution shall affect the oath, tenure, term, status, or compensation of any person holding any public office, position, or employment in the Commonwealth, nor affect the date of filling any State or local office, elective or appointive, which shall be filled on the date on which it would otherwise have been filled.

Section 3. *Laws, proceedings, and obligations unaffected.*

The common and statute law in force at the time this revised Constitution goes into effect, so far as not in conflict therewith, shall remain in force until they expire by their own limitation or are altered or repealed by the General Assembly. Unless otherwise provided herein or by law, the adoption of this revised Constitution shall have no effect on pending judicial proceedings or judgments, on any obligations owing to or by the Commonwealth or any of its officers, agencies, or political subdivisions, or on any private obligations or rights.

Section 4. *Qualifications of judges.*

The requirement of Article VI, Section 7, that justices of the Supreme Court and judges of courts of record shall, at least five years prior to their election or appointment, have been members of the bar of the Commonwealth, shall not preclude justices or judges who were elected or appointed prior to the effective date of this revised Constitution, and who are otherwise qualified, from completing the term for which they were elected or appointed and from being reelected for one additional term.

Section 5. *First session of General Assembly following adoption of revised Constitution.*

The General Assembly shall convene at the Capitol at noon on the first Wednesday in January, nineteen hundred and seventy-one. It shall enact such laws as may be deemed proper, including those necessary to implement this revised Constitution. The General Assembly shall reapportion the Commonwealth into electoral districts in accordance with Article II, Section 6, of this Constitution. The General Assembly shall be vested with all the powers, charged with all the duties, and subject to all the limitations prescribed by this Constitution except that this session shall continue as long as may be necessary; that the salary and allowances of members shall not be limited by Section 46 of the Constitution of 1902 as amended and that effective date limitation of Section 53 of the Constitution of 1902 as amended shall not be operative.

Index to the Constitution of Virginia

(References are to Articles and Sections)